CHILE

highlights

Tim

D0462030

Edition 1

Bradt Travel Guides Ltd, UK
The Globe Pequot Press Inc, USA

About this book

There are many heavyweight guidebooks to Chile bloated with long lists of budget hotels and overviews of public transport targeted at backpackers and independent travellers. This 'highlights' guidebook is more selective in the information it offers, and is written for the traveller on (or planning to go on) an organised tour. The book has two main aims: first, to help those considering a vacation to decide what they'd like to see and do, and therefore to construct their itinerary or liaise with tour operators in an informed way; and, second, to provide an entertaining, colourful and informative guide to carry on the trip itself. With that in mind, the book provides overviews of every town, national park and city that ranks as a possible highlight, a quick summary of practicalities and a short list of recommended accommodation. The selections are made by Tim Burford, who has been writing guidebooks to Chile since 1997. In addition, we have called upon the expertise of local and international tour operators – those that know best what the country has to offer – to recommend their favourite itineraries and activities. Those tour operators were invited to contribute on the basis of their reputations for excellence; they also made a payment towards the production of this book (see pages 60–1).

These pages are unique in bringing together the selections of a top writer and experienced operators, ensuring that this is a useful guidebook available to those planning an organised tour to Chile.

List of maps

Author

Tim Burford studied languages at Oxford University. In 1991, after a brief career as a publisher, he began writing for Bradt Travel Guides, first covering hiking in eastern-central Europe and then backpacking and ecotourism in Latin America. He has now written ten books for Bradt (including Bradt's Chile travel guide) and also leads hiking trips in Europe's mountains. He lives in Cambridge, loves train travel in Europe and flies only across oceans.

Author's story

Australis cruises let you get up close and personal with glaciers. (CA)

I have been visiting Chile for over 15 years, and it remains one of my favourite destinations. Originally I came to lead hiking trips, in Patagonia and the Lakes District, and then I found myself updating hiking guidebooks. Before too long I was able to discover the whole country while writing a general guidebook to Chile, and began to appreciate its astonishing variety of scenery, culture and activities. I even got to visit Easter Island.

I went white-water rafting for the first time, and look forward to an extended sea kayak trip sometime soon off Chiloé.

The growth in wine tourism has been a revelation (as has the increasing availability of beers called what sounds like 'Parlez Arlez' and the like!) – the accompanying food is fun too!

I've taken the Navimag ship between Puerto Montt and Puerto Natales three times now – it's one of my favourite journeys, where the misty atmosphere, the camaraderie and the occasional whale more than compensate for the lack of cruise-liner luxuries.

As the country has become more developed, the range of outdoor activities on offer has become wider, and the standards of accommodation and other services have risen sharply, so that Chile now compares – and competes – with the world's best-known destinations.

Contents

Introduction

Chile is famous as that absurdly long, thin country squeezed between the Andean cordillera (range) and the Pacific Ocean; the contrasts between its northern and southern extremities are quite mind-boggling. Its southern extremities form part of Patagonia, but in contrast to the bare pampas of Argentine Patagonia this is one of the wettest parts of the world, with amazingly thick coastal rainforests between mighty glaciers and fiords. To the north is the Lakes District, much loved by tourists with its perfect conical volcanoes reflected in the lakes; further north there is a near-perfect climate producing fruit and wine exported worldwide. To the north of the capital, Santiago, the country is increasingly arid, with many archaeological remains preserved by the climate in the world's driest region, the Atacama Desert.

Santiago itself is a teeming modern city with many attractions, both by day and by night, but also less hectic and mentally exhausting than other more 'Latin' cities.

Covering 748,800km² (without its claim to part of Antarctica), Chile is one of South America's smaller countries; but it's over 4,300km long and embraces almost 40°of latitude (over 70° if you include Antarctica), and thus encompasses more climates, landscapes and ways of life than any other country of its size in the world. It's also one of the most prosperous countries in Latin America, with a very efficient transport system and other necessities such as plenty of good hotels and an efficient and incorruptible police force.

Chile is pretty affordable due to a gradual 20% devaluation over the past couple of years. There's very little crime apart from a bit of the usual big-city pickpocketing and mugging in parts of Santiago.

Incidentally, the name 'Chile' is probably derived from the Aymara for 'The end of the Earth', or perhaps 'Snow'; the Aymara, still (with the Quechua) the dominant population of Peru and Bolivia, also live in a few villages high on the Chilean altiplano.

Feedback request

If you have any comments about this guide (good or bad), we would welcome your feedback. Please email us on Ⓔ info@bradtguides.com. Alternatively you can add a review of the book to Ⓦ www.bradtguides.com or Amazon.

Introducing Chile

History 5

People and culture 18

1 Background

Chile was first populated around 15,000 years ago (although this date keeps being pushed back) by people who crossed from Asia by the Bering land bridge; a wide range of cultures evolved to match the natural environments, from the world's driest desert to the relentless wind and rain of the south. The Incas briefly ruled northern Chile, but to the south the Mapuche people managed to resist both them and, from 1535, the Spanish conquistadores. Nevertheless, a mixed (*mestizo*) populace and culture evolved, and with independence from Spain in 1818 Chile - separated by desert, mountains and glaciers from its neighbours - became a distinctive society that is now one of the most prosperous and efficient states of the continent. Some unique native cultures survive and are now reasserting themselves.

Chile at a glance

Location West coast of southern South America

Neighbouring countries Argentina, Bolivia, Peru

Area 748,800km^2 (excluding a claim to part of Antarctica)

Climate Mostly temperate (increasingly wet and cold to the south); dry tropical in the far north

Status Presidential Republic

Population 17.3 million (2011)

Life expectancy 78 years

Capital Santiago (population 6 million based on 2011 figures)

Other main towns Arica, Iquique, Antofagasta, La Serena, Valparaíso, Concepción, Temuco, Valdivia, Puerto Montt, Punta Arenas

Economy Free-market capitalism

GDP US$247 billion (US$300 billion at Purchasing Power Parity [PPP]), 2011

GDP growth 5%

Language Spanish

Religion 70% Roman Catholic

Currency Peso; written as $ in Chile, P in this book

Exchange rate £1 = P866; US$1 = P480; €1 = P612 (Nov 2012)

National airline LAN (formerly LanChile); main airport Santiago (SCL)

International telephone code +56

Time GMT -3

Electrical voltage 220V, 50Hz

Weights and measures Metric

Flag One white and one red horizontal band, blue square at hoist end of upper (white) band, five-pointed white star in centre of blue square

National anthem *Puro, Chile, es tu ciel azulado* ('Chile, your sky is pure blue') by Eusebio Lillo and Ramón Carnicer, 1827

Public holidays 1 January New Year (Año Nuevo); Good Friday (Viernes Santo), Easter Saturday (Sábado Santo) and Sunday (Pascua); 1 May Labour Day (Día del Trabajo); 21 May Navy Day (Glorias Navales); 29 June Saints Peter and Paul (San Pedro y San Pablo); 16 July Our Lady of Mount Carmel (Virgen del Carmen); 15 August Assumption of the Virgin (Asunción de la Virgen); 18 September Independence Day (Día de la Independencia); 19 September Army Day (Día del Ejercito); 15 October Colombus Day (Día de la Raza or Día del Descubrimiento de Dos Mundos); 1 November All Saints (Todos los Santos); 8 December Immaculate Conception (Inmaculada Concepción); 25 December Christmas (Navidad); 31 December New Year's Eve (El Fin del Año)

History

Prehistory

Humans first reached the Americas from Asia, crossing the Bering land bridge to Alaska and heading south; the oldest human remains so far found in Chile date from almost 15,000 years ago. Between then and 10,000 years ago a **Palaeo-Indian** culture developed in what is now the Norte Chico, killing the last mastodons around 11,000 years ago. From about 5,000 years ago maize, beans and squash were cultivated, and people moved to higher altitudes where they domesticated llamas and alpacas. By 500BC the San Pedro or **Atacameño** culture had developed in the oases of the Atacama Desert, producing ceramics and textiles, and was influenced by the Tihuanaco culture in present-day Bolivia. Other groups lived along the coast and fished the immensely rich Humboldt Current, notably the **Chinchorro** people in the far north whose mummified corpses (2,000 years older than Egyptian mummies) are still being discovered, preserved by the desert climate.

A mummified Chinchorro baby (IA/R/C)

Fine **ceramics** were produced by the El Molle (between AD0 and 800) and Diaguita (1000 to 1500) cultures, both in central-northern Chile. By the 15th century, the far north was settled by the Aymara people, with the Atacameños to the south of the Río Loa, and the Diaguita and Aconcagua cultures in the Norte Chico, while south of present-day Santiago were the Araucanian peoples, the ancestors of the modern **Mapuche**. In the wetter southern climate few artefacts have survived, but the Pitrén (from c600) and El Vergel (from 1000) cultures lived by hunting and growing maize and potatoes; from the 14th century they mixed with incomers from what is now Argentina to form the Mapuche, of whom about a million survive. To the south of the icefields lived various small groups, such as the Kaweskar, Yámana and Selk'nam, leading very simple lives in the harshest of conditions.

The **Inca** invaded in the second half of the 15th century and conquered the northern half of Chile, but they were unable to defeat the Mapuche, who were not finally absorbed into Chile until the 19th century. The Inca left few physical or cultural traces.

The colonial era

Inca dominion was not to last long, as the **Spanish conquistadores** made their first incursion from Peru between 1535 and 1537, when Diego de Almagro led what might be called a military exploration, enduring a disastrous winter crossing of the Andes. In 1540, **Pedro de Valdivia** set out from Cuzco on a more serious invasion. He founded the city of Santiago in 1541; it was burnt down by the Mapuche later that year and then rebuilt as a fort. There was another uprising in 1553 – during which Valdivia was killed – and further revolt between 1598 and 1608. The Spanish subsequently left Araucanía in semi-autonomy for the next 250 years.

In 1641 a frontier was established along the Río Biobío, and Valdivia was resettled in 1645. The colony, consisting of little more than seven towns between La Serena and Castro, stagnated due to trade restrictions designed to benefit Spain and stifle its colonies. Some gold was found, but it was largely exhausted by the late 17th century. This resulted in cattle-ranching becoming the colony's main economic activity, and the formation of huge estates which belonged to an oligarchy of about 300 families. The native peoples were decimated by Old World diseases such as measles, smallpox and influenza, but a *mestizo* (mixed-blood) population rapidly replaced them, boosted by settlers from the Basque country and elsewhere. More gold was found, and reforms permitted Chile to trade with other Spanish colonies such as Argentina, though not with other countries. Perhaps the best known of Chile's colonial governors was the Irish-born **Ambrosio O'Higgins**, who rose through the Spanish service to become governor of Chile in 1788 and then Viceroy of Peru in 1796. Among his other reform projects, he built the Santiago–Valparaíso road and resettled Osorno.

It was, however, too little too late. Chile's *mestizos* and *criollos* (native-born Hispanics) resented their exclusion from power and their country's exploitation by Spain, and things came to a head after Napoleon's invasion of Spain in 1808 left the colonies uncertain who was supposed to be ruling them. The local elite, who had economic but not political power, set up a junta or governing council on 18 September 1810, led by **Mateo Toro y Zambrano**, who had been appointed as Chile's first *criollo* governor. In 1811, a Royalist revolt began, while radicals led by **José Miguel Carrera** set up their own junta and dissolved the congress. In 1813, **Bernardo O'Higgins**, son of Ambrosio, took command of the Patriot Army, just in time to save Santiago from the Royalists. A treaty would have granted Chile some autonomy, but was rejected by the viceroy in Lima, who marched on Santiago again; the patriots, split between Carrera and O'Higgins, patched up their differences,

An artist's depiction of the Battle of Chacabuco (PSE/MNBA)

but not well enough. O'Higgins made a heroic stand in Rancagua, but reinforcements never arrived from Carrera, and both leaders had to flee to Argentina with about 2,000 men.

The Royalists took Santiago and abolished the junta's reforms. Repression naturally fuelled the desire for independence, and in 1817 the Argentine **José de San Martín** led an army across the Andes and caught the Royalists off-guard, defeating them in the **Battle of Chacabuco**. His second-in-command O'Higgins consequently took charge of Chile, finally declaring independence after another Spanish army was defeated by San Martín in April 1818 at Maipú, although the south remained under Royalist rule.

Independence

At the end of 1818 the British **Lord Thomas Cochrane** arrived in Chile, after rather too colourful a career in the Royal Navy, and took command of Chile's small fleet. He won control of the sea and in 1820 captured Valdivia in a brilliant feat of daring during which he launched a surprise attack at night from the inland side of the massive forts protecting the harbour. By 1826 the Spanish had been driven out of Peru and from Chiloé, their last toe-hold in South America. O'Higgins introduced a new constitution in 1822 but abdicated when it was rejected by the political establishment, and went into exile. The economy did better, with big new silver mines opening in 1825 and 1832; foreign trade in the mid-1830s was twice the level it had been in 1810.

In 1830 the conservative establishment seized power and kept it for three decades. The ruler of Chile was now **Diego Portales**, an enigmatic character who introduced a republican-influenced constitution in 1833, but also established a strong state with an indirectly elected president. Elections were routinely rigged, but the system proved remarkably stable, lasting until 1890. The budget was balanced and exports boomed, but Portales was murdered by mutinous troops in 1837; a war with the Peruvian–Bolivian confederation was finally won in 1839, and the victorious general Manuel Bulnes became president in 1841. His designated successor **Manuel Montt** had to overcome a revolt before establishing himself in power in 1851. He was a great promoter of education and public works; driven by silver mining, the economy grew fast, with foreign trade increasing fivefold from the mid-1840s to the mid-1870s. The **Californian** and **Australian gold rushes** of 1848 and 1851 at last provided a market for the Central Valley's wheat, and put its surplus land and labour to use, with modern mills and irrigation canals soon constructed. Railways, the telegraph and gas lighting all appeared early in the 1850s, and large colonies of foreign merchants and engineers, including the British, arrived. German colonists set up south of the Biobío River.

However, the conservative ascendancy fell apart over the issue of the Roman Catholic Church's role in public life. In 1858, an alliance of liberals and dissident conservatives took power, ruling for the next 15 years. The Mapuche attacked again in 1859, as settlements were now steadily creeping into their territory, and the army began the so-called **Pacification of Araucanía**, with lines of forts being steadily moved south until 1881 when a final Mapuche offensive was easily defeated. In 1866, the first **caliche** (nitrate fertiliser) was found in the Atacama, and

The fighting Cochranes

Lord Thomas Cochrane, the tenth earl of Dundonald, has achieved new fame since being identified as the model for the character of Jack Aubrey (played by Russell Crowe in *Master and Commander: The Far Side of the World*) in Patrick O'Brian's historical novels.

It's ironic, as he was such a great basher of the French, that his great-great-grandson Commander The Honourable Michael Cochrane should have received the Croix de Valeur

Admiral Lord Cochrane (JR/DL)

Militaire (and an OBE) in 2002 after commanding HMS *Somerset* under a French admiral off former Yugoslavia. At the end of 2002 the *Somerset* was sold to Chile and was named the *Almirante Williams*. In 2003 Cochrane reappeared, in charge of protecting Iraq's offshore oil terminals, freshly captured by the Anglo-American coalition, and was promoted to Commodore in 2012.

The sinking of the *Esmeralda* at the Battle of Iquique, 1879 (TS)

a massive new industry was born. Although this was largely in Peruvian and Bolivian territory, it was funded and run by Chilean companies, and the new city of Antofagasta had an almost entirely Chilean population. Bolivia raised taxes on Chilean nitrates companies, triggering the **War of the Pacific** with both Bolivia and Peru from 1879. It started badly, with the sinking of the *Esmeralda* and the capture of a loaded troopship, but public outrage led to a re-organised army capturing what is now the Norte Grande, and then between 1880 and 1881 invading Peru and capturing Arica and Lima.

In 1883 cemeteries were secularised, and in 1884 civil marriage and registration of births and deaths was introduced, stirring up huge opposition among the Church's supporters. José Manuel Balmaceda, president from 1886, brought about compromise with the Church, and began to use Chile's huge revenues from nitrates taxes for public works. However, increasing use of presidential patronage was unpopular, while labour unrest was brewing in the nitrate industry and elsewhere. In 1891, the conservative opposition triggered a civil war during which between 10,000 and 15,000 were killed and Balmaceda was overthrown.

Admiral **Jorge Montt** (who had led the mutiny) served as president from 1891 to 1896, overseeing the birth of the Parliamentary Republic; Federico Errázuriz Echaurren took over in 1896, forming a Liberal–Conservative Coalition that was to last until the 1920s. By 1904 border disputes with Argentina and Bolivia had been settled through peaceful arbitration.

20th-century development

Pedro Montt (son of Manuel) became president in 1906; he was hardworking but suffered from poor health and had to contend with a massive earthquake in Valparaíso (which killed 3,000 people), as well as a fall in copper and nitrate prices. Labour unrest spread, leading to the massacre of perhaps 1,350 strikers in Iquique in 1907. The development of synthetic fertilisers undermined the nitrates industry, and the opening of the **Panama Canal** in 1914 took a lot of shipping away from Chile's ports. Chile's share of world copper production had fallen from about a third to less than a 20th; however, the American Guggenheim, Kennecott and Anaconda companies provided investment to develop vast new reserves at El Teniente and Chuquicamata. World War I boosted copper exports, but this was followed by a recession, more strikes, and the rise of the Radical Party and the Socialist Workers Party (which became the Communist Party in 1922).

The charismatic and populist **Arturo Alessandri** was elected president in 1920, urgently seeking reforms to avoid a revolution as in Mexico or Russia; his unstable coalition was blocked, however, by the conservatives. In 1924 he won control of both houses, introduced an income tax, and was overthrown by a military coup and then invited back; the new constitution of 1925 returned the balance of power to a directly elected president. After some infighting **General Carlos Ibáñez del Campo** (one of the coup leaders) was elected president in 1927, imposing an authoritarian regime with a huge public works programme, including airports and the colonisation of Aysén. Massive foreign debt and the world depression caused economic collapse by 1930, with copper exports falling from US$111 million in 1929 to US$33 million in 1933, and nitrate production halved. Spending cuts, tax increases and defaulting on debt repayments all came too late, and the government resigned.

Alessandri returned to run for president again in 1931 but the popular Radical Juan Esteban Montero won easily; the next year supporters of Ibáñez staged a coup by a military junta who briefly established a socialist republic. Alessandri won elections and governed from 1932 to 1938, restoring stability and, thanks to his brilliant finance minister Gustavo Ross (and higher copper prices and output), balanced the budget and cut unemployment with a public works programme. By 1938 industrial production was a third above 1929's level. Demonstrations by Ibáñistas and Nazis preceded the 1938 elections, won by Pedro Aguirre Cerda, candidate of a left-wing alliance led by Gabriel González Videla.

The state became increasingly involved in the economy, a process accelerated by the massive **Chillán earthquake** of 1939, Chile's worst-ever natural disaster which left at least 28,000 dead and led to the establishment of Corfo – a state body charged with industrial development. In 1941 Aguirre Cerda resigned due to illness and died two weeks later. Juan Antonio Ríos Morales of the Radical Party was elected president but he himself resigned in 1946 due to terminal cancer. With unstable minority governments, Chile largely sat out World War II, declaring war on the Axis only in February 1945.

In 1946 the Radical Gabriel González Videla won the presidency with the support of communists (the first 'eurocommunist' party, having renounced violence and committed itself to follow democratic norms), but his government fell apart and under US pressure he decided to form an anti-communist government, banning the party and arresting its leaders. **Pablo Neruda**, the communist poet, fled abroad and vituperated against the betrayal; perhaps in compensation, female suffrage was introduced, but communist agitation continued. The war had boosted the economy, but a post-war slump was ended only by the Korean War. Finance Minister Jorge Alessandri cut spending and raised taxes, almost halving inflation, but then from 1950 the economy shrank as inflation, unemployment and the cost of living all rose. The heavily taxed copper companies were reluctant to invest until 1955 when a 'new deal' allowed them to boost production by a third. **Ibáñez** (a populist with dictatorial tendencies similar to his Argentine contemporary Juan Perón) was easily elected president again in 1952, and he imposed wage and price controls and sent strike leaders to a camp in the desert. Inflation fell, but drought and a slump in the price of copper pushed it up again in 1957, leading to riots in Santiago. In 1960 the capital's population reached two million – four times higher than in 1940 – as Chile rapidly became urbanised.

In the 1958 elections – the first after reforms that ended vote-buying and increased the electorate by a third – **Jorge Alessandri** was elected president largely due to his economic record. He balanced the budget, boosted production and cut unemployment, but in 1960 the **most powerful earthquake ever recorded** hit south-central

People examine an enormous crack in a street in Valdivia after the earthquake that struck the area on 21 April 1960 (STF/AFP/G)

Chile and knocked the economy sideways and left two million people homeless (although the death toll was relatively low, less than 1,700). Limited agrarian reforms were introduced in 1962, together with electoral reforms that more than doubled the number of voters. In the 1963 municipal elections the centrist Democracia Cristiana (Christian Democracy), formed in 1957, became the largest party, and in 1964 their leader **Eduardo Frei Montalva** was elected president. The socialist leader Salvador Allende had lost the 1958 presidential race (his second) in a tight three-way race with Frei and Alessandri, and Frei, funded by the CIA, fought hard to beat him again. His reforms were at first held up in congress but in the 1965 elections he demanded and got 'a Congress for Frei', allowing him to push through serious reforms at last. Most significant, and controversial, was the campaign to 'Chileanise' la Gran Minería, the big copper mines. Between 1958 and 1964 copper exports rose from $232 million to $363 million and tax revenues nearly doubled, but popular pressure demanded more; in 1969 the state took a 51% share of both Kennecott and Anaconda.

Construction of the Panamerican Highway began in the late 1960s. (BPR/USNA)

Nevertheless, other multinationals invested in Chile and prosperity spread; construction of the Panamerican Highway and Santiago's new airport and metro began. Overall, Frei's reforms raised hopes he could not meet, while doing enough to infuriate the upper classes, creating an increasingly polarised society.

The coup and dictatorship

The presidential election of 1970 was perhaps the most momentous in Chile's history, and even harder fought than that of 1964, with **Allende** leading the Unidad Popular (UP) alliance, offering probably the most radical platform ever set before the Chilean electorate. Allende won by 40,000 votes, triggering a fall in shares and a run on the banks. Allende himself was a sensible politician (although a terrible administrator, and harmed by his very public friendship with Fidel Castro), but there were extremists in his own Socialist Party who were well to the left of the communists and wanted revolutionary change at once. A CIA-backed plot to kidnap the army's commander-in-chief in order to provoke a coup was bungled, twice, and the only result was outrage, leading to Allende being easily confirmed as president by congress.

Agrarian reform and spontaneous land occupations gathered pace, and businesses were handed over to worker co-operatives; the copper industry was fully nationalised in 1971. Copper productivity plummeted (just as the price of copper fell) as lots of new staff were given jobs for political reasons, and strikes constantly broke out. Production also fell in other nationalised companies, and a drought hit agriculture. With prices frozen and wages rising the standard of living rose but so did inflation and the trade deficit ballooned; by 1973 the economy was close to self-inflicted collapse. After the 1973 congressional elections the UP controlled just a third of the senate and two-fifths of the congress. Small businesses and truck drivers went on strike, and the army attempted a mutiny in June 1973. Allende tried in vain to find a compromise, while the Supreme Court warned of the government's 'open and wilful contempt of judicial decisions'. The right wing was stockpiling guns, while the left-wing Movement of the Revolutionary Left (MIR) was staging bank robberies, and the CIA subsidised the opposition and trained the military in Panama. In August 1973 the army's commander-in-chief resigned and was replaced with the supposedly 'constitutionalist' **Augusto Pinochet** (see box, overleaf).

11 September

In 2001, the date of 11 September was appropriated as a day of infamy by the USA, but it already had a bad track record in Chile. Not only was this the date of the 1973 coup, but an earlier junta also took power on 11 September 1924.

It was a national holiday under Pinochet and was marked with demonstrations against his regime, especially on the avenue of the same name in Providencia, but the holiday has now been abolished. The build-up to the 30th anniversary of the coup (followed by the 30th anniversary of Neruda's death and the 15th anniversary of the 1988 plebiscite) was marked by proposals from both government and opposition to compensate the families of the 'disappeared'. In 2003, there was also a reunion on Dawson Island, off Tierra del Fuego, of survivors of the Allende ministers and others imprisoned there after the coup.

Allende and Pinochet

The twin faces of Chilean politics in the late 20th century were both born in Valparaíso and were both partly of Basque origin, but other than that they could not have been more different. **Salvador Allende Gossens** (1908-73) came

Staff from the presidential palace captured during Pinochet's 1973 military coup. (WHA/A)

from an upper-class liberal family of doctors and social reformers. He too became a doctor and was elected a deputy in 1937, becoming Health Minister from 1938 to 1942. He was elected to the senate in 1945 and was the socialist candidate for the presidency in 1952, 1958 and 1964, being kept from power by the left-wing vote that was always conveniently split. He was president of the senate from 1966 to 1969, and in 1970 he finally became the first Marxist to be democratically elected president of a Latin American country.

Augusto Pinochet (1915-2006) was a career army officer who became the army's chief of staff early in 1972 and its commander-in-chief on 23 August 1973. Having led Allende to believe that he was a strict 'constitutionalist' who would not challenge the government he then led the military overthrow on 11 September 1973 (see below).

The presidential palace was bombed, Allende committed suicide and Pinochet unleashed a reign of terror on the country. During his time in power up to 4,000 people were killed and 'disappeared', and the secret police co-ordinated a campaign to kill opponents of Latin American military regimes worldwide.

On **11 September 1973** the armed forces staged a **coup** that culminated in jets attacking La Moneda with rockets, and Allende killing himself with a Kalashnikov given to him by Castro. The golpe (coup) itself was no surprise, but the savagery that followed certainly was. Up to 95,000 suspected leftists were rounded up and 3000–4000 were killed, while many more went into exile. The new **DINA secret police** eliminated leftists internally and also set out (in co-operation with other military regimes) to kill possible leaders of a counter-coup abroad. DINA was replaced by the **CNI** (National Information Centre) in 1977, and the number of 'disappearances' dropped (although they continued until

1987). Although the military at first claimed they would be in power merely for a matter of months, a feeling of gloom soon settled over the country, the only effective resistance coming from the Roman Catholic Church. Immediately after the 1973 coup several churches created the Committee for Co-operation for Peace (COPACHI), to protest against disappearances and support the families of those who had disappeared. The government effectively closed down the committee in 1975, but the Roman Catholic Church took the lead and established the Vicariate of Solidarity (La Vicaría de la Solidaridad) which operated from 1976 to 1992. Entry to the headquarters was via Santiago's cathedral which created a fair degree of secrecy thus allowing the vicariate to support around 700,000 people and provide vital information to human rights campaigners abroad.

With copper prices low and oil prices high, the economy remained a mess; Pinochet opted for shock therapy, giving control to monetarists trained under Milton Friedman at the University of Chicago. Public spending was cut by a quarter and interest rates tripled, causing industrial production to fall by a quarter and unemployment to rise to nearly 20%. Tariffs were cut to a flat 10% and consumer imports and foreign debt boomed; from 1976 to 1981 the economy grew by 7% every year, and inflation fell to 9.5%. Then, in 1982, worldwide recession caused economic collapse; unemployment rose to 30% and riots and strikes forced Pinochet to return to a minimum wage and instigate a job creation programme. A more pragmatic finance minister brought stability and then growth; private pension funds (AFPs), now worth more than US$29 billion, proved the key to continuing investment, together with foreign companies exploiting massive new copper finds. With higher public spending, Chile came to resemble a modern Westernised nation, with impressive improvements in public health.

A new constitution creating a strong presidency, elected for eight-year terms, and with a third of the senate nominated rather than elected, was passed by a plebiscite in 1980; Pinochet became president and moved into the rebuilt Moneda palace. The old political parties, brought together by the new Archbishop of Santiago, became increasingly active, as did organised labour. Pinochet called another plebiscite in 1988, expecting to be granted another term as president but a brilliant campaign by the Concertación de Partidos por la Democracia (Coalition of Parties for Democracy), despite the arrest of 2,000 activists, won a 54% 'no' vote. Elections were held in December 1989, in which the Concertación's presidential candidate, Christian Democrat leader **Patricio Aylwin**, won 55% of the vote, and they also took control of the congress and senate.

The return to democracy

In March 1990 Aylwin took office, treading very carefully but nevertheless setting up a **Truth and Reconciliation Commission**, reporting in 1991 on over 2,000 deaths (see box opposite). Export-led growth allowed social spending to grow by a third from 1989 to 1993, and the proportion of the population living in poverty fell from two-fifths to a third.

In 1994, the Concertación's **Eduardo Frei Ruiz-Tagle** (son of the earlier Frei) became president, continuing with the same free-market policies, though with increased public spending to boost employment. Pinochet was arrested in 1998 in London on a Spanish warrant but allowed to return to Chile in 2000; he was indicted there but didn't come to trial before his death in 2006. This episode and the jailing of various generals and others for killings and abuses hugely weakened the army; thus it was felt safe for a socialist, the Blairite **Ricardo Lagos**, to stand as the Concertación candidate in 1999. His campaign was surprisingly complacent, only just beating a right-wing candidate. His government continued to use export-driven economic growth to reduce poverty. Housing and education were the major focuses, as well as contentious health and legal reforms; unemployment insurance was introduced, the death penalty was abolished for peacetime offences and divorce was allowed.

Lagos was succeeded in 2006 by another socialist, **Michelle Bachelet**, who was soon beset by student protests demanding changes to the astonishingly unequal education system created under Pinochet. Other problems included corruption scandals and the introduction of the capital's new integrated public transport system, an embarrassing fiasco. Bachelet herself remained popular, but the Concertación was clearly tired, while the opposition Alianza por Chile, consisting of the centre-right Renovación Nacional and the far-right Unión Demócratica Independiente (UDI), was growing stronger.

In 2010, the Alianza's **Sebastián Piñera** became president; although fairly moderate himself he depends on support from the UDI. Just before his inauguration, the sixth-largest **earthquake** ever recorded, at moment-magnitude 8.8, hit the Maule region. Good preparation meant that only 525 people died, but the earthquake and the tsunami it triggered caused massive damage. Then, in August 2010, 33 miners were trapped 625m underground near Copiapó, and rescued 69 days later after a massive international effort that held the world's attention throughout. Having been boosted by this, Piñera was then damaged by ongoing protests against education policy and the construction of massive dams in Patagonia. The economy, however, remains sound, with growth of about 5% in 2012.

Since the 19th century Chileans have seen themselves as 'the British of South America', this was partly due to the role of British mercenaries in liberating Chile and that of British merchants in developing it (sharing 'class-consciousness and bad teeth', as Isabel Allende puts it). The country's **self-image** is of a less Latin and more Nordic people than the rest of South America, with a strong government and a temperate climate.

Truth and Reconciliation Commission

The wall of memory at Santiago's Cementerio General (CB)

After the return to democracy in 1990, a Truth and Reconciliation Commission was set up and an apology and compensation were paid to the families of those murdered or disappeared under the Pinochet regime. In 1993, the names of 4,000 of the 'disappeared' were recorded on a wall of memory at Santiago's Cementerio General, and the commander of DINA, Manuel Contreras, and his deputy were jailed. However, the military blocked attempts to identify those responsible for abuses, until Pinochet's arrest in Britain in 1998 changed the dynamic; after that, the process of justice gradually gained momentum.

In 2004 a second commission took evidence from over 35,000 survivors of torture (and it was estimated that a similar number felt unable to come forward), and further compensation was authorised, at about twice the level of the state pension. Pinochet supporters largely ignored the process, insisting that the abuses were a communist myth, and pointing to a few cases where compensation had been paid to the family of someone who later turned up alive and abroad.

People and culture

In 2010 Chile had a **population** of approximately 17 million, of whom six million are in Santiago and the surrounding metropolitan region. In the far north and south almost everyone lives in major cities such as Arica and Punta Arenas; between Santiago and Puerto Montt far more people live in villages and isolated rural settlements. It's a largely urbanised society and virtually all homes have mains electricity and water. **Life expectancy** is over 77 years, and population growth has fallen to a near-First World level of 0.84%.

Minorities

At the time of the Spanish conquest the indigenous population of Chile was between 800,000 and 1.2 million, though this had shrunk by around 80% by the end of the 16th century due to European diseases rather than war and deliberate abuses. Now the majority of Chile's population is of *mestizo* (mixed Hispanic and indigenous) stock, although later immigrant groups such as the Germans and Croats have remained fairly homogenous.

There are around 15,000 **Aymara** on the northern altiplano, and around 3,000 **Rapanui**, the Polynesian inhabitants of Easter Island. More recently tiny groups such as the **Kolla** (in the mountain valleys of Chañaral province) and the **Diaguita** (in the east of Coquimbo region) have been officially recognised, as well as the 100-odd surviving **Kaweshkar** in the far south.

However, the **main minority**, about a million strong, are the **Mapuche** of south-central Chile, centred on Region IX (La Araucanía). Although

Mapuche women dressed for a traditional ceremony. (Tit/D)

their culture is now resurgent (there's now a Mapudungun version of Microsoft Windows), the Mapuche ('People of the Earth') have long been a marginalised minority in Chile, with low educational levels and incomes, and high unemployment. Only 88.6% of the Mapuche are literate, their income is half the national average, and their unemployment rate is at least double the average. In an overwhelmingly urban country, the Mapuche are unusual in being largely rural; even so, there are over 400,000 in Santiago, where they earn about twice as much as those in Araucanía.

Pehuenche people (POAG)

The Mapuche territory lay between Coquimbo and Chiloé, subdivided into groups including the Picunche ('People of the North'), north of the Biobío; the Lafkenche coastal fisher-gatherers; the Pehuenche hunter-gatherers in the Andean foothills and the Lakes District; the Huilliche ('People of the South') further south and in Chiloé; and the Cunco marine nomads who first lived on the coast south of Osorno but were driven further south by other groups to beyond the Éstero de Reloncaví. Interestingly, what is now known as the Mapuche culture developed largely after the arrival of the Spanish, when they began to breed horses and cattle, and developed their distinctive style of silver jewellery.

The **Pehuenche** are the people of the *Araucaria* (monkey-puzzle) tree (*pehuen* meaning the Araucaria nut, eaten raw, toasted or boiled, ground up to produce flour, or made into the sacred drink *chavid*). They are being driven off their ancestral lands by dams being built on the upper Biobío, but non-profit groups are launching some interesting ethno-tourism projects.

Problems are more intractable in the Mapuche heartland around Temuco, where it is the forestry industry that is driving the people from their lands. Under laws passed by the Pinochet regime, forestry companies were able to take over large tracts of land and, with a subsidy of up to 90% of the cost of tree-planting, began clearing native forest to plant Monterry pine and eucalyptus. Despite the end of the military regime, the rate of loss of native forest increased. The Mapuche claim that their lands are being taken in defiance of the 1881 agreement ending the so-called Pacification of Araucanía, and that the plantations are drying out and acidifying the land. In the 1990s they were driven to take direct action, staging brief occupations of forestry estates and destroying logging equipment; police repression, using 'anti-terrorism' laws introduced by the Pinochet regime, has led to further violence. The government hopes to buy around 120,000ha to return to the Mapuche, bringing their lands back to roughly the same area as in 1973, but the perception is that the government is still standing by big business and that democracy has nothing to offer the Mapuche. There is a chance of compromise, but conflict continues. In January 2012 arson attacks on plantations near Temuco led to the deaths of seven firefighters.

Culture

For a country of just 17 million, Chile doesn't do badly on the world cultural stage, with two Nobel Prizes for Literature as well as artists of the calibre of Claudio Arrau and Roberto Matta.

In the field of **classical music**, Claudio Arrau (1903–92) was one of the 20th century's greatest pianists, leaving a huge catalogue of recordings, especially of the Austro-German repertoire. The leading current pianist is Alfredo Perl. Chile also produces fine **opera** singers.

Popular music began with the great success of **La Nueva Canción** ('The New Song'), a leftist folk/protest movement that arose in the 1950s and helped propel Allende's Unidad Popular alliance to power. Its leading lights were Violeta Parra, Patricio Manns, Victor Jara and Rolando Alarcón. Parra killed herself after recording her *Ultimas Composiciones* ('Last Compositions') in 1967. Jara was tortured and killed by the army after the 1973 coup, and the others went into exile. They and groups such as Quilapayún, Illapu and Inti Illimani – also heavily influenced by folk music, especially from the Andes – lived and toured abroad, playing an important role in rallying opposition to Pinochet. They all returned to Chile in the late 1980s and are still active and very popular.

Chile's **national dance**, seen at every festival, is the *cueca*, derived from the Spanish *fandango*. It represents a cock stalking a hen, a *huaso* cornering a filly, or simply a couple flirting. You'll need two clean handkerchiefs if you want to try it yourself.

Chilean literature

Chilean literature begins with Alonso de Ercilla y Zúñiga, who arrived in Chile in 1557 and wrote an epic poem about the conflict with the Mapuche, *La Araucana*. In the 20th century there were many fine short story writers and three remarkable poets. **Gabriela Mistral** (1889–1957) was awarded the Nobel Prize for Literature in 1945; she's seen as a frumpy conservative figure but was in fact quite radical in her feminism and her fusion of native American and European cultures. **Vicente Huidobro** (1893–1948) spent most of his career in Paris; his key collection is *El Cuidadano del Olvido* ('The Citizen of Forgetfulness'). The youngest and most famous of the three was **Pablo Neruda** (1904–73), born Neftalí Ricardo Reyes Basoalto in Parral.

Portrait of Pablo Neruda (ss)

He led a remarkable double life, as a poet he won the Nobel in 1971, and as a diplomat/politician/activist he brought intellectuals fleeing the Spanish Civil War to Chile. He served as a Communist Party senator, and was Allende's ambassador to France. He lived life to the full and married three times; love was the subject of his early poems but his style and subject matter later evolved in many directions. The so-called **'Generation of '57'** (because they all came to public notice then) includes José Donoso (1924–66), a deliciously dark novelist, and Jorge Edwards (born 1931), winner of the Cervantes Prize (the leading award for Spanish-language literature) in 2000. Poets Gonzalo Rojas (1917–2011) and Nicanor Parra (born 1914; who calls himself an 'anti-poet' because his minimalist poems are so unlike those of Neruda) have also won the Cervantes Prize.

Perhaps the finest contemporary novelist is **Antonio Skármeta** (born 1940), who in 2003 won both the UNESCO Children's Literature Prize and Spain's Planeta Prize. He's best known for *Ardiente Paciencia*, filmed as *Il Postino*, which garnered one Oscar and four nominations.

A younger generation (born between 1949 and 1953) includes novelists Luis Sepulveda, Hernán Rivera Letelier, Marcela Serrano and the very acid Roberto Bolaño, who achieved worldwide success after his early death in 2003.

The oldest art in Chile is **rock art**, for example the outline paintings of hands near Villa Cerro Castillo. The Diaguita culture (see pages 5 and 18) in the 11th century produced ceramics beautifully painted with geometric decorations. The **first notable artist** in Chile was in fact a Peruvian, José Gil de Castro y Morales (c1786–1850), who spent the crucial period of 1814–22 in Chile, painting all the leading figures of the newly independent country. British and French artists came to teach and to record local life before Chilean artists really began to make an impact, and even these were mostly trained in Paris. They included Ramón Subercaseaux (1854–1936), Pedro Lira Rencorcet (1845–1912) and Alfredo Valenzuela Puelma (1856–1909), not to be confused with Alberto Valenzuela Llanos (1869–1925). Juan Francisco González (1853–1933) and Pablo Burchard (1875–1964) were more in the Fauvist or post-Impressionist vein.

It was students from the Universidad Católica's architecture school, notably Roberto Matta (1911–2002) and Nemesio Antúnez (1918–93), part of the surrealist set in Paris, who became **Chile's most successful artists**. Roberto Matta is the only Chilean artist to have achieved worldwide recognition; leaving Chile in 1933, he lived in Paris, the US and Italy, returning to Chile in 1970–72 to work on collective murals for the Allende government. A leading surrealist, though seen as shallow by some, his works feature strange predatory shapes.

In the 20th century Chile produced a remarkable generation of **sculptors**, and many of the best were women, notably Rebeca Matte Bello (1875–1929), Laura Rodig (1900–72), Marta Colvin (1917–95) and Lily Garafulic (born 1914).

Santiago has a very lively **drama scene**, with many alternative venues in Bellavista especially, and the excellent **Teatro a Mil Festival** in January.

Despite early experiments in Porvenir (Tierra del Fuego), **Chilean cinema** came of age only in the 1960s. The industry is far smaller than Argentina's, and most films on release are imports, especially Hollywood blockbusters.

The **national sport** is, of course, *fútbol* (football or soccer), although by Latin American standards Chile is not very good. The domestic season runs from March to December, with two championships, the Apertura and the Clausura (or Campeonato Oficial). In February and from June to August, the international club games of the Copa Libertadores are played. Tickets can be bought at the gate or at agencies such as Ticketmaster or Feria del Disco. Home internationals are played at Santiago's Estadio Victor Jara.

Huasos show their equestrian skills at a rodeo. (MiCM)

Equestrian sports

Horseracing is popular and in the countryside it is traditionally just two horses racing on a straight course known as a *carrera*. In the 1860s there was a move to a circular track or *hípico*, at least in the cities, due to an infatuation with the English way of doing things. **Rodeo** is the great sport of rural Chile, deriving from the round-ups of cattle for branding, sale or slaughter on the colonial *fundos*. The cattle were often almost wild and it was necessary to break a young cow or *novillo* by catching it between a horse and a wall and forcing it to the ground to be branded.

Although it no longer serves an agricultural purpose, the competitive display of equestrian skills is still very popular, and a rodeo is always the centrepiece of a town's fiesta, especially in the Central Valley, where almost every town has a *medialuna* or arena. This is a great opportunity to see *huasos* in their traditional finery of ponchos, wide-brimmed hats and silver spurs, and to enjoy a great family day out with plenty of traditional food and drink. The season starts with the *fiestas patriotas* in mid-September and climaxes with the national championships in Rancagua in March.

Stretching for over 4,200km (2,650 miles) from tropical deserts to sub-Antarctic bogs whipped by the gales of the 'roaring forties', Chile has perhaps the world's widest range of geographical and climatic settings. The far north is dominated by the Atacama Desert, but there's a chain of Andean volcanoes along the border and Aconcagua, the highest peak outside Asia, is only a few miles to the east. Nearer Santiago the climate is still dry but with irrigation plentiful, crops can be produced. South of the capital is Chile's agricultural heartland, the broad Central Valley, lined with vineyards and orchards, and with the Andes never far to the east. Perhaps the most beautiful part of the country is the Lakes District, dotted with lakes, volcanoes and cows, beyond which a colder climate and heavy rain produce near-jungle and huge icecaps. The far south is wild and windy, with little other than sheep and penguins flourishing, although spectacular peaks and wildlife make it popular with visitors.

Geography and climate

What is now Chile's **Norte Grande** began to emerge from the sea about 390 million years ago, the rest of the country gradually following; 52 million years ago the south sank as Antarctica began to separate from South America, and 35 million years ago the Andes rose, pushed up as the Nazca and Antarctic plates thrust below the South American plate. This process continues, at a rate of about 6cm per year – **Araucanía** and the **Lakes District** are dotted with volcanoes and are particularly susceptible to earthquakes. The Andes are very young in geological terms, but the heavily eroded remains of far older mountains survive as the coastal cordillera (meaning 'range').

Over the last seven million years there have been perhaps 40 glacial periods in the far south, the last a mere 18,000–15,000 years ago, when the **South Patagonian Icefield**, still huge today, was 300–700m thicker. About 11,000 years ago a warming climate caused a loss of grazing for the **megafauna**, such as the American horse, paleo-llama, mastodon and milodon, leading to their extinction soon after man appeared, having crossed the Bering land bridge from Asia to Alaska, and migrated southwards through the Americas.

The **Antarctic Circumpolar Current** or West Wind Drift (Deriva del Viento Oeste) circulates through the Southern Ocean clockwise around the world reaching the Chilean coast at the Taitao Peninsula, midway between Puerto Montt and Puerto Natales. It then splits, with the Cape Horn Current flowing south and the Humboldt Current flowing north to Peru. This huge body of cold water, among the richest in minerals of any oceanic water, produces the world's most fertile fishing grounds.

Global warming has seen sea temperatures rise 2°C in just 40 years and the **southern icefields** – now 14,000km² and 4,200km² in area – have already shrunk by 500km² in the last 50 years, and the rate of shrinkage is twice what it was between 1975 and 1995. However, the Patagonian glaciers are particularly dynamic, some receding at no less than 20m a year, and others actually growing rapidly at the moment.

Condor over a glacier flowing off the South Patagonian Icefield. (NP/S)

Over the country as a whole, the 'greenhouse effect' (*el*

efecto invernadero) is expected to reduce rain in the centre and south of Chile by 10–30% (reducing harvests), thereby increasing the effect of the *invierno boliviano* (Bolivian winter or the summer rains) and extending it southwards. The average temperatures are expected to increase by a degree or two over the next 40 years.

Slow and furious: Chile's earthquakes

The 20th century's strongest earthquake, and the strongest yet recorded, hit southern Chile on 21 May 1960. It rated 9.5 on the Moment Magnitude scale (8.6 on the Richter scale) and caused a tsunami with 30m waves that reached Easter Island, Hawaii, Japan and New Zealand which created almost as much damage as the earthquake itself. In the region of Valdivia the coast dropped 1.5m, 18,000 homes were destroyed and around 3,000 people died.

A succession of quakes estimated at magnitude 8.5 have hit Chile every century or so, notably in 1575 (Valdivia), 1647 (Santiago), 1730 (Valparaíso), 1751 (Concepción), 1868 (Arica) and 1922 (Vallenar), although those of 1906 in Valparaíso (magnitude 8.2), and 1939 in Chillán and 1985 in Santiago (both magnitude 7.8) did much more damage. On 27 February 2010 an 8.8 magnitude quake hit the Maule region, one of the ten most powerful ever recorded. Chile's second city, Concepción, was moved 1.2m upwards; Santiago was moved about 28cm to the southwest; Chile's area grew by 1.2km², and the day was shortened by about 1.26 microseconds due to a shift in the earth's axis.

Between 2008 and 2011 the Llaima, Chaitén, Hudson and Puyehue-Caulle volcanoes have all erupted, disrupting air travel and possibly affecting the weather around the southern hemisphere. The reason for all this violent activity is that the relatively small **Nazca Plate**, part of the bed of the Pacific Ocean, is being driven (subducted) under the **South American Plate**, forming the deep **Chile-Peru Trench**.

In 2002 scientists, with the aid of Global Positioning Systems, made a breakthrough in their understanding of earthquakes when it was realised that they were often triggered by hitherto undetectable 'slow earthquakes' (which can last years, or just minutes) far below the recognised stress zone (up to 300km below ground). At these depths rocks being forced against each other begin to soften and stick, building up stress which is then released by a sudden earthquake of the type we've always known. In the case of the 1960 Chilean earthquake, it's estimated that there was an interplate slip of up to 10m in the hour before the main quake, and that some of the drop in the coastline may in fact be attributable to the slow earthquake. As sensors are developed to monitor slow earthquakes, it will become easier to predict the big shocks.

Climate

In winter the climate is detestable and in the summer it is only a little better. I should think there are few parts of the world, within the temperate regions, where so much rain falls.

Charles Darwin (referring only to southern Chile)

Most of Chile, south of La Serena, has a **temperate climate** with four distinct seasons whose timing is the exact reverse of those in Europe. Spring is roughly November and December, summer January and February, autumn April and May, and winter June to October. Spring is usually wet, summer is clear and sunny with occasional rainy days, autumn is crisp and cool, and winter is cold and damp. As you travel south, summers become cooler and a persistent wind blows, but winters are never really cold anywhere, except in the far south, where wind and rain are more of an issue.

In **Patagonia** and **Tierra del Fuego**, summer temperatures reach a maximum of 25°C. The region is notorious for relentless **wind and rain**, and at higher altitudes it may **snow** even in January or February. One advantage, however, is that during this season the **days are very long** and it does not get dark until nearly midnight; in June, however, there are only five hours of light per day in Puerto Williams. Autumn (late February and March) is a good time to visit the Torres del Paine, as there will be less wind and rain than in the summer.

The **coastal lowlands** north of La Serena form **one of the driest regions** in the world; it's a typical 'cold-water-coast desert' with relatively cool weather and frequent morning fog all year round, even if it virtually never rains. Inland, at higher altitudes, it's warmer but there's more water, thanks to the Andes blocking the passage of clouds. Here there are the distinct rainy and dry seasons such as those found in Peru and Bolivia; the rainy season, known as the *invierno boliviano* (Bolivian winter) is from December to March (the southern hemisphere's spring and summer), and the driest months are from May to October.

Southern Chile lies directly beneath an **ozone hole** (or more accurately an area of ozone depletion), which has appeared over populated areas since the early 1990s. This leads to an increase in ultraviolet radiation from September to mid-October and coupled with altitude and dry, unpolluted air, an increase in the risk of cataracts and skin cancer. Chilean scientists say that the situation is improving, and over the next 30 to 50 years it should return to the level of the 1960s. However, after some warmer years in 2006 the ozone hole covered a

The Central Valley is where most of Chile's fruit, exported worldwide, is grown - including the grapes that produce world-class red wines. (FJLC/G)

Climatic zones

From north to south, the country falls into five sharply contrasting zones, plus the Pacific islands:

Gran Norte

The 'Great North' is a virtually rain-free desert with huge deposits of nitrate and copper and occasional oases.

Norte Chico

The 'Little North' is a semi-desert with irrigated valleys.

The Heartland

This is where most of Chile's population live. Huge farms and vineyards cover this very beautiful area, which includes the country's three largest cities: Santiago, Concepción and Valparaíso, as well as the Central Valley, Chile's most fertile land.

Araucanía and the Lakes District

Forests, mountains and lakes between Concepción and Puerto Montt.

Chile Austral or The Far South

Islands, forests, fiords, mountains and icefields between Puerto Montt and Cape Horn. This area is sparsely populated with some of the country's finest and wildest scenery.

Pacific islands

Juan Fernández and Rapa Nui (Easter Island). The former is only a couple of hours offshore while the latter is part of the Polynesian world and is exotic even to Chileans.

El Niño

El Niño (or, scientifically, ENSO, the El Niño Southern Oscillation) is the name of a sporadic weather system, usually occurring in the southern hemisphere's summer, when the cold waters which usually flow north from Antarctica up the west coast of South America are diverted to the west, and warm water reaches the Pacific Coast. Seas up to 8°C warmer than usual produce more evaporation, therefore more cloud and more rain. When you hear this has happened (roughly every four to seven years), you'd do well to reconsider plans to visit the north of Chile, which will generally be battered by heavy rains. The rest of the country will have a hot dry summer, with good weather in the south extending into April as a rule, followed by a bad winter.

However, in other areas El Niño can lead to the rains failing. Fires in the Brazilian state of Roraima blazed out of control when the 1998 wet season failed. Over 60,000km² were burned, including large areas of virgin Amazonian rainforest, home to the Yámana and other indigenous peoples.

The phenomenon was first identified on Christmas Eve 1982 (hence its name – 'El Niño' is 'The Christ Child'), but it's nothing new. In 1925 almost 2m of rain fell on Lima (compared with its usual 5cm) and in 1965, 27 million seabirds died when anchoveta fish stocks crashed. After three years of drought, the 1997–98 El Niño delivered three times the usual average rainfall to Chile, leaving 30 people dead.

El Niño is followed by its counterpart, known as **La Niña**, when there's next to no rain in the winter and spring. The results are that hydroelectric dams run low (with a risk of power cuts) and rafting is bad, although the weather is otherwise nice.

Relatively mild El Niño cycles in 2002-03 and 2006-07 were followed in 2011 by the strongest in 35 years, almost halving rainfall in some areas and leading to power cuts, very poor harvests, and terrible forest fires at the start of 2012.

record 29.6 million km² due to unusually cold air over Antarctica, close to the record 29.9 million km² of 2000; it also lasted longer than usual. Since then it has been shrinking, to 22.6 million km² in 2010, although it rose to 26 million km² in 2011.

There are similar but less widely reported problems in the north, as the air is clear and dry and the sun's rays take a shorter route through the atmosphere. Be sure to use high-factor suncream and good sunglasses, plus UV filters on cameras.

Habitats and vegetation

Given Chile's position, squeezed in-between the Andes to the east, the Pacific to the west, the arid puna (high-altitude desert covered with patchy grasslands) and Atacama to the north, and the icecaps to the south, it's not surprising that there are many endemic species – the Pacific islands are even more isolated, so have even more endemic species. Species diversity declines towards the south and in the temperate zone rodents have begun to dominate (including introduced hares and rabbits, see below). This is partly as a result of human action which has decimated their predators, notably the puma.

Man has transformed the landscape to a vast extent, with **alien species** now found in the most unlikely places. The puna in the north and the sub-Antarctic zones in the far south are relatively untouched, but everywhere in-between you'll find European herbs as well as broom, wild roses and brambles; large areas of Chile are covered with plantations of pine and eucalyptus. The first horses and cows were brought to the River Plate in 1537 and left to run free when the colony was abandoned. Their population exploded, and by 1580 horses had reached the Straits of Magellan.

Similarly, European hares and rabbits are now omnipresent, and form the core diet of many native predators such as pumas and foxes.

On the high puna of the far north, on the border with Bolivia, llamas and alpacas gather on *bofedales* or **bogs**, which also support wildfowl;

Vicuñas grazing on *bofedales*, Lauca National Park. (JB/A)

Get active in Chile

JOURNEY LATIN AMERICA

Chile is seemingly designed for lovers of the great outdoors, a place where the staggering scale of nature's attractions is often best appreciated on foot. But even aside from iconic trekking, such as the W-Circuit in Torres del Paine, you can climb volcanoes, go white-water rafting or horseriding in stunning scenery or even get your skiing fix in the middle of British summer. Adrenaline junkies should base themselves in Pucón for an array of adventure activities.

these seem natural but are in fact largely created by irrigation channels. The **scrub forests** of *queñoa* (*Polylepis tarapacana*), which may have covered the puna until the 16th century, are now found only in the damper gullies. This should not be confused with quinoa (*Chenopodium quinoa*), a very nutritious native grain still grown by the indigenous Aymara population. The *llareta* (*Laretia compacta*) forms a mound up to 1m high and 30m² in area, comprising many thousands of tiny rosette leaves; it can be several thousand years old, growing just 1.5mm per year. Beneath the surface is dead material which makes good fuel. At **lower levels** there's tussock grass with cacti (notably the wonderful candelabra cacti on the Arica–Putre Highway) and small Prosopis trees which once covered large areas of what is now desert.

Llareta plants at Cerro Rojo, Salar de Surire National Monument (I/FLPA)

South of the Atacama Desert, the Norte Chico and central Chile are dominated by sclerophyllous (waxy-leaved) shrubs adapted to conserve water, with some Nothofagus (see box, opposite) at higher altitudes in the coastal ranges. In most areas, hot, dry summers and cool, moist winters produce a Mediterranean (or Californian) scrub (*matorral*) with small cacti or low evergreen trees. In the damper southern part of this region, you'll find Maulino forest between 100 and 900m, dominated by hualo (*Nothofagus glauca*).

The **biologically richest zone** is the Selva Valdiviana, with **temperate rainforest** extending through Araucanía, the Lakes District and Aysén to the Northern Patagonian Icefield. At lower levels, predominantly south of Puerto Montt, this is mostly evergreen forest dominated by the tall *coihue* (*Nothofagus dombeyi*), and with a very dense understorey. A cypress, the *ciprés de las Guiatecas* (*Pilgerodendron uvifera*), thrives in the wettest areas.

There's little **low-level forest** left to the north of Puerto Montt, the higher levels are covered by a largely deciduous forest dominated by *lenga* (*Nothofagus pumilio*); in exposed sites the *ñirre* (*N. antarctica*) does well. High, dry areas are home to Andean *cypress* (*ciprés de la cordillera*; *Austrocedrus chilensis*), and to the *pehuen* or **monkey-puzzle tree** (*Araucaria araucana*). There used to be huge stands of the latter throughout southern Chile but it is now confined mostly to the Lakes District, Nahuelbuta and the upper Biobío, though you may see scattered examples elsewhere, with many planted in towns throughout Chile. Its seeds are eaten by the Mapuche, as well as by the *choroye* parakeet, and about 70 species of insects are found only on the monkey-puzzle. It lives for up to 3,000 years, and can grow to 50m in height and 3m in diameter. Further south is the similarly long-lived *alerce* (*Fitzroya cupressoides*), which seeds only when 200 years old and lives for up to 4,000 years – second only to the bristle-cone pine. Both of these have been heavily logged and now survive mainly in national parks.

The southern or false beeches

There are ten Chilean species of *Nothofagus*, a genus also found in Australia and New Zealand. Three are evergreen: *coihue* (or *coigüe*; *N. dombeyi*), *coihue de Magallanes* (or *guindo*; *N. betuloides*) and *coihue de Chiloé* (*N. nitida*). These normally grow at lower altitudes or in milder climates.

The deciduous species flourish at higher elevations, further south and in harsher conditions, sometimes in almost unrecognisable stunted forms. In good conditions they can be massive trees, up to 40m in height. In April and May their leaves turn gold, giving autumn hiking a special tinge. Of these, the most widespread are *lenga* (*N. pumilio*), a beautiful, tall tree with a copper tinge to its leaves; and *ñirre* (*N. antarctica*), a small, often stunted tree with characteristically crinkled and irregular leaves. Others are roble (or *roble pellin*; *N. obliqua*), *hualo* (*N. glauca*), *raulí* (*N. alpina*), *ruil* (*N. alessandri*) and *roble maulino* (*N. nervosa*). There's also *huala* (*N. leonii*), which is now thought to be a hybrid of roble and *roble maulino*.

Chusquea bamboos and shrubs such as *arrayán* form a dense understorey that's a great impediment to hiking. Many have red flowers to attract hummingbirds, such as the aptly named 'fire bush' (*notro* or *ciruelillo*; *Embothrium coccineum*), fuchsia (*chilco*; *Fuchsia magellanica*), and *ourisia* (*Ourisia alpina*), which grows in the spray of waterfalls.

Chile's **national flower** is the *copihue* (*Lapageria rosea*), a creeper with deep-pink, elongated, bell-shaped flowers which clings to trees and bushes. By the water you'll also see *nalca* (*Gunnera chilena*), similar to rhubarb (and equally edible), which produces huge umbrella-like leaves. *Canelo* (*Drimys winteri*), known as 'Winter's bark' (or 'cinnamon tree'), also likes water. Sacred to the Mapuche, it has branchlets with elongated, green leaves, and from November to September these have white flowers at their tips.

To the south of Lago General Carrera, the species-poor **Magellanic**

Eating wild

Devotees of wild food will be in seventh heaven here. Southern Chile has an abundance of edible berries, greenery, fungi, eggs and seafood, but of course you should not eat wild food until you have positively identified it. Here are a few of the tastier possibilities.

The barberry (*Berberis* spp) grows in great profusion in Patagonia and Tierra del Fuego – particularly the box-leafed barberry (*calafate*; *B. buxifolia*) and holly-leafed barberry (*michay*; *B. ilicifolia*) – and the spiney bushes bear fruit similar to the blackcurrant or blueberry. In Patagonia there is a saying '*Quien come el calafate vuelve por más*' or 'Whoever eats the *calafate* berry will come back for more', showing just how addictive this fruit can be. The berry ripens between January and March, and also happens to be a good laxative.

The wild strawberry or rainberry (*frambuesa silvestre* or *frutilla* (*de Magallanes*); *Rubus geoides*) grows across southern Chile, most abundantly in Tierra del Fuego. With its tiny lumps, it looks like a small raspberry but is the

Diddle-dee berries (SS/I/FLPA)

Forest is dominated by *coihue de Magallanes* (or *guindo*; *Nothofagus betuloides*), with *lenga* and *ñirre* also common. Except in the inaccessible parts of the Pacific Coast, the forest is generally open, with herbs and over 400 species of moss. In more open areas, there are many small, flowering trees and bushes, such as the various barberries (*calafate*; *Berberis* spp) with yellow flowers and edible berries.

In Chile's small enclaves on the eastern side of the Andes, there's a **semi-desert steppe** of *coirón grass* (*Stipa* and *Festuca* spp), thorny 'saltbush' *mata barrosa* (*Mulinum spinosum*) and *mata guanaco* (*Anartrophyllum desideratum*).

Finally, in the **sub-Antarctic** climes of the far south, little grows except for low bushes and bogs of sphagnum mosses. In fact one could argue that the most successful plant in this area is kelp, the fastest growing plant on Earth, which can grow to over 100m in length in sheltered waters.

source of the modern cultivated strawberry. The *lahueñe* (or *frutilla silvestre*; *Fragaria chiloensis*) also produces reddish edible fruit but don't confuse this with the nasty-tasting false strawberry (*frutilla del diablo*; *Gunnera magellanica*).

The Magellanic blackcurrant (*parrilla de Magallanes*; *Ribes magellanicum*) grows extensively in Tierra del Fuego and Patagonia, and is an effective laxative. The European blackberry (*mora*; *Rubus* spp) was introduced as hedging, and soon spread throughout the Lakes District, where there are masses of blackberries in March and April.

The diddle-dee berry (*sepisa*; *Empetrum rubrum*), found across Tierra del Fuego, is rather bland compared with the rainberry. There are two types: the black berries are sweeter than the bright red ones.

The *murtillas* (*Gaultheria caespitosa*, *G. pumila*, *Ugni molinae*) have small red berries that make delicious jam. If you visit the Lakes District around Easter, you will almost certainly see people selling them from buckets at the roadside.

Wild celery and cress grow in damp areas, sorrel in sunny meadows and mint everywhere. In damp areas of the Valdivian forest is the huge rhubarb-like *nalca*, which can be eaten in a similar way – peel with a knife and then stew the stalks.

The southern climate is ideal for fungi and there's an amazing variety. The giant puffballs that are common in Torres del Paine National Park are very tasty: fried, mixed with soup, or thinly sliced and dried in the sun, after which they are as crunchy and tasty as crisps. Similar yellow-orange fungi (*llao-llao* or *pan del indio*; *Cyttaria darwini*) are found in Tierra del Fuego. They were a mainstay of the indigenous people, but are pretty tasteless.

Land mammals

Seventy million years ago the only mammals in South America were ungulates, marsupials (including sabre-toothed 'cats') and palaeanodonta, such as the taxodont, a hippo-sized guinea pig. Sloths, anteaters and armadillos evolved, including now-extinct variants such as 6m-long ground sloths and the heavily armoured glyptodont. About 40 million years ago rodents and monkeys crossed the island chain from North America, and two to three million years ago the Panama land bridge was completed, allowing raccoon, deer, mastodon, weasel, tapir, skunk, peccary, dog and bear to move south from North America.

The camelids were among those moving from North America and are now extinct there. Of the four surviving in South America, the **guanaco** (*Lama guanicoe*) is the most successful, ranging from the high-altitude grasslands of the north to Tierra del Fuego. This slender, elegant animal lives in family groups with one male guarding from four to 12 females. The young, called *chulengos*, are often kept as pets but they tend to become vicious as they grow up. The guanaco's domesticated cousin is the **llama** (*L. glama*) of which 40,000 live on the Chilean puna, and many more to the north. Llamas serve as pack animals, provide meat for food, skin for shoes and faeces for fuel.

The **vicuña** (*Vicugna vicugna*) is superbly adapted for life on the arid puna. It's the only ungulate with continuously growing lower incisors (like rodents), allowing it to eat the hard *festuca* (bunchgrasses), and it has 14 million red corpuscles per $1mm^3$ of blood (man has five to six million) and a heart 50% larger than the average for similar-sized mammals, helping it to cope with the low oxygen levels at altitude. It produces the finest wool on earth, but only 500g of it a year, against the 3kg of its domesticated cousin the alpaca. Unfortunately, it's easier just to kill the vicuña rather than attempt to shear it, so the Chilean

Vicuña are now a common sight on the altiplano. (J/S)

population fell from perhaps two million at the time of the Conquest to around 1,000 in 1969; it has now recovered to perhaps 20,000, perhaps one-sixth of the world population, most in the Lauca National Park. The vicuña is now the rarest of the Americas' camelids, and is considered globally threatened. The **alpaca** (*L. paca*) is a domesticated camelid related to the vicuña. It produces a relatively rough wool and also meat; it won't work as a pack animal and breeds relatively slowly.

Three native species of **deer** can be found in Chile, although your chances of seeing them are low: the **pudú** (*Pudu pudu*) is a dwarf deer that lurks in the thickest parts of the Valdivian forest, and the **Patagonian huemul** (*Hippocamelus bisculus*) is a desperately endangered deer, which it was thought only survived on the higher and more remote slopes between Chillán and Paine. In 2003, however, more were found in the very remote Bernardo O'Higgins National Park. Despite this, the total population is still only about 2,000 (some in Argentina). To the north, the **Peruvian or northern huemul** (*taruca*; *H. antisensis*), discovered only in 1944, is now classified as a separate species. Like its northern counterpart and the pudú, it is considered globally threatened. **Red deer** (*Cervus elaphus*), a European species, was introduced to Argentina for sport hunting, and has spread into montane forests of Chile. Another European species, **fallow deer** (*Dama dama*) has also been introduced to private forests in Valdivia.

Large tracts of montane forest are being preserved as habitat for the desperately endangered southern or Patagonian huemul. (IW)

Darwin fox hiding in nalca plants. (KS/MP/FLPA)

There are three species of **fox** in Chile. The **South American grey fox** (*zorro chilla*; *Lycalopex griseus*) is common from La Serena south to the Magellan Straits, and has been introduced into Tierra del Fuego, encroaching on the Fuegian fox, one of the four subspecies of the rarer and much larger **culpeo** (*zorro culpeo* or *colorado*; *L. culpaeus*), which has reddish tints to its grey coat. There's also the **Darwin's fox** (*zorro chilote; L. fulvipes*), found in Chiloé and for some reason in Nahuelbuta. This critically endangered canid is endemic to Chile.

In addition to the **puma** (*Felis concolor*), found the length of the Andes and a sought-after resident of Torres del Paine National Park, five species of **wild cat** include **Geoffroy's cat** (*gato montes*; *Leopardus geoffroyi*) and the Chilean cat or **guiña** (*huiña* or *kodkod*; *L. guigna*).

There are two **otters**, the **marine otter** (*chungungo*; *Lutra felina*) and the **southern river otter** (*huillín*; *L. provocax*); despite its name, the latter also occurs amidst coastal rocks, so do not assume that every otter swimming in salty water is the former. Smaller predators in the same family (mustelids or weasels) include the **lesser grison** (*hurón*; *Galictis cuja*) and **Patagonian hog-nosed skunk** (*chingue* or *zorrino*; *Conepatus humboldtii*).

Rodents are plentiful. There are nine species of akodont (field mice and grass mice), two species of rice rat, and a score of mainly large-eared, High Andean mice. These include Bolivian pericote (*Auliscomys boliviensis*) which lives almost as high as any mammal in the Americas (up to 6,000m altitude). The **mountain vizcacha** (*chinchillón*; *Lagidium viscacia*) looks like a rabbit with a long tail but is related to the chinchilla; it can be seen in arid rocky areas from Patagonia to Peru, particularly at high altitude. Two rarer vizcachas, **Wolffsohn's mountain vizcacha** (*L. wolffsohni*) and **northern mountain vizcacha** (*L. peruanum*) occur, respectively, at the northern and southern extremities of the country.

Chile's two species of chinchilla are pint-sized versions of vizcachas: **short-tailed chinchilla** (*Chinchilla breivcauda*) occurs in montane northern Chile and is the more likely to be seen. There are also two species of chinchilla rat, agile rock climbers that ascend bushes when feeding.

Cavies are the ancestor of the domesticated guinea pig. In the High Andes, however, they are also a source of meat. Four species of cavy occur in Chile, the best-known being **montane guinea pig** (*Cavia tschudii*). There are four species of **tuco-tuco** (*Ctenomys*

Mountain vizcacha (JL)

spp), a stocky, burrowing rodent. The common name stems from the mammals' call, which echoes resoundingly from their underground lairs. Holes in the ground surrounded by recently excavated soil are a clear sign of tuco-tuco presence: wait near the hole and one should pop up. Octodonts are large-headed, rat-like, terrestrial or burrowing mammals in the Andes. Nine species include two that were unknown to scientists before the 21st century.

Armadillos have an armour of horny plates connected by flexible skin. Chile's three species are all noticeably hairy. The most widespread is **big hairy armadillo** (*Chaetophractus villosus*); it is sometimes kept as a pet.

There are four **marsupial** species in Chile: two species of **fat-tailed mouse opossum** (*yaca*; *Thylamys* spp.) in the north, with big eyes and enormous ears; the **long-nosed caenolestid** (*comadrejita trompuda*; *Rhyncolestes raphanurus*), one of the rarest mammals in Chile, discovered in the 1920s in the Valdivian forests; and the **monito del monte** (*Dromiciops australis*), also a nocturnal inhabitant of the Valdivian forests.

Better-known nocturnal mammals are **bats**. In Chile the species count just creeps into double figures. The ranges of several species, such as the Mexican free-tailed bat (*Tadarida brasiliensis*), extend into North America. Others, such as Chilean mouse-eared myotis (*Myotis chiloensis*), occur solely in Chile. The most infamous Chilean bat is the common vampire bat (*Desmodus rotundus*), which feasts on the blood of domestic animals, seals, seabirds and – occasionally – humans...

Finally, in addition to the deer mentioned above, a handful of mammals have been introduced to Chile, whether intentionally or inadvertently.

These include aquatic mammals such as **beaver** (*Castor canadensis*) and **coypu** (*Myocastor coypus*) and ground-dwelling creatures such as **European hare** (*Lepus europaeus*). **European wild boar** (*Sus scrofa*) is another interloper, having reached southern Chile from Argentina following deliberate introductions there. Some interlopers are welcome; others less so.

Marine mammals
The seal family

Seals evolved some 30 million years ago, and fall into two groups: Otariidae (eared seals), descended from a bear-like animal; and Phocidae (true seals), whose ancestors were otter-like carnivores. Seals are far more at home in the sea than on land, and have hind limbs that have evolved into tail-like appendages, forelimbs like flippers and a thick layer of insulating blubber. In Chile, you can see representatives of **sea lions**, **fur seals** and **elephant seals**, which share the same seasonal timetable. In spring the bulls arrive on shore to establish their territories; then the cows join them, and those that are pregnant give birth within days. Males guard their harem and mate with members shortly after they have given birth. As soon as the pups are independent, the adults return to the sea to feed, coming back to shore in the autumn again to moult before leaving until the following spring.

Numbers of South American fur seals are slowly increasing in Chile. (CR/MP/FLPA)

Fur seals

A long pointed snout distinguishes **South American fur seals** (*lobo fino austral* or *lobo marino de dos pelos*; *Arctocephalus australis*) from sea lions. A luxurious coat almost led to their extinction through hunting, but now they are fully protected and their numbers are increasing. Their fur is in two layers: a soft, dense undercoat, and an outer layer of coarse hair which traps bubbles of air to increase insulation. In fact, fur seals often seem to get too hot, and you will see them wave their flippers around in an attempt to cool off. **Juan Fernández fur seal**

(*A. philippii*) occurs on the archipelago of the same name; although scarce, its numbers are increasing through protection.

Sea lions

Southern sea lions (*lobo común* or *lobo marino de un pelo*; *Otaria byronia*), found the length of the Chilean coast, have small, clearly visible external ears. They are much more mobile on land than true seals, being able to rotate their rear flippers sideways to propel their bodies forward. A fully grown bull is over 2m long, and weighs up to half a tonne. His enormous neck is adorned with a shaggy mane, hence the name 'sea lion', which also refers to his roar. The elegant limpid-eyed females that make up his harem (up to 100 of them) weigh only a quarter as much, but then they expend less energy. Between coming ashore in December and leaving in March, the bull sea lion neither eats nor sleeps for more than a few minutes at a time. Guarding his harem and procreating is a full-time job.

Elephant seals

These massive animals can measure as much as 6m and weigh around three tonnes (the record is nearly 7m long and four tonnes). The bull **southern elephant seal** (*elefante marino del sur*; *Mirounga leonina*) has an elongated nose which can be inflated and extended, although the bulls only give this spectacular display when in rut. Normally they content themselves with letting it overhang their mouths as they roar a warning. The females are half the size of the bulls, with no 'trunk'. While stragglers can occur anywhere along the Chilean coast, the only breeding colony is at Ainsworth Bay on Tierra del Fuego.

Only male elephant seals have the trademark 'trunk'.
(YM & JE/MP/FLPA)

Cetaceans

Various **whales** can be seen from ships off the coast of Chile, in Patagonian fjords east of Punta Arenas and from shore at the northern end of the island of Chiloé, where they are attracted by the cold and food-rich Humboldt Current. Species found in different areas include blue (*Balaenoptera musculus*), fin (*B. physalus*), sei (*B. borealis*), dwarf minke (*B. acutorostrata*), humpback (Megaptera novaeangliae) and southern right whales (*Eubalena australis*). In 2003 a blue whale nursery was discovered in the Golfo Corcovado, to the southeast of Chiloé, and soon declared a Marine Protected Area. The island has become one of the best places to see Earth's largest creature, particularly between February and April.

Dolphins and porpoises are far more common and frequently seen. More than a dozen species occur in Chilean waters, the most attractive being Commerson's dolphin (*tonina overa*; *Cephalorhynchus commersoni*), usually found around Tierra del Fuego. Chilean dolphin (*delfín chileno*; *C. eutropia*), ranging from Concepción to Cape Horn, is little known. Peale's dolphin (*delfín austral*; *L. australis*) is also found around Tierra del Fuego. Dusky dolphin (*L. obscurus*) is relatively frequent along the entire Chilean coast.

Birds

Just shy of 500 species of birds have been recorded in Chile (5% of the world total), including ten or so endemics (although the total keeps reducing as species are discovered in neighbouring Argentina!). Unsurprisingly for a country that spans so many latitudes, there is not much overlap between the avifauna of the far north and that of the

Peruvian thick-knee (ID)

far south – and the majority of endemic species occur in central Chile. Perhaps the most wide-ranging species is also one of the most iconic: the **Andean condor** (*cóndor*; *Vultur gryphus*) which ranges the entire length of the country.

The **Pacific slope** of Peru and Chile, including Chile's two northern provinces, Arica and Parinacota, is considered a priority for biodiversity conservation due to its large number of species that are globally threatened and/or have a very restricted distribution. These include horned coot (*Fulica cornuta*), Chilean woodstar (*Eulidia yarrellii*), white-throated earthcreeper (*Upucerthia albigula*), Chilean seaside cinclodes (*Cinclodes nigrofumosus*) slender-billed finch (*Xenospingus concolor*) and Tamarugo conebill (*Conirostrum tamarugense*). Other interesting birds in the northern lowlands include two hummingbirds – Peruvian sheartail (*Thaumastura cora*) and oasis hummingbird (*Rhodopis vesper*) – and Peruvian thick-knee (*Burhinus superciliaris*). On the altiplano there are three species of flamingo, lesser rhea (*suri*; *Pterocnemia pennata*), giant coot (*Fulica gigantea*) and the remarkable and striking diademed sandpiper-plover (*Phegornis mitchellii*).

To the south, three birds that are omnipresent are the black-faced ibis (*bandúrria*; *Theristicus melanopis*), southern lapwing (*tero* or *queltehue*; *Vanellus chilensis*) and the chimango caracara (*tiuque*; *Milvago chimango*). These have benefited greatly from man's clearing of natural habitat to create agricultural land, but paradoxically the first two take great exception to human intruders – the honk of the ibis and the squawk of the lapwing will be the soundtrack to your visit. Other birds of southern Chile are quite unperturbed by humans, and it's easy to get within 5m of Magellanic woodpeckers (*carpintero negro* or *gigante*; *Campephilus magellanicus*) and Austral pygmy-owls (*chuncho*; *Glaucidium nanum*) in southern forests, and ringed kingfishers (*martín pescador*; *Ceryle torquata*) along rivers.

Waterfowl are also very noticeable. You may come across up to five species of geese (*cauquén*) – in fact sheldgeese, closer to Old World shelducks than to true geese, and almost inedible – and a variety of ducks (*patos*), some sporting plastic-looking blue bills. The Andean ruddy duck (*Oxyura jamaicensis*) is the most common. You'll probably see torrent ducks (*pato cortacorrientes*; *Merganetta armata*) by fast-flowing rivers. These attractive, small ducks feed on stonefly larvae, which can exist only in highly oxygenated water, hence their reckless dives into the rushing torrents. Equally distinctive are the two species of steamerduck, one flightless and frequenting salt water only (flightless steamerduck; *pato vapor* or *quetru no volador*; *Tachyeres*

The Magellanic woodpecker can be seen in the far south of Chile. (JL)

A flightless steamer duck flaps its wings in vain. (DD/FLPA)

pteneres), and the other capable of flight and inhabiting both fresh and salt water (flying steamerduck; *pato vapor volador*; *T. patachonicus*). When alarmed, they paddle across the water surface in a cloud of spray, in a manner recalling steamboats, from whence their name, but the myth (dating back to Darwin) that they beat their wings alternately has been disproved by filming. Black-necked swans (*cisne de cuello negro*; *Cygnus melancoryphus*) are also frequently seen, from sea level to over 4000m, often on the same freshwaters as coscoroba swan (*cisne coscoroba*; *Coscoroba coscoroba*) with its bubblegum-pink bill.

In the dense **Valdivian forest** there are quite a few birds that you're more likely to hear than see. Tapaculos are infamous for their skulking nature. The chucao tapaculo (*chucao*; *Scelorchilus rubecula*) is a ventriloquist with a musical chuckle from which it takes its name; if it calls from the right side of the path it is said to mean good luck, while a call from the left portends bad luck. The black-throated huet-huet (*hued-hued de sur*; *Pteroptochus albicollis*), almost black with a red cap and breast, also takes its name from its call. In more open forests in north-central Chile, these two species are replaced by moustached turca (*turca*; *P. megapodius*) and white-throated tapaculo (*tapaculo*; *S. albicollus*). The latter's local name refers to its habit of holding its long tail erect; Darwin translated the name as 'cover your posterior'.

Forest residents that are somewhat easier to see, fortunately, include striped woodpecker (*Picoides lignarius*) and Patagonian sierra-finch (*Phrygilus patagonicus*). The thorn-tailed rayadito (*rayadito*; *Aphrastura spinicauda*), a smart treecreeper-like bird with a spiky tail, often seen hanging upside-down, has particularly strong views about its territorial rights. On the woodland fringe and surrounding open areas look for the dove-sized giant hummingbird (*Patagona gigas*).

While **woodpeckers** are traditionally associated with trees, two of Chile's contingent primarily feed on the ground. Andean flicker (*Colaptes rupicola*) occurs in the rocky and grassy puna of the far north, whereas Chilean flicker (*C. pitius*) occurs in sparsely wooded country from central Chile southwards. **Small birds** that you're bound to notice are rufous-collared sparrow (*chincol*; *Zonotrichia capensis*), and in the south the Patagonian yellow-finch (*chirihue austral*; *Sicalis lebruni*) and black-chinned siskin (*jilguero*; *Carduelis barbatus*).

The most distinctive **large bird** is the flightless lesser rhea – one of the South American versions of Africa's ostrich. Ornithologists bicker over whether the lesser rhea is actually two species. Those in favour argue that Darwin's rhea (*ñandú*; *Pterocnemia pennata pennata*) of the Patagonian steppe differs from rheas found in the northern altiplano grasslands (puna rhea; *suri; P. pennata tarapacensis*). Female rheas are thoroughly liberated, playing no part in the raising of her offspring. The male mates with a variety of females, then assumes responsibility for brooding up to a score of eggs that the females lay in his nest, incubating them entirely unaided, and then caring for the lively chicks or *charitos*.

Also on the Patagonian steppe, the elegant crested tinamou (*martineta*; *Eudromia elegans*) scurries about wearing a ridiculous pointed hat, and is much prized as a game bird. The long-tailed meadowlark (*Sturnella loyca*), grey-hooded sierra-finch (*cometocino*; *Phrygilus gayi*) and dark-faced ground-tyrant (*dormilona tontita*; *Muscisaxicola macloviana*) are also common in such open habitats of the south.

The flightless lesser rhea tending his young. (JL)

The Austral parakeet is the world's southernmost parrot. (RL/S)

Even in Tierra del Fuego you will be able to see two members of bird families normally associated with tropical climates: **hummingbirds** (*picaflores*) and **parrots** (*loros*). The green-backed firecrown (*picaflor chico*; *Sephanoides galeritus*) is a hummingbird with brilliant green upperparts and an iridescent red crown, and the Austral parakeet (*cotorra austral* or *cachaña*; *Enicognathus ferrugineus*), the southernmost parrot in the world, is dark green with a reddish belly and tail. The globally threatened slender-billed parakeet (*choroy*; *E. leptorhynchus*) visits *Araucaria* forests during the fruiting season, using its specially adapted beak to probe for seeds in monkey-puzzle trees.

Birds of prey are very common, the largest being the black-chested buzzard-eagle (*águila mora*; *Geranoetus melanoleucus*), which feeds on rodents and small birds. The most commonly seen raptors are southern caracara (*carancho*; *Caracara plancus*), chimango caracara and variable hawk (*aguilucho*; *Buteo polysoma*). More familiar species are osprey (*aguila pescadora*; *Pandion haliaetus*) which is largely coastal in Chile and peregrine falcon (*halcón peregrino*; *Falco peregrinus*), which has recently colonised some cities.

The caracaras are carrion-eaters, as are turkey vultures (*jote*; *Cathartes aura*), and both often hang around sheep stations and fishing ports. But the most impressive carrion eater is the huge Andean condor, which is quite common in the southern Andes all the way to Cape Horn, and may come to look at hikers (so keep moving...). It can be recognised in flight by its long, evenly broad wings and the 'fingering' of the primary wing feathers. Adults are further marked by their white, fluffy neck ruff and white upperside to the wings.

The Andean condor has the largest wing area of any bird (almost 2m²), but the 3m span is surpassed by one of Chile's **seabirds** – the **northern royal albatross** (*albatros real*; *Diomedea sanfordi*), which has the joint-longest wing span of all. These marvellous birds are occasionally seen near the shore during their wanderings in the southern seas: joining a whalewatching trip off central Chile is your best bet to see one.

You are more likely to see black-browed albatross (*albatros de ceja negra*; *Thalassarche melanophrys*), which is commonly spotted in the channels around Tierra del Fuego as well as in the Humboldt Current. More widely, Chile is marvellous for seabirds – from the tiny Wilson's storm-petrel (*Oceanites oceanicus*) to the stocky Hall's giant petrel (*Macronectes halli*) – but most will require you to take an offshore boat trip to see them. From the shore, you should look instead for kelp gull (*Larus dominicanus*), South American tern (*Sterna hirundinacea*) and Chilean skua (*Stercorarius chilensis*). The latter, resembling a large brown gull, are opportunists and scavengers, ever ready to grab an egg or young bird. In northern Chile, look for Peruvian pelican (*pelícano*; *Pelecanus thagus*) while five species of cormorant (*Phalacrocorax* spp.) inhabit various stretches of Chile's coast.

The **penguin** (*pingüino*) commonly found around the southern coast is Magellanic penguin (*Spheniscus magellanicus*). It nests in burrows near the shore and when alarmed runs on all fours, using its flippers as an extra pair of legs, and achieving remarkable speeds with no apparent concern for physical safety. The very similar Humboldt penguin (*S. humboldtii*), greatly reduced in numbers, overlaps with the Magellanic penguin in the region of Chiloé, and replaces it further north. Both of these 'jackass' penguins are globally threatened as are southern rockhopper penguin (*Eudyptes chrysocome*) and macaroni penguin (*E. chrysolophus*), which both breed on islands off Tierra del Fuego. Rarer in Chile, but commoner in global terms is the king penguin (*Aptenodytes patagonica*), which nests in small numbers on Tierra del Fuego.

Magellanic penguins can be confused with Humboldt penguins, which have a pink base to the bill and only one black stripe at the top of the chest. (ER/S)

Reptiles and amphibians

About 90 species of reptile occur in Chile. By far the largest grouping are the 20-plus **neotropical ground lizards** in the genus *Liolaemus*. Most have a body length of 5–8cm, with the tail the same length again. They tend to be cryptically patterned; most are covered in coarse scales but some are spiny. All bar two are terrestrial; painted tree lizard (*L. pictus*) and thin tree lizard (*L. tenuis*) are both strikingly coloured tree-climbers. Species' ranges tend to be relatively small and to be complemented by a degree of habitat specialisation. Only one reaches Tierra del Fuego – Magellanic lizard (*L. magellanicus*) is the most southerly reptile in the world.

In **northern Chile**, there are also half-a-dozen lava or desert lizards (*Microlophus* or *Tropidurus* spp.) and four dragon lizards (*Phrynosaura* spp.). Two rare species of mountain lizard (*Phymaturus* spp.) occur in the Andes and Patagonia. There are also three grumblers (*Diplolaemus* spp.), four anoles (*Pristidactylus* spp.), one whiptail (Chilean iguana; *Callopsites maculatus*) and a handful of geckos (*Homonota*, *Phyllodactylus* and *Lepidodactylus* spp.) in the arid north.

Painted tree lizards are tree-climbers. (JL)

There are only six **snakes** (excluding the sea snake of Easter Island), all in northern Chile. Although some may be long, almost all are slender and small-mouthed and do not pose a serious threat to humans. You'd pretty much have to stick a finger into a snake's mouth for the fangs to connect. The largest snake is **long-tailed** green racer (*Philodryas chamissonis*), which can reach 1.8m long. This is a graceful, active serpent that moves rapidly through bushes and trees.

There are 60 or so species of **amphibians**, all **frogs** (*sapo*) **or toads** (*rana*). Many are rare and/or restricted to a single locality. The population of some species is declining rapidly, as is the case with many amphibians worldwide. There are five species of true toad (*Chaunus* spp.), four of which are globally threatened. A group of four 'false toads' (*Telmatobufo* spp.) includes sapo hermoso (*T. venustus*) which is so rare that its rediscovery in 1999 followed a century-long disappearing act. Chile's largest toad is the helmeted water toad (*rana chileno gigante*;

Caudiverbera caudiverbera). At 25cm in length, females are twice the size of males. Its size renders it vulnerable to humans catching it for food; to save wild populations, there has been some attempt at local 'raniculture'.

Frogs fall into several groupings. The trio of four-eyed frogs (*sapito de cuatro ojos*; *Pleurodema* spp.) derive their name from prominent glands on the hips. A quartet of wood frogs (*Batrachyla* spp.) mostly inhabit cool rainforests, from which males chorus during the southern autumn. Five species of water frog (*Telmatobius* spp.) inhabit streams in northern Chile, mostly in the Andes. Seven species of ground frog (*Eupsophyus* spp.) live in damp terrain in *Nothofagus* forest. There is a single emerald forest frog (*Hylorina sylvatica*), arguably the most attractive of Chilean amphibians, and five types of spiny-chest frog (*Alsodes* spp.).

The most interesting of all Chilean amphibians is the tiny Darwin's frog (*ranita de Darwin*; *Rhinoderma darwinii*), discovered by the great man in the Valdivian forest. The male guards the eggs, and when they begin to move he appears to eat them. In fact they're safely held in his vocal sac, which extends right down the underside of his body, and are later born through his mouth. Its scientific name means 'rhinocerus-nosed' and refers to the protrusion on the forehead which gives this frog a triangular-headed appearance.

Although four species of **turtle** (*tortuga*) occur in Chile, three do so rarely and, even then, usually far offshore. The exception is green turtle (*Chledonia mydas*) which congregates in summer at the mouth of the Río Loa in northern Chile. There are no breeding colonies in the country.

Darwin's frog (seen here attending its young on the forest floor) is camouflaged to blend with leaves. (MF & PF/MP/FLPA)

Invertebrates

There's a considerable variety of invertebrates in Chile but none that causes much harm. The **brown recluse spider** (*araña de rincón*; *Loxosceles laeta*) has a mildly toxic bite, while the **Chilean rose tarantula** (*araña peluda*; *Gramostola rosea*) is the most common pet spider, the size of a newly hatched chick. There are also some spectacular **stag beetles**, and the much less obvious stick insects. In the Lakes District you should watch out for biting **horseflies** (*tabanos*) and **blackflies** (*jején* or *petro*).

More likely to cause excitement than irritation are Chile's **butterflies** and, to a lesser extent, **moths**. More than 160 species of butterfly occur in the country, spanning the spectrums of size and colour. At the smaller and dowdier end of the scale are butterflies such as the funereal duskywing (*Erynnis funeralis*), a sombre-looking creature just 3cm in length. This is one member among 20 in the spread-wing and grass skipper subfamilies. There is just one swallowtail, Aristolochia swallowtail (*Battus polydamas*), but it is relatively common from the Atacama Desert to Biobío.

There are more than 30 species of whites, sulphurs and yellows (family Pieridae), a handful of hairstreaks and ten or so blues (both in the family Lycaenidae). Several of the blues are grouped together as 'Nabokov's blues', in honour of the Russian-American author of *Lolita*,

Vladimir Nabokov, a dedicated lepidopterist who studied this group of Chilean butterflies. The 17 or so satyrs (subfamily Satyrinae) are largely drab coloured, but the half-dozen fritillaries brightly garbed. Perhaps the most instantly recognisable Chilean butterfly is the South American monarch (*monarcha*; *Danaus erippus*), which closely resembles its well-known North American sister species.

Although most moths are small dowdy creatures, some of Chile's contingent are large and striking. Cases in point are sphinx moths (*Hyles annei*), often mistaken for hummingbirds as they hover by flowers while feeding. The Saturniidae family includes spectacular day-flying species such as venusta moth (*Cercophana venusta*) and four-eyed moth (*Polythysana rubrescens*). Look for them on stone walls and trees.

Chilean rose tarantula (AS-B/S)

Montane araucaria forest – the natural setting for the monkey-puzzle tree. (TDR/MP/FLPA)

The forestry industry

Forestry protection has a long history in Chile: the Araucaria (monkey-puzzle tree) has been protected since the 18th century, originally in order to ensure a supply of timber for the Spanish navy. Nevertheless, other trees have been mercilessly logged and burned.

Forestry is booming in southern Chile, with the industry producing 8% of Chile's exports and 2% of employment (130,000 direct jobs). Of an original 45 million hectares of native forest, at least 30 million have been lost. A survey in 1998 put the total of native forest at just over 13.4 million hectares (17.8% of the national area, and 76.5% of the total forested area). A law to protect native forest was introduced in congress in 1992 and finally passed, in a watered-down form, in 2007, due to obstruction by logging interests.

Plantations of exotic species now cover 2.5 million hectares, thanks to generous subsidies. About 90% of this is Monterrey pine (*pino insigne; Pinus radiata*), which was introduced in the 1880s and grows faster here than anywhere else (in the Lakes it's ready for harvesting in 15 years). There's also eucalyptus and Oregon pine, and CONAF is now planning to plant large areas of poplars further to the north.

This area of plantations is home to many Mapuche, whose villages have become islands in exotic forests of pine which acidifies and dries the land; this is the poorest area in Chile, with 36% living in poverty. Not surprisingly, there is increasing agitation for indigenous land rights, fuelled not just by plantation forestry but also by dam-building on the Biobío.

Forest fires are an increasing problem, mostly in the pine plantations of Araucanía, where arson by Mapuche land-rights activists is blamed. However, some of it is due to arson by land-owners themselves who would rather sell fire-damaged alerce trees (worth US$20,000 each) than have protected trees growing on their land.

3 Planning a Trip

Planning a trip to Chile need not be complicated. Quite apart from the simplicity of its north-south alignment ('Shall I turn left or right at Santiago?'), there's a wide range of local and international companies that offer tours here. This guide includes recommendations from some of the main operators, but a quick search online will find plenty of packages that range from minibus trips to chauffeur-driven luxury tours. There are, however, various factors to be taken into account when planning your trip - from the best time of year to visit, whether to fly or drive the length of the country, whether to sleep in a boutique guesthouse, an all-inclusive resort or a handy hotel - and this chapter runs through these and similar questions. See also our list of Chile's 12 top attractions, showcasing the country's varied natural and cultural highlights.

When to visit

Northern Chile is best visited in **winter** (May to October) since the summer rains (*invierno boliviano*) wash out roads and trails. The **southern summer** (December to March) is the best time for almost all **outdoor activities** (other than skiing). The best times to visit the **rest of the country** are from November to April. In high summer (January and February) it can be a bit too crowded, but school begins at the beginning of March, so you will then have many places completely to yourself. The reverse applies in **Santiago**, which empties in January and February, when great bargains are available at hotels. In April, tourist facilities start to shut down and public transport is reduced, but in July and August everything springs to life again in the Lakes District for the winter sports season. However, some of the passes to Argentina are closed by snow in winter, and you may find other minor roads impassable, too.

Birdwatchers will want to catch the **spring and autumn migrations**, with birds following the Pacific Coast, often all the way to or from North America and even the Arctic.

Public holidays

The main public holidays or **Fiestas Patriotas**, combine **Independence Day** on 18 September and **Army Day** on 19 September, as well as an unofficial 'bridge' to the nearest weekend, allowing most people to take the best part of a week off. It's a bit early in the season for most foreign visitors, but is a good start to the spring for Chileans. **Easter Week** (Semana Santa) is also a big event, with many people taking their last

Statues and festivals

RAINBOW TOURS

The iconic *moai* statues of Rapa Nui are universally recognised. The island's unique blend of Latin and Polynesian culture alone makes this a fascinating trip, but it's worth visiting during one of the festivals, Tapati (early February) being the most important. You will see traditional sporting contests and  processions with music and dance. Every trip should include a visit to the quarry (Rano Raraku) where the *moai* were originally carved. See page 266.

Average maxima and minima

For **Santiago**, average maxima and minima in January are 29°C and 12°C, in April 23°C and 7°C, in July 15°C and 3°C and in October 22°C and 7°C; average precipitation for the same months is 3mm, 13mm, 76mm and 15mm, with humidity of 38%, 46%, 60% and 50%.

In **Pucón** the maxima and minima in January are 23°C and 8°C, in April 16°C and 3°C, in July 9°C and 1°C and in October 16°C and 3°C. Average precipitation for the same months is 68mm, 151mm, 395mm and 144mm.

In **San Pedro de Atacama** the maxima and minima in January are 24°C and 17°C, in April 21°C and 14°C, in July 17°C and 12°C and in October 19°C and 14°C with average precipitation of 1mm, 4mm and 0 in July and October.

Finally, in **Punta Arenas** a **heatwave** every five or six years can push temperatures up to about 25°C, but even here it has reached 29.9°C.

break of the summer, and hotel reservations are advisable. **Christmas** is less important in religious terms than Easter, with supermarkets open from mid-afternoon – there's more of a shut-down on **New Year's Day**. Schools are on holiday from mid-December until the start of March, and for two weeks in July.

The festival of La Tirana in the Norte Grande peaks on the night of 15 July. (Tif/D)

Itinerary planning

Chile's geography lends itself to a longitudinal journey from north to south, or vice-versa. However, as you're likely to arrive in **Santiago**, in the middle, you may have to split the trip into two halves, or if constrained by time go only north or south. The **north** is pretty arid, and if you don't like desert you probably shouldn't bother, unless to simply visit the beach resorts. The **south** is far lusher, with a variety of lakes, volcanoes and activities such as world-class white-water rafting; however, if you want to reach the far south, you have to decide whether to fly, take a three-day voyage by ship, or pass through Argentina.

Flying out to **Easter Island** (Rapa Nui) is usually available as an extension, rather than as an integral part of tours of Chile. Two or three nights here will be enough for most people, but you could stay longer to enjoy some surfing, or the Tapati Festival in early February. You should be sure to make time for a side trip from Santiago to Valparaíso, and maybe for a wine tour starting from Santiago or Valparaíso.

It's worth noting that Patagonian trips often combine Chile and Argentina, with flights down from Santiago or Buenos Aires.

It's easy and affordable to take **internal flights** (although you almost always have to change planes in Santiago), so it's quite possible to visit the Atacama then head south to the lakes and glaciers, but if travelling by road you'd want more than two weeks to do this comfortably. See *Chapter 4*, page 95 for further information on internal flights.

Various companies offer **overland tours** of Chile, including local firm Pachamama By Bus (see opposite for contact details), whose trips – with northern and southern circuits operating at least weekly –

Self-drive holidays

Although this book is aimed primarily at people planning organised tours, Chile is also very well suited to self-drive holidays – distances are great, especially in northern Chile, but roads and infrastructure are generally excellent. Navigation is easy once you're out of Santiago. Many tour companies will set up a full package for you, providing a car as well as hotel and other bookings. You'll find the usual car rental agencies in all major cities and airports, plus other tourist centres. See *Chapter 4*, pages 94–5 for further information.

(EP/S)

operate on a hop-on hop-off basis. This means that rather than having to stick with one group throughout or indeed do the whole circuit, it's possible to take back roads and loop into national parks rather than just belting down the main roads. Other companies offer overland tours in converted trucks, on international routes such as Lima–Santiago or Santiago–Buenos Aires–Rio de Janeiro, but these are fixed groups of young backpackers, with none of the flexibility offered by Pachamama by Bus (ⓦ www.pachamamabybus.com).

Cruising has become a very popular way of sampling Chile (as nowhere is very far from a port), including voyages around Cape Horn and even to the Antarctic Peninsula. The main port for beginning or ending cruises is Valparaíso (about 90 minutes from Santiago's international airport); Puerto Montt and Punta Arenas are also busy, with Arica, Iquique, Antofagasta, Coquimbo, Talcahuano, Valdivia, Ancud, Castro and Puerto Chacabuco also seeing some ships. Easter Island is an obvious call for South Pacific cruises, although you spend a lot of time at sea getting there. A full range of excursions is provided by the cruise lines, with wine tours a favoured add-on before starting or after finishing a cruise at Valparaíso.

Accommodation

Accommodation, like transport, has more in common with Europe or North America than with the rest of Latin America, so that there are plenty of attractive high-quality hotels, and even the cheapest family homestays are clean and decent.

You will come across a bewildering variety of names to describe places to sleep: a top-end place is usually a *hotel*, although this term can be used across the price range. A *hostal* is also generally of good quality (and not to be confused with a *hostel*, which is a backpacker place with shared dorms).

Most hotels have cable TV in the room, and Wi-Fi; a frigobar (minibar or refrigerator) and safebox are less common. If there's a basket by the toilet, be sure to leave used paper there rather than flushing it, which will allegedly block the system and cause a massive methane explosion.

Special-interest holidays

In addition to general cultural/scenic tours, operators also offer tours focusing on a variety of activities: birdwatching, botanising and other wildlife viewing; rafting, kayaking, hiking, climbing, cycling, horseriding, skiing and other outdoor activities; wine tasting, and even astronomy, which is booming due to Chile's clear skies. These can be stand-alone tours or extensions to other tours or cruises. Operators can also book you onto local cruises through the southern fiords, of which the most luxurious includes a visit to Cape Horn (see page 253).

Booking

Trips can be booked through your home travel agency – which will be bonded and will probably be more flexible and have access to cheaper flights – or through a local operator on the ground in Chile, which might have more local knowledge and contacts. A Chilean operator will, however, not be covered by any British or American bonding scheme, and you will probably want to buy additional travel insurance for the unlikely possibility of being left stranded somewhere.

See pages 60–1 for details of our recommended tour operators.

Horseriders exploring Patagonia. (SS)

Wine-tasting holidays

The Viña Mar winery, Casablanca (VM)

Vineyards are spread over 500km, from north of Santiago to Chillán. From north to south the main districts are: the Aconcagua Valley (north of San Felipe), the Casablanca Valley (northwest of Santiago, known for fine whites), the Maipo Valley (southwest of Santiago), the Rapel Valley (Rancagua to San Fernando), Colchagua (around Santa Cruz), the Curicó Valley (also known as Lontué, from Curicó to Talca), and the Maule Valley (south of Talca). Most of the more prestigious houses (Concha y Toro, Cousiño-Macul, Santa Carolina, Undurraga) are based in Santiago and just south in the Maipo Valley, but the bulk of their grapes are actually grown to the south in the Rapel, Curicó and Maule areas.

Nearly all those near Santiago can easily be visited, and it's worth seeing their 19th-century French-designed parks and cellars made of *calicanto* (or *cal y canto*, stone cemented with lime and egg white). Some of those to the south have got together to create a **Ruta del Vino** in each area, with an office to organise tours. Independent drop-in tastings are relatively rare, though most vineyards have a salesroom. See pages 176–83, 183–4 and 184–5 for details of the Colchagua, Curicó and Maule Rutas del Vino. Harvest time is February and March, which is the best time to visit.

Since the early 1990s the Casablanca Valley, west of Santiago, has become Chile's premier area for white wines; in addition to local houses, the big companies such as Concha y Toro are also expanding into the area.

Wine Travel Chile (Ⓦ www.winetravelchile.com) will lay on tours for a day, a week, or however long you wish.

See the industry's website for further information: Ⓦ www.winesofchile.org. See pages 90–1 for Chilean wine varieties.

Recommended tour operators

Aysén Patagonia

ⓣ +56 (0)672 33302 ⓔ rosario@aisen.cl
ⓦ www.queulatlodge.com

Aysén offers accommodation (Fiordo Queulat Ecolodge) and activities in Queulat Park: hikes in the forest (Hanging Glacier, Morrena, waterfall, Enchanted Forest), trips to Poyeguapi Island, sea-life observation (austral dolphins and sea lions), sea kayaks, and birdwatching (chucao and huethuet). Also airport transfers and tailor-made programmes in the region.

Huella Andina Expeditions

ⓣ +56 (0)9 754 87967
ⓔ info@huellandina.com ⓦ www.huellandina.com

Huella Andina is the result of more than a decade of exploration in the Andes. They are a family business offering professional service in adventure tourism. José Miguel and Matías operate several trekking journeys in nearby national parks and wilderness areas, guiding the major volcanoes of southern Chile, such as Osorno and Calbuco.

Journey Latin America

ⓣ +44 (0)20 8622 8376 ⓔ tours@journeylatin
america.co.uk ⓦ www.journeylatinamerica.co.uk

Journey Latin America are the UK's number one specialists in travel to Central and South America. Having dealt exclusively with Latin America for well over 30 years, they offer practical advice based on personal experience. For the journey of a lifetime, let them show you the Latin America they know and love.

Rainbow Tours

ⓣ +44 (0)207 666 1272
ⓔ info@rainbowtours.co.uk ⓦ www.rainbowtours.co.uk

RAINBOW TOURS

Rainbow Tours' award-winning Latin America specialists have been providing expert advice and tailor-made tours to the region for over a decade. Focusing on comfortable adventure, Rainbow's trips in Chile are aimed at enabling visitors to discover the very best of the region's natural wonders with opportunities to soak up the local culture.

Senderos Nativos

☏ +56 (0)2 8973761 Ⓔ info@senderosnativos.com
Ⓦ www.senderosnativos.com

Senderos Nativos is a local tour operator specialised in tailor-made trips to Chile. Founded and run by qualified and experienced tourism professionals who know the region deeply and care about each detail, they invite you to discover and explore dazzling scenery, encouraging interaction with nature and the local culture.

SouthAmerica.travel

☏ +44 (0)20 3026 0287 (UK); +1 800 747 4540 (US)
Ⓔ chile@SouthAmerica.travel Ⓦ www.SouthAmerica.travel

SouthAmerica.travel is the 4* and 5* South America specialist to Chile, Peru, Brazil, Ecuador, Argentina, Bolivia, Paraguay, Uruguay, and Colombia. They've been sharing their passion for South America since 1999 through offices in Seattle, Buenos Aires, Lima, Rio de Janeiro, and Stuttgart. Call from anywhere in the world! See their website for local phone numbers in 44 countries.

travelArt Chile

☏ +56 (0)2 2378 3440
Ⓔ info@travelart.com Ⓦ www.travelart.com

Since 1994, travelArt has offered high-quality tailor-made tours throughout Chile and Patagonia, including cultural excursions, active travel, wine tours, wellness holidays, cruises and much more. Our creativity, local contacts and experienced bilingual guides make travelArt your perfect partner for a unique travel experience at the 'End of the World'.

Vidandes Tour Operator

☏ +56 (0)2853 4419
Ⓔ info@vidandes.com Ⓦ www.vidandes.com

For the honeymoon of your dreams in the most exotic and wonderful landscapes, such as Easter Island, Atacama Desert and Patagonia, Vidandes offers you a personalised service; each of their programmes is created according to their clients' specific needs. Gay-friendly. German also spoken.

Your itinerary: 12 top attractions

An important first step in planning an itinerary to any country is deciding which sights you absolutely *must* visit, and Chile is no exception, even though its long, thin nature does make it easier to choose a route than in many other countries. Having identified those must-sees, you might want to tailor the rest of your itinerary around them, focusing on places of interest that don't require too much of a detour. In order to help you with this decision, a brief synopsis of my 12 top attractions in Chile is listed below, divided thematically into culture, landscapes and activities. You'll also need to consider the balance between spending time in major cities, the exceptional range of stunning scenery, sports and other outdoor activities, and wine tourism.

Culture

Santiago
Chile's capital has all the facilities of any modern city but has also preserved its historic core, and the pace of life is less frenetic than in most Latin American capitals.

(I/S)

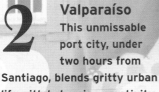

2 Valparaíso

This unmissable port city, under two hours from Santiago, blends gritty urban life with bohemian creativity in an unforgettably exciting cocktail.

(SS)

Landscapes

3 Atacama Desert

In San Pedro de Atacama, an oasis in the heart of the world's driest desert, fine boutique hotels offer excursions to Inca ruins, astronomical observatories, hot springs and much more.

(M/S)

4 Torres del Paine National Park

Hike through the continent's most stunning scenery, with a choice of guiding options and fine accommodation.

(JT)

5 Carretera Austral

A long lonely road through the pioneer country, between thick wet rainforest and the icecaps that cut off the far south of the country – this is an experience like no other.

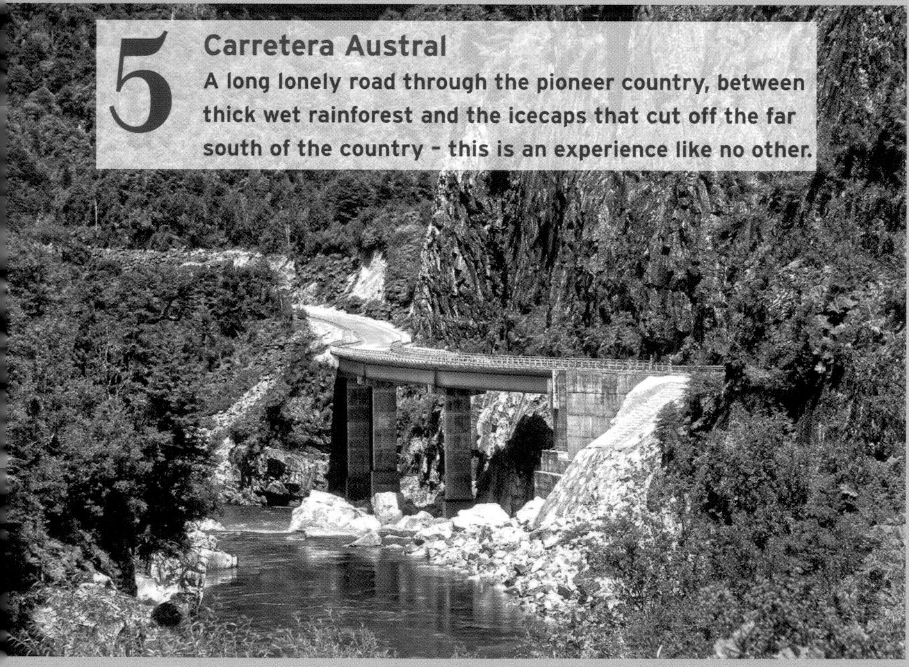

(EZ)

6 Cruce de los Lagos
Buses link boats across a chain of lakes, carrying you across the Andes from Chile to Argentina.

(IP/S)

(MG)

7 Desierto Florido
In rainy years, the arid Norte Chico bursts into life as colourful flowers erupt from the desert.

8 **Visiting vineyards**
Chile's winemaking industry, well known for its affordable but characterful blends, is increasingly welcoming tourists, with fine restaurants and guesthouses on the vineyards. For white wine-lovers, the area to head for is Casablanca, between Santiago and Valparaíso; for red wine-lovers, head south for a couple of hours to Colchagua (and beyond).

(LF/A)

(SS)

9 **White-water rafting**
A wide variety of rivers can be run in Chile, some with well-organised tourist operations.

10

Condor-watching in the Andes

Just to the east of Santiago, it's a short excursion to the modern ski resorts where you can hike up to the snowline and look down on condors soaring in vast gorges.

(G/S)

11

Fly-fishing

(MDW)

In the far south of Chile, introduced brown trout grow to a massive size and give great sport to aficionados staying in remote but luxurious lodges.

12

Hiking in the temperate rainforest

Central-southern Chile has some of the world's densest and most species-rich rainforest, offering superb hiking.

(I/FLPA)

Tourist information

The national tourism authority is Sernatur, which has a useful website (⑩ www. sernatur.cl) and produces a good range of publications. Their head office in Santiago (Avenida Providencia 1550, Providencia, Santiago 7500548 ① (+56) 2 731 8336/7) makes an excellent starting point for a tour; offices in regional capitals are stronger on local information than on other parts of the country. Abroad, you can pick up some publications in Chilean embassies but are best off referring to the Sernatur website, and also ⑩ www.chile-travel.com and ⑩ www.gochile.cl.

Red tape

Almost no-one requires a visa to visit Chile, with most foreign visitors routinely receiving on entry a **tourist card** valid for a 90-day stay. However, citizens of the USA, Canada, Australia and Mexico have to pay a '**reciprocity fee**' of up to US$160 on arrival at Santiago or Easter Island airports. This might be described as a 'retaliation fee', because Chileans have to pay equivalent fees to apply for visas to those nations, with no refund if it's not granted. The fee is valid for the lifetime of each passport, and is not charged at other airports or at land borders; there's a counter before immigration where those concerned have to pay in US dollars, with cash or a credit card.

The tourist card can be extended for more than 90 days but there's often no need, as you'll get another 90 days every time you go into Argentina and return, something which happens a lot in the disconnected southern parts of Chile. The Policia Internacional, which staffs most border posts, is as efficient and upright as the Carabineros (the regular Chilean police), who in fact staff the most minor border posts; these are likely to be open only limited hours, while the most important are open 24 hours a day.

Tourist cards can be extended during their last 30 days of validity – take two colour photos and US$100 to the Departamento de Extranjería y Migración, San Antonio 580, Santiago (⑩ www.extranjeria.gov.cl ☉ 09.00–16.00 Mon–Fri), or the equivalent in the capital city of each region. The process takes between two to three days, in the same time it takes to pop over to Mendoza and return with a new tourist card for much the same price.

Loss of a tourist card should be reported to the Policia Internacional at Morandé 672, Santiago (Ⓣ (+56) 2 737 1292 Ⓔ jenaex@investigaciones.cl ⊙ 08.00–14.00 Mon–Fri), or the Sección de Extranjería de Policía de Investigaciones in any regional capital.

Getting there

By air

LAN (Ⓦ www.lan.com), Chile's flag-carrier airline (though privately owned since 1989), is consistently rated the best airline in Latin America. It's a member of the oneworld airline alliance with American Airlines, British Airways, Iberia, Cathay Pacific, Qantas and half-a-dozen others.

You're most likely to arrive in Chile by **flying into Santiago**. **In Europe**, LAN flies daily to Madrid (either direct or via Buenos Aires or Sao Paulo) and on to Paris or Frankfurt; LAN and **Iberia** each fly nightly from Madrid to Santiago, with shared codes so that each seems to have two flights. Connections from Barcelona, Rome, Zurich, Amsterdam, Dublin and London are operated by Iberia; British Airways serves London, Birmingham and Manchester. From London you can fly via Sao Paolo with TAM. All these options take at least 17 hours.

In the **USA**, the main LAN routes are from Miami and New York followed by Los Angeles; there are onward connections with American Airlines (also providing service to Asia); code-shared flights operated by American are available from Santiago to Dallas. LAN also have flights from San Francisco to Lima (Peru), connecting to Santiago.

It's easy enough for **Europeans to travel via Miami** (and the baggage allowance is larger), but it's simpler to avoid this routing, as even passengers in transit have to clear US immigration and customs. Generally though, the contraction of the airline industry and the growth in alliances and code-sharing worldwide have simplified the routing possibilities.

By road

It's quite common to include Chile in a multi-country tour, most often with Argentina. It's easy to arrive in or leave Chile overland, although crossing **from Argentina** involves crossing the Andes (except from Río Gallegos to Punta Arenas or in Tierra del Fuego). The most common transfer is from Mendoza to Santiago via the Libertadores tunnel and Portillo. The Bariloche–Osorno route is the next most popular, with the Junín–Pucón route also useful. In the far north the most useful link from Argentina is from Jujuy and Salta to San Pedro de Atacama and

Calama. The main route **to Bolivia** is from Arica via Putre and the Lauca National Park, although tour groups from San Pedro de Atacama use the Laguna Verde border post. Virtually all traffic **to Peru** crosses from Arica to Tacna, a quick and easy journey.

These roads are paved on the Chilean side, but there may still be unpaved stretches on the Argentine side, although these do not require anything more than a standard car. With hire cars there is some extra cost and paperwork involved in crossing borders, but the rental agency should take care of this. For car-hire companies, see page 94.

By sea

It's entirely possible to arrive in Chile at the end of a **cruise** and either spend a day or two visiting vineyards and Valparaíso and Santiago, or even start a full tour of the country. Otherwise, there are no regular ferry services to Chile, with the exception of a couple of lake crossings in the south, notably the spectacular **Cruce de Lagos** from Bariloche in Argentina. From Ushuaia, in Argentine Tierra del Fuego, there is as yet no regular service to Puerto Williams or Puerto Navarino, on Chile's Isla Navarino, though this should develop before too long. At the moment you have to fly or take a 36-hour ferry from Punta Arenas, or hitch a ride on a yacht. The Mare Australis luxury cruise from Punta Arenas to Cape Horn will drop you off in Ushuaia, but this is an expensive way around the problem.

Health and safety
With Dr Felicity Nicholson

Healthcare standards are remarkably high in Chile, although you should have full insurance as it can be expensive; see page 73 for details. Your best health protection is to be fit and well before you set off; have your teeth checked pre departure and carry your prescription if you wear glasses (or save it as a Hotmail/Gmail message). For more details on staying healthy in Chile, see *Chapter 4*, pages 78–80.

Inoculations

No vaccinations are legally required, but make sure you're up to date with **tetanus** and **diphtheria** – which these days comes with polio as the all in one Revaxis – and **hepatitis A**. **Typhoid** will also be recommended for most trips unless you're going for a week or less and there is no time for immunity to develop. **Hepatitis B** may be recommended for those

Travel clinics and health information

A full list of current travel clinics worldwide is available on Ⓦ www.istm.org. For other journey preparation information, consult Ⓦ www.nathnac.org/ds/map_world.aspx. Information about various medications may be found on Ⓦ www.netdeoctor.co.uk/travel. Other useful sites include Ⓦ www.fitfortravel. scot.nhs.org (a useful source of general travel health information) and Ⓦ www. nc.cdc.gov/travel (with updates on specific destinations and information for those with limited mobility and those travelling with children). Both the British and US governments also provide dedicated travel health information online (Ⓦ www.nhs.uk/nhsengland/healthcareabroad and Ⓦ www.travel.state.gov).

working in hospitals or with children. Three doses of vaccine should be given ideally over a minimum of three weeks for those aged 16 or over. Longer is needed for younger travellers. **Rabies** vaccine is advised for people working with animals, but ideally all travellers should be offered a course of three pre-exposure vaccines, as Chile is considered a high-risk rabies country and treatment is not always readily available. Yellow fever is not present in Chile and there is no requirement for proof of vaccination even if you are entering the country from yellow fever infected areas.

Long-haul flights, clots and DVT

Any prolonged immobility, including travel by land or air, can result in deep-vein thrombosis (DVT), which can be dangerous if the clot travels to the lungs to cause pulmonary embolus. The risk increases with age, and is higher in obese or pregnant travellers, heavy smokers, those taller than 6ft/1.8m or shorter than 5ft/1.5m, and anybody with a history of clots, recent major operation or varicose vein surgery, cancer, a stroke or heart disease. If you think you are at increased risk of a clot, ask your doctor if it is safe to travel.

Women travellers

Chile is a very conservative society, but it's not as ridiculously macho as some Latin American countries. Women travelling in Chile can relax, as this is one of the safest and most hassle-free countries in Latin America. Men may shout and whistle, but as a rule that's as far as it goes. There are certainly bars where women should not go alone, or in some cases at all, but they're pretty obvious. Dressing and behaving reasonably modestly is simply good manners here.

Personal first-aid kit

Depending on where and how you travel, and for how long, a minimal first-aid kit might contain the following:

• A drying antiseptic, eg: iodine or potassium permanganate
• A few small dressings (Band-Aids)
• Suncream
• Insect repellent
• Antihistamine tablets/cream
• Aspirin or paracetamol
• Anti-inflammatories, eg: Nurofen or Ibuprofen
• Antifungal cream, eg: Canesten
• Ciprofloxacin or norfloxacin, for travellers' diarrhoea
• Antibiotic eye drops
• A pair of fine-pointed tweezers
• Alcohol-based hand rub or a bar of soap in a plastic box
• Thermometer

Disabled travellers

Arriving at Santiago airport, you may think that all is perfect for disabled travellers in Chile. There are wheelchair-accessible lifts, phones and bathrooms, and tactile indicators and Braille signs. Once outside in the real world, however, you'll realise that all is far from ideal. Although modern hotels are required to provide level access, this tends not to be thought through; elsewhere access is often impossible, and pavements are narrow, often blocked and have high kerbs. The Santiago Metro's lines 1 and 2 are not accessible, but more recent lines have lifts, and new buses have powered ramps. The tour operator Korke (Ⓦ www.korke.com) has a division, AMAPI, dedicated to accessible travel, and should be able to cater to your needs.

What to take

Travelling in Chile requires pretty much whatever you'd take on a trip to Europe or North America, the only real proviso being to pack a variety of clothing, a hat, good sunglasses and plenty of suncream. It can be very wet and windy in the south, but you can just as easily freeze at altitude in the far north. A Latin-American Spanish dictionary or phrasebook may be useful, as the language differs a bit from European Spanish.

Electric voltage is at 220 volts 50 Hertz, so visitors from North America will require transformers (which are best bought at home) for their appliances. Plugs have two round pins, or three for earthed appliances (the smaller southern European type, not the larger northern European ones).

Be sure to take out adequate **travel insurance** before leaving home. This should include both medical insurance and a travel protection plan to cover costs incurred if your trip is cancelled, interrupted or delayed. Likewise, if driving, be sure to have adequate insurance, including cover for windscreen damage. In addition to the standard suppliers (your tour operator, the Post Office, M&S, Boots), travel insurance can be purchased in the UK from Age UK (℡ 0845 600 3348 ⓦ www.ageuk. org.uk), who have no upper age limit, and Free Spirit (℡ 0845 230 5000 ⓦ www.free-spirit.com), who cater for people with pre-existing medical conditions. Most insurance companies will insure disabled travellers, but it is essential that they are made aware of your disability. For information on how to make a claim if you are a victim of crime, see *Chapter 4*, page 81.

Hospitals and pharmacies are generally excellent, but do take a good supply of your **prescription medications** with you, and it is advisable to pack this in your hand luggage during flights in case your main luggage gets delayed. For a suggested first-aid kit, see opposite.

Be sure to take binoculars if you want to spot condors soaring over the Torres del Paine National Park. (GK/S)

Few people would consider travelling without a **camera and/or video recorder**. Photos taken on a mobile phone just won't cut it, and that's even more true of video. For the best results, take an SLR camera rather than a compact 'point and shoot', and a pair of good zoom lenses. If you use a digital camera, make sure you have all the **batteries**, **plugs**, **connectors** and **storage devices** you need, as well as a **universal adaptor**. If you use **film**, be aware that this may not be readily available, so bring as many rolls as you're likely to need.

Binoculars are also essential for viewing wildlife, especially birds.

Organising your finances

Visiting Chile on an organised tour, you won't as a rule need to carry much cash as most expenses will be covered by your operator, including airport and cruise transfers, ground transport with driver or guide, domestic flights, national park and other entrance fees, and accommodation. As far as meals are concerned, the most common arrangement is for breakfast only to be provided in cities and beach destinations, with lunch and dinner included in more remote locations. However, some tours provide full board throughout, or just with the odd free evening, so be sure to check with your operator. You will need enough cash to cover **everyday expenses** such as drinks, tips and souvenirs, which are unlikely to run to more than US$50 a day.

There are some superb **all-inclusive resorts** in Chile (mainly in San Pedro de Atacama and the Torres del Paine National Park), but the emphasis is not on free drinks and pampering so much as on a range of excursions (mainly activities such as hiking, biking and kayaking).

The very cheapest beds cost around P7,000 (US$13), but you can easily pay over US$100 a night. Similarly, you can shop in markets and supermarkets, and use the kitchen in a hostel or *residencial*, or you can plunge right in and enjoy fantastic seafood every night as well as taking every available tour. Thus it's possible to travel on a budget of just US$20–30 a day, or you can max out your credit cards. There are many discounts for those over 60.

Credit cards (Visa and MasterCard above all, especially in smaller towns) are widely accepted in the better hotels and restaurants and by car-rental companies.

You'll need some Chilean **cash** – readily available from ATMs in just about all towns – for smaller expenses and in more remote locations such as national parks. **Travellers' cheques** are not easy to change, but a small supply of US dollars, euros or pounds sterling may be useful as a back-up.

The **Chilean peso** (P in this book, though the usual symbol is $) is a stable currency, trading at about P870 to the pound sterling and P480 to the US dollar.

For more information on banking and foreign exchange, see *Chapter 4*, page 82.

Entry fees

National park entry costs between £1.20 and £5 (US$2 and US$8) in most cases, but the crown jewels of the Torres del Paine and Rapa Nui (Easter Island) parks cost considerably more for foreigners – around £18.50 (US$30) for Torres del Paine, or £6 (US$10) for local guides and transport staff. The whole of Easter Island is a national park, with a pass costing foreigners £38 (US$60) for access to four sites. The parks authority CONAF has recently introduced an annual pass, also costing £38 (US$60), including four children under 18, but this excludes Torres del Paine and Easter Island.

Museums are usually very cheap, with entry fees around £1; there are only a few exceptions to this, such as the major museums in Santiago and the Museo de Colchagua in Santa Cruz. **Wine tours** can be pricey although they should be included in the fee of most organised tours.

Many museums in Chile are free, like the Museum of Memory and Human Rights in Santiago. (CP/MMDH)

4 On the Ground

On an organised tour, your ground operator will handle day-to-day practicalities such as checking into hotels, paying entry fees, and finding places to eat or to exchange money. Chilean guides are very efficient and eager to help, but you may need a little local knowledge if you are on a self-drive trip or taking an extension before or after an organised trip or a cruise. Therefore, this chapter covers a few key topics such as health and safety, foreign exchange, eating and drinking, shopping and communications. It may seem challenging, but Chile's infrastructure is generally excellent and local guides and anyone else you meet will be friendly and keen to help.

Health and safety in Chile
With Dr Felicity Nicholson

Chile is a remarkably hygienic and risk-free destination, with high standards of healthcare across the country. **Tap water** is drinkable across Chile, although mineral water is almost always available. **Food poisoning and cholera** are not a great problem, but uncooked *ceviche* (shellfish) should be avoided (see below). **Dengue fever** has occurred on Easter Island, so try and avoid being bitten by mosquitoes there, especially during daylight hours.

Pharmacies are probably more common than food shops, and some stay open until midnight. **State hospitals** are good and not too expensive, though staff are unlikely to speak foreign languages. **Private hospitals**, mainly in Santiago, do have doctors who speak English and other languages.

There are **no poisonous snakes**, although the **recluse spider** (*araña de rincón*), found in many homes, has a venomous bite which can kill. There are **biting insects** in summer in the south (and sometimes around Arica) but they don't carry disease.

Depletion of the ozone layer, coupled with dry, unpolluted air, has led to increased levels of ultraviolet radiation in southern Chile, causing **sunburn** and increasing the risk of cataracts and **skin cancer**. The same applies in the north, where the air is clear and the sun's rays take a more direct route through the atmosphere. Be sure to wear good sunglasses and plenty of sunscreen. For details on pre-departure inoculations and other health advice, see *Chapter 3*, pages 70–1.

Shellfish
The Marea Roja or 'Red Tide' is an accumulation of **toxic algae** which concentrate in shellfish and can cause death in humans; it occurs in southern Chile in hot weather. Shellfish is very closely monitored in markets and restaurants, but you should be extremely careful about any you gather yourself.

Hanta virus
The **hanta fever** virus (or hantavirus pulmonary syndrome) does best in dark unventilated areas, so there's a higher risk in huts and *cabañas* that have been shut up over the winter. It's transmitted mainly by the long-tailed mouse, so don't touch food that's been chewed or defecated on by a rodent, and don't leave it where this might happen. The symptoms are flu-like fever, muscle pains, headache and fainting,

followed by breathing difficulties and possible heart failure. Hanta fever is not responsive to drugs but with good care the body usually fights it off.

Altitude sickness

Altitude sickness is only likely to affect you only on the altiplano of the far north. San Pedro de Atacama is low enough that you should need only to take it easy for a few hours, if that. However, the Lauca National Park is another story, as far too many tours involve driving directly from Arica, at sea level, to the park, at over 4,000m. In most cases the basic symptoms of thumping heart and gasping breath will pass in an hour or two; some people will also experience headaches, fatigue, dizziness, loss of appetite or nausea (similar to a hangover). The combination of two or more of these symptoms should have you consulting your guide and if there is any doubt then you should descend at least 500m.

Travellers' diarrhoea

Travelling in Chile carries a moderate risk of getting a dose of travellers' diarrhoea. It is estimated that around half of all visitors will suffer and the newer you are to exotic travel, the more likely you will be to succumb. By taking precautions against travellers' diarrhoea you will

Treating travellers' diarrhoea

Dehydration from diarrhoea can make you feel awful, so drink lots of clear fluids. Sachets of oral rehydration salts give the perfect biochemical mix to replace all you are losing, but other recipes taste nicer. Any dilute mixture of sugar and salt in water will do you good: try Coke or orange squash with a three-finger pinch of salt added to each glass (if you are salt-depleted you won't taste the salt). Drink two large glasses after every bowel action, and more if you are thirsty. These solutions are still absorbed well if you are vomiting, but you will need to take sips at a time. If you are not eating you need to drink three litres a day plus whatever is pouring into the toilet. If you feel like eating, take a bland, high carbohydrate diet. Heavy greasy foods will probably give you cramps.

If the diarrhoea is bad, if you are passing blood or slime, or you have a fever, you will probably need antibiotics in addition to fluid replacement. Seek medical help in a timely manner. If the diarrhoea is greasy and bulky and is accompanied by sulphurous (eggy) burps, a likely cause is giardia. This too will need the relevant treatment.

also avoid other infections such as typhoid, etc. Travellers' diarrhoea and the other faecal-oral diseases come from getting other peoples' faeces in your mouth. This results most often from cooks not washing their hands after a trip to the toilet, but even if the restaurant cook does not understand basic hygiene you will be safe if your food has been properly cooked and arrives piping hot. The most important prevention strategy is to wash your hands before eating anything. The maxim to remind you what you can safely eat is:

PEEL IT, BOIL IT, COOK IT OR FORGET IT.

Fruit you have washed and peeled yourself, and hot foods, should be safe but be careful with raw foods and foods kept lukewarm in hotel buffets, as they can be dangerous. Dairy products such as yoghurt and ice cream are best avoided unless they come in proper packaging. That said, most good hotels and restaurants have good standards of hygiene and travellers should be able to enjoy a variety of foods.

HIV/AIDS

The risks of sexually transmitted infection are moderately high in Chile whether you sleep with fellow travellers or locals. In 2009, 0.4% of the adult population were HIV positive but this is probably an underestimate. Be safe and use condoms or femidoms, which help reduce the risk of transmission. If you notice any genital ulcers or discharge, get treatment promptly since these increase the risk of acquiring HIV. If you do have unprotected sex, visit a clinic as soon as possible – this should be within 24 hours or no later than 72 hours – for post-exposure prophylaxis.

Crime

Chile is a very safe destination, but in a city the size of Santiago there will always be some **pickpockets** and **con artists**. It goes without saying that you should take the usual, sensible precautions, especially in major cities. Lock your car and avoid looking like a wealthy tourist: keep your bag under your arm or over your shoulder, and leave

Emergency phone numbers

Ambulance ℡ 131
Carabineros (police) ℡ 133
Fire ℡ 132
Forest fire ℡ 130
Investigaciones (detectives) ℡ 134
Marine rescue ℡ 137
Mountain rescue ℡ 136

jewellery and other such valuables at home. If your passport is too bulky to carry comfortably and safely, keep handy some other form of identification, such as a driving licence, or photocopies of the key pages of your passport. Note down the numbers of your travellers' cheques, credit cards, passport, and flight bookings; it's smart to leave them as a Hotmail (or similar) message to yourself. You can even attach digital photos of your passport and air itineraries.

Carabineros (police) motorcyclists on parade (PC/B)

Chile's **main police force** is the Carabineros, who are well respected and not at all corrupt. Their vehicles and buildings are green and white. In addition, there's the Gendarmería, who run prisons, and the Policia de Investigaciones or detectives, which includes the Policia Internacional, found at most border crossings and airports, alongside personnel of the SAG or Livestock and Agriculture Service, whose mission is to stop pest-laden food products entering the country.

If you are **robbed** and wish to claim on insurance, ask the police for a copy of the official report (*la denuncia*); similarly, in the case of a **road accident**, ask for *la constancia*. You may just be given a reference number, which should satisfy your insurer.

Earthquakes

Chile, hit in 1960 by the most powerful earthquake ever recorded, and by plenty of other big ones (see page 27), is well prepared for the inevitable. Modern buildings are constructed to international standards of earthquake-proofing, with power and gas automatically cut off in some towns by motion sensors, and the emergency services are competent.

Above all, don't panic if the earth starts to shake; don't use the lift, and stay indoors in a doorway. In modern cities falling glass from high buildings is the main cause of injuries, so resist the temptation to rush into the street.

Banking and foreign exchange

The Chilean peso ('P' in this book, though the usual symbol is '$') is a stable currency, trading at about P480 to the US dollar, P870 to the pound sterling or P212 to the euro. There are coins from P1 to P500, and notes from P1,000 to P10,000, many of them in both old and new forms. You may also see references to two other rather odd monetary units, the UTM or Monthly Taxation Unit (currently about P39,138) and the UF or Unidad de Fomento (about P22,365) used, for instance, for levying statutory fines and for house prices.

The cheapest and easiest way to obtain pesos is from the **ATMs** (*cajeros automáticos*) found in virtually every town and airport. The major banks all belong to the RedBanc consortium, whose machines accept virtually all foreign cards; similarly, RedCompra swipe-card terminals are found in many shops. Smaller towns may only have a branch of Banco Estado, whose machines only accept MasterCard.

Exchange offices (*casas de cambio*) will take US dollars and Argentine pesos, and usually euros, sterling and Canadian dollars, too; other currencies may prove more difficult, especially outside Santiago.

Tipping

Knowing when to tip, and how much, is always a potential minefield when travelling. In restaurants, a tip of 10% for the waiters is usual and if this has been included in the bill it's customary to leave much the same again on the table. In smaller family-run *comedores* no tip is expected, but as with taxis you should round the bill up.

Upmarket lodges and hotels often operate on an all-inclusive basis, but you can always leave a cash tip for individual staff. It's probably better not to charge it to your room or add it to a credit card bill, as there may be no mechanism for ensuring that the tip reaches the intended beneficiary. Lodges may also have a tips box at reception, which is a good way of ensuring that some of the largesse reaches the behind-scenes workers.

A few exchange offices, mainly in Santiago, will change **travellers' cheques**, but as a rule you'll need a **bank** (⊘ 09.00–14.00 Mon–Fri). You'll have to pay a commission of about 3%, or accept a differential rate which comes to about the same thing. If you have **American Express travellers' cheques**, you can take them to an AmEx agent, change them to US dollars without commission, and then exchange the cash at a *cambio* as required.

The *impuesto de valor agregado* (**value-added tax**, or IVA), is usually included in bills where relevant, although it's sensible to check (*¿IVA incluido?*). The exception is hotel bills, where tourists are exempt – rates quoted in US dollars are without IVA, whereas peso rates usually include it.

Eating and drinking

Food

Not surprisingly, in a country which exports fruit, fish and other foods around the world, there's plenty of good produce in Chile, ranging from tropical fruit from the north to fish and lamb from the south, not to mention the fine wines. It's easy to eat well and healthily, but sadly the average Chilean diet is getting less healthy, as a result of increasing prosperity. Exercise levels are falling and consumption of meat, alcohol, fat and artificial sugars is increasing, while consumption of fish and vegetables is falling fast. At least Chileans eat plenty of fruit.

Chilean cuisine blends **Spanish** and **Mapuche influences**; it's not particularly spicy (although table sauces such as *ají* and *pobre* liven things up, and salt, sugar and mayonnaise are heavily used), but a wide range of vegetables and even seaweeds are used, so that although simple there's plenty of flavour and colour in Chilean dishes. Chileans eat only two-thirds as much meat as Argentines (84kg per head per year), and it's mainly chicken and pork rather

Vegetable market in Santiago (TS/S)

than beef. Even so, **vegetarianism** is hard going here, as vegetarian restaurants are rare outside Santiago and there's a general assumption that chicken, ham and tuna don't count as meat. In Santiago you can find more or less any cuisine under the sun; elsewhere there are at least pizzerias and, in the north particularly, *chifas* or Chinese restaurants, which are cheap and a welcome change.

Given the riches of the Humboldt Current, **seafood** is a mainstay – both fish (*pescado*) and shellfish (*mariscos*) – and the variety available is enormous. Be sure to have fish *al vapor* ('steamed') or *a la plancha* ('grilled') rather than *frito* ('fried in batter'). *Congrio* is probably the most common type of fish, often served as *caldillo de congrio*, a tasty soup. It's usually translated as conger eel, but is in fact a ling, with succulent white flesh. Salmon is usually from fish farms and a bit tasteless; there's plenty of good wild trout in the southern rivers. Others to look out for include *merluza* (hake), *corvina* (Patagonian toothfish) and *reineta* (pomfret or bream).

The array of **shellfish** includes *cholgas*, *mejillones*, *choros* and *choritos* (types of mussels), *almeja* (clam), *picoroco* (a giant barnacle with white crablike meat), *piure* (like a strongly flavoured sponge), *ostione* (scallop), *ostra* (oyster) and *erizo* (sea urchin). Crustaceans include *langosta* (crayfish), *langostino* and *camarone* (shrimp), *calamar* (squid), *pulpo* (octopus), *jaiva* and *cangrejo* (crab), and *centolla* (southern king crab). The latter is a speciality of the far south and can measure a metre from leg to leg, weigh as much as 2kg, and tastes sublime. *Locos* (abalone) are common as a starter and also as a casserole or *chupe de locos*; *machas* (razor clams) are good *a la parmesana*, baked with parmesan cheese melted on top.

Seafood is often prepared in mixed dishes such as *sopa marinera*, *paila chonchi* or *paila marina* (fish and shellfish stew, like bouillabaisse), *mariscal* (similar but with raw fish and seafood), *arroz marinera* (a seafood paella) and *chupe de mariscos* (a porridgey shellfish soup often topped with cheese). The best of these is *curanto* (or *pulmay*), a speciality of Chiloé and nearby areas, consisting of smoked pork, chicken or sausage, vegetables and various types of clams and mussels on a potato base, all cooked for a few hours on hot stones in a hole in the ground. It's served with bread and a bowl of rich buttery soup and some spicey *ají*. In addition, there's *ceviche* (or *cebiche*), fish or shellfish traditionally marinated raw in lemon juice and served chilled, although nowadays it has to be lightly cooked to guard against cholera and parasites.

Of the **non-seafood dishes** perhaps the most typical is *cazuela*, a broth of rice, potato, corn and maybe onions, squash and green peppers,

Preparing *curanto*, a Chilote stew cooked in a hole in the ground. (PMA)

plus a piece of beef or chicken. Other dishes include *pastel de choclo* (ground beef with olives, chopped onions and hard-boiled egg baked in a clay bowl with a topping of mashed corn and brown sugar), *pastel de papas* (cottage pie), *charquican* (stewed vegetables and minced beef, sometimes with *chochoyuyo* seaweed and topped with a fried egg), and *pollo arvejado* (chicken with peas).

There's a wide choice of steaks and other cuts of **meat**; the most common is beef, known generically as *carne*, as well as *carne de vacuno* or *bife*; *lomo a la pobre* ('poor man's steak') is the ironic name for steak with everything, including two fried eggs on top. An *asado* or *parrilla* is a mixed grill of prime cuts and various by-products, such as kidneys. *Cerdo* (pork) is also fairly common; *ave* (bird) generally means chicken, or occasionally turkey (*pavo*). *Cordero* (lamb) is traditionally associated with the far south, where it is spit-roasted on an open fire. *Cecinas* and *choricillos* are sausages; *prieta* is a sausage with cabbage and carrot, plus blood to bind it together.

Meat-free dishes include *paila de huevos* (scrambled eggs in a metal dish), *humitas* (boiled corn paste wrapped in corn leaves), *budin de acelga* (leafy greens or chard in a cheese casserole), *porotos granados* (thick bean and pumpkin soup), *porotos con riendas* (beans cooked with spaghetti), *arroz primavera* (rice and spring vegetables), *tomatican* (tomato and onion), *salpicon* (carrots, potatoes and boiled eggs) and *tomate relleno* (stuffed tomato). Dishes of lentils (*lentejas*) are traditional at New Year.

The standard **salad** or *ensalada chileno* is simply sliced tomato and onion with herbs, and a dressing of oil, lemon and salt rather than

When and where to eat

Chileans eat a light breakfast (*desayuno*), just tea or coffee and toast or a bread roll, but in hotels you'll find jam, cheese, ham and maybe even eggs. Normally you'll find instant coffee and teabags, and hot water in a vacuum flask. The main meal of the day is lunch (*almuerzo*), when restaurants serve fixed menus which are great value (as long as you eat meat). You may also find a high tea known as *onces* (because it used to be served at 11.00), which can include sandwiches or cakes (*kuchen*), and can be quite a feast. Dinner (*cena*) is more formal, and expensive, with no fixed-price menus.

The simplest eating places are called *comedor* or *cocinería*; a *picada* tends to be slightly more interesting, often family-run and with some effort at style. A *casino* is a canteen – those attached to fire stations are particularly popular. A *cafetería* doesn't usually offer table service, while a *restaurante*, which can range from something pretty basic to the very classy, does. The *fuente de soda* (soda fountain) is the staple for snacks, juices and light lunches, with counter service and sometimes tables. *Comida de chatarra* (literally 'junk food') is ubiquitous, usually in the form of chicken, hot dogs or burgers.

The *menú* refers to the set lunch, and the *oferta* is the dish of the day. For a fuller choice, ask the *garzón* for the *carta*. When you're done ask for *la cuenta* or the bill.

Roadside restaurant in the Atacama Desert (SS)

vinegar; an *ensalada surtida*, also containing green beans, beets and *quesillo* (soft cheese), makes a decent vegetarian dish. Potatoes (*papas*) are a staple, not surprisingly as they're native to this part of South America; in most cases they come as *papas fritas* (chips or fries). Another native staple is quinoa, a grain from the northern altiplano and little known elsewhere in Chile, although it's immensely nutritious.

Chile's trademark **dessert** is *kuchen*, German cakes, commonly found in the Lakes District. More authentic Chilean desserts are *alfajor* and *cuchufli*, or wafers and *manjar* (sweet and sticky caramelised milk). Other popular options are *arroz con leche* (chilled rice pudding with cinnamon), *semola con leche* (a cornflour flan topped with manjar), *flan* (egg custard) and *pie de limon* (lemon pie). Ice cream is very popular, but only a few shops sell handmade *helados artesanales*.

You'll find some fascinating **fruits**, such as *chirimoya* (custard apple), *alcayota* (which looks like melon but is more like a squash), *carica* (mountain papaya), *lúcuma* (eggfruit), *guanábana* (soursop) and *nalca* (a rhubarb-like plant that you'll see by the roadside in the south). *Palta* (avocado) is common in salads and sandwiches, and many other introduced fruits are grown in the north, where wonderful juices are available at most cafés and restaurants – ask for *puro jugo sin azúcar* (pure juice without sugar) if you want it unsweetened.

The most popular **snack**, almost the national dish, is *el completo*, a hot dog in a bun with avocado and tomato topped with trademark squiggles of mayonnaise, mustard and ketchup. There's also a wide range of semi-toasted sandwiches (*sánguche*) such as *barros jarpa* (ham and melted cheese), *barros luco* (steak and melted cheese), *chacarero* (steak, tomato, chili peppers and green beans) and *churrasco* (beef strips). Usually the only **veggie option** is *queso caliente*, plain melted cheese, but you can usually get tomato or avocado added or even *palmito* (palm heart). *Sopaipilla* is deep-fried pumpkin dough, eaten hot with butter, mustard or *pobre* (a tomato, onion, garlic and herb sauce). An *empanada* is a turnover or pasty usually filled with *pino* (beef and onion) and then fried (*frito*) or baked (*de horno*); they can also be filled with cheese (although these are usually fried and greasy). On the central coast they can be made with *marisco* (shellfish) and in the south with *manzana* (apple).

Drinks

Chileans are possibly the world's greatest consumers of *bebidas* or **soft drinks**, each person guzzling an average 100 litres a year; they're available everywhere and are usually included in set meals (Bilz and Pap are uniquely horrid Chilean concoctions). Nectars are good bottled

Yerba maté

Yerba maté (*Ilex paraquariensis*) is a bitter, tea-like herb that is drunk with a silver tube or *bombilla* from a gourd (also known as a *maté*) that circulates among a group of friends. Originally consumed by the native peoples of northern Argentina and neighbouring parts of Uruguay, Paraguay and Brazil, it was cultivated by the Jesuit missions and became popular across the region.

fruit juices, but the fresh juices served in many cafés and *fuentes de soda* (especially in the north) are far tastier. On hot summer days carts on the street sell *mote con huesillo*, peaches with husked wheat, which looks bizarre but is one of the most refreshing drinks imaginable. **Mineral water** is widely available; it's mostly *con gas*, so if you want it still, specify *agua mineral sin gas*. **Tap water** (*agua de la llave*) is fine just about everywhere.

Coffee afficionados tend to suffer outside Santiago, as instant coffee is deemed quite good enough. Likewise, **tea** is not great – regular tea is *té negro*, and if you want it white you should ask for cold milk, as *té con leche* is a teabag dipped into warm milk, or (horror!) hot water with milk powder. **Herbal teas** are a better bet, with many Chilean varieties such as *boldo* or *llantén*, as well as *menta* or *hierba buena* (mint) and *manzanilla* (camomile). In the south many people drink *maté*, an Argentine ritual as much as a drink; see above.

Pisco sours (BM)

As for alcoholic drinks, Chilean **wines** (see box, pages 90–1) are an obvious choice. **Beer** (*cerveza*) is very popular and pretty drinkable; draught lager is known as *schopp*, and is cheap and refreshing. There's been a huge growth in craft breweries, with Kunstmann, Kross, Szot, Puerto and others producing a great range of tasty darker beers.

Pisco is a clear grape **brandy**; the national drink, *pisco sour*, is made with egg white, icing sugar and lemon juice. Young people drink it as *piscola*, with Coke, or with Sprite; they also drink *jote* (wine and cola). *Chicha* is partly fermented grape juice made and consumed locally, and *chicha de manzana* or *sidra* is cider.

Shopping

Supermarkets and hypermarkets account for 90% of food sales in Santiago, the highest rate in Latin America; elsewhere smaller shops are still important but they tend to have a pretty limited choice of foods. Shops are normally open 09.00–20.00 Monday–Friday, 09.00–14.00 Saturday, although malls are open daily from 10.00 to 21.00. In the smaller towns most shops will close for an hour or two at lunchtime.

Large well-stocked **malls** in Santiago (especially the affluent eastern suburbs) and in most other cities offer globalised consumer goods much like those at home. Smaller towns offer less choice but you should still be able to find any essentials you've forgotten to bring with you. Isolated hotels will probably be able to sell you toothbrushes, batteries and the like at reception, but little more.

Larger cities have a **daily market**, but this will largely deal in food and agricultural supplies; **crafts** can be found in smaller *artesanía* markets in tourist centres. There's a wide variety of crafts; from the Aymara **weavings** of the northern altiplano to the Mapuche silverware of Araucanía and the *moai*-style carvings in wood and stone of Easter Island. On the altiplano, **llama and alpaca wool** is used to produce hats

Artisanal market in Castro, Chiloé (Carlos Ivovic O)

Chilean wine

According to researchers at Glasgow University, Chile's red wines have the highest levels of flavonols (which reduce heart disease and cancer) of any wines in the world. Even if this news hadn't reached you, the odds are that you are already aware of the ideal blend of quality and low cost offered by Chilean wine. Within Chile itself the prices are even better, although the choice is more limited than you'll be used to. Not many restaurants have much of a wine list, and usually only by the full bottle – the possibilities of getting wine by the glass are increasing, however, although it's an expensive option. Still, even Gato Negro (or the white equivalent, Gato Blanco) poured from a Tetrapak box can taste pretty good after a busy day in the summer heat of Santiago.

Chile's reputation was originally built on red wines (*vino tinto*); now elegant, but good-value, Chardonnay and Sauvignon Blanc whites (*vino blano*) are gaining the same recognition. New red wine varieties (such as Merlot and Pinot Noir) are improving with every vintage, producing reviews like 'pure pungent gum-staining fun', and taking over from CabSauv. Other varieties such as Zinfandel, Malbec and Syrah (Shiraz) are also coming into their own, but the most exciting development is the rediscovery of the Carmenère grape, assumed to have been wiped out by Phylloxera. A Bordeaux grape (part of the Cabernet family) and taking its name from the Spanish *carmín* (crimson) for the intense red of its wine and its autumn leaves, it was brought to Chile in 1850 but then lost, and only rediscovered in 1996, growing among Merlot vines. Intensely fruity, with hints of spices, vanilla and chocolate, and smooth tannins, it's softer than Cabernet Sauvignon but less so than Merlot. It is an ideal accompaniment for cheese, pasta, poultry and game birds. Another unusual variety which Miguel Torres is currently working with is Cariñena, a Spanish grape introduced in the colonial period.

The secret is in the weather: it's easy to grow grapes in a hot climate, but they tend to have a slightly stewed feel to them, whereas they have a better

and pullovers, although much of what you'll find in markets is made in Bolivia or Peru. To be sure of what you're getting you should buy from people in the Lauca National Park. In southern Chile you'll find similar goods, but made of sheep's wool (much of what is sold in the Angelmo market in Puerto Montt is also from Bolivia and Peru).

Wooden stirrups pictured here hanging in a stable. (TLB)

The Casa Silva winery in the Colchagua Valley (vcs)

structure and purer fruit flavours if chilled slightly overnight. Chile's wine-growing regions are cooled by early-morning breezes (and fogs) from the Pacific, and by an evening breeze from the Andes.

Over time, winemakers have become more skilled and more ambitious, accepting lower yields to capture fresh fruit flavours and producing quintessential 'New World' wines that leap out of the glass – full fruity wines at a good price – leading to a boom in exports. Having mastered the art of producing quaffable wine for under £5/US$8, they are now producing excellent value in the £5-15/US$8-25 range and are preparing for a serious assault on the higher-priced market. However, domestic consumption is falling rapidly, from 60 litres a year to 28 litres (just three bottles a month), as Chileans prefer beer and *pisco*.

In the Chilean heartland (the Norte Chico and the Central Valley) you'll find some wonderful *talabartarías* or **saddlery shops**, selling a great variety of leather harnesses as well as carved wooden *huaso* stirrups, like big clogs. Although some craft and souvenir shops sell saddlery, it's more interesting to seek out the regular shops used by working *huasos*.

Mapuche **silverworking** developed only after the arrival of the Spaniards; using silver coins and taught by Spanish prisoners, they developed their own ways of working silver, which matured as a fully

Mapuche silverwork ornaments from the collection of the Universidad Católica de Temuco (JZV)

fledged craft in the second half of the 18th century. The Mapuche also practise **basketry** and **weaving** with vines such as *voqui*, as well as horse-hair. You'll probably find items such as the *ñillwaka* (a bag made from a cow's udder) and the *trong-trong* (made from a bull's scrotum) only in museums, but you may be able to buy a *kulko* (wicker basket), *llepu* (wicker tray), *trariwe* (woven sash), *makuñ* (poncho) or *kultrung* (drum).

Lapis lazuli, a blue semi-precious stone, is found only in Chile and Afghanistan. Stones and jewellery can be bought in La Serena and the Bellavista district of Santiago.

Haggling is not part of the culture, although there may be some leeway in craft markets.

Media and communications

Media

Chile has a lively range of media, but unfortunately virtually all have a very right-wing viewpoint. *El Mercurio*, founded in 1827, is the oldest continuously published Spanish-language newspaper, and is still owned by the Edwards family. *Las Ultimas Noticias*, *La Segunda* and *La Tercera* are tabloids but sound sources of news. The main English-language outlet is the *Santiago Times*, only available online (ⓦ www. tcgnews.com/santiagotimes or via ⓦ www.chip.cl).

There are five national **television stations**, of which the most popular are the state-owned TVN (Channel 7) and the Universidad Católica's Channel 13; the evening peak begins with the *telenovelas* or soap operas, with intense competition between the channels to capture the largest audience share for the rest of the evening. There are at least 200 cable channels – it's easy to find international football, Hollywood films and CNN en Español. There are plenty of **radio** stations, playing various varieties of popular music.

Post

Chile has an efficient postal service (Correos), with letters taking a week or two to reach Europe or North America. Post offices are generally open 09.00–17.00 from Monday to Friday, and 09.00–12.00 on Saturdays. See ⓦ www.correos.cl for post office locations, as some larger offices are being closed and replaced by branches inside shops.

Telephones

Chile has one of the most competitive telephone systems in the world, with a dozen companies operating, of which the largest are CTC Telefónica (ⓦ www.telefonicadechile.cl) and Entel (ⓦ www.entel.cl).

From a **public phone**, just use coins for local calls (P100, or P200 to a mobile); for a long-distance or international call you have to select a carrier company, using a price list posted by the phone. For long-distance calls, dial the three-digit carrier code, the area code and the number. For international calls dial the carrier code, 0, then the country code, area code and number. It's much easier to use **call centres** (*centros de llamadas*), found in most towns, and often open until midnight.

Phonecards are common, but cards are company specific, except for the Tarjeta Línea Propria, which works via a free-phone number and a scratch-off code on the back of the card. Instructions are in Spanish only, but you have to dial 800 800802, then 1, then your code number, then wait, then dial a carrier code, country and area codes and the number. You'll also find that you get slightly less time for your money than with company-specific cards.

There are now over 21 million **mobile (cellular) phones** in Chile, the highest penetration rate in Latin America, and four competing

Business and time

Business hours are similar to those in much of Europe, although with a more leisurely lunch and a later finish, around 18.00-18.30; punctuality is appreciated. Bank hours are 09.00-14.00 Monday-Friday. The peak hours for public transport are 07.15-09.00 and 18.00-19.30. For shopping hours, see page 89.

Chilean time is three hours behind GMT but clocks currently go forward an hour on the second Saturday of March and back on the second Saturday of October. Thus in summer, Chile is in the same time zone as Argentina. Easter Island is two hours behind the mainland. You'll often hear a siren, or in Santiago a cannon fired on Cerro Santa Lucía, at midday.

providers. There's coverage almost everywhere you're likely to need it, including the Santiago Metro. The European GSM standard is used; phones can be rented at Santiago airport or through travel agencies. For advice on buying a Chilean SIM, see below.

The **international code** for Chile is 56.The phone code for **Santiago** is 02, followed by seven digits; numbers in other areas have six digits, except for some rural numbers with seven digits. **Mobile** (cellphone) numbers begin with 09 and have seven digits. What is listed as a fax may in fact be just as valid as the main telephone number – don't be shy about calling it if the other number no longer works.

Internet

Almost all businesses have websites and email contact addresses, and Wi-Fi is widespread. Most hotels and guesthouses, even the cheapest *hospedajes*, now offer internet access. This will usually be through a Wi-Fi connection, although some will just have a PC for guests to use; there may be connections in every room, or only in the foyer. This is usually free, although some places will charge. There are also cybercafés in many towns, and *centros de llamadas* (phone call centres) also often have a PC or two.

Alternatively, if you have a smartphone, you can buy a Chilean SIM card and then browse at a very reasonable rate (SMS text messages are even more affordable) – be sure to check that your phone has been unlocked and the settings will permit this before you leave home. In many remote areas you'll find yourself without mobile (cell) phone reception, so be sure that no-one at home will panic if you vanish for a few days.

Car rental and internal flights

Car hire

It's easy enough to organise car hire for yourself in Chile. Franchises of all the major international chains can be found in most cities and airports; local operators are usually cheaper but will probably not provide support in other cities. Note that rental rates and fuel costs are not particularly good value and you will need a valid **driving licence (with photo)** and a **credit card**. International chains set a **minimum driver age** of 25, while local Chilean companies may go as low as 22. There's additional cost and paperwork if you want to take the car into Argentina. Compact and family cars are easily available, but pickups are also popular, often with four-wheel drive. The following international

Freedom of the open road

Self-driving offers the chance to slow down and get to know the country. Our favourite routes include the wine region, Lakes District and the Carretera Austral, slicing through virgin Patagonian wilderness straight from your imagination. We organise your car hire and accommodation, but it becomes your own adventure the moment you hit the road: pause for as many pictures as you like, discover local hidden gems and arrive at your lodgings when it suits you.

companies are well represented: **Hertz** (Ⓦ www.hertz.cl), **Europcar** (Ⓦ www.europcar.cl), **Avis** (Ⓦ www.avis.cl) and **Budget** (Ⓦ www.budget.cl).

The spine of the country is Ruta 5, the **Panamerican Highway**, of which over 1,500km (close to a thousand miles) from Puerto Montt to north of La Serena (via Santiago), is now a dual-carriageway toll road with a 120km/h (77mph) limit. Other main roads are also paved and in good condition, with a 100km/h (64mph) limit, but minor roads may still be *ripio* (dirt). The speed limit in towns is 50km/h (32mph), and most streets are one-way – watch out for the tiny arrow painted with the street name on the sides of buildings at intersections. The Carabineros (**police**) enforce speed limits and seat-belt laws politely but firmly; the drink-driving limit is lower than in most European countries.

Internal flights

Internal flights are operated by the national flag-carrier, LAN (Ⓦ www.lan.com) and competing domestic airlines Sky (Ⓦ www.skyairline.cl) and PAL (Ⓦ www.palair.cl) – these all use modern jets and offer decent in-flight service, while remaining affordable. Internal flights are an unavoidable part of many tour itineraries, but modern airports move you quickly and efficiently between flight and transfer.

Cultural etiquette

Chileans are fairly conservative and formal people, usually **greeting** you with *Buenos días, Buenas tardes* or *Buenas noches* and shaking hands (or kissing a woman). If doing business, you'll probably start by exchanging cards. Likewise people tend to be fairly well but conservatively dressed (shorts are not as common as in other Latin American countries).

It's best to ask before taking portrait photos, especially of indigenous minorities, although normally they'll be perfectly happy. Haggling is not part of Chilean culture; similarly, you should not offer bribes, especially not to the police. There are few public toilets, but you can use those in cafés, paying a small contribution towards cleaning.

There are some fairly macho men, whistling or aiming kissing noises at women (unless they're with a man) – this is annoying but generally harmless, and is best ignored. There's not a lot of public drunkenness in Chile although domestic violence, often alcohol-related, is a big problem.

Because Chile is a conservative society, **homosexuality** is only slowly becoming acceptable. There are no specific laws against it, but police and other authorities can make their displeasure clear – behave discreetly and avoid public displays of affection. As you might expect, Santiago is more gay-friendly than other places, with Bellavista leading the way. The capital's nightclub scene is very gay-oriented, and there are even gay saunas here. A magazine called *Opus Gay* satirises the rabid prejudice of Opus Dei, the very powerful Roman Catholic group that many of the political and business elite belong to. Not surprisingly, it turned out Opus Dei had trademarked the name and sued for infringement, although the verdict was that the two groups were unlikely to be confused.

Crowd at a rodeo in Chile's Central Valley (SS)

Chile Highlights

5 Santiago

Opinions vary on Chile's capital city: some find it thrilling while others, especially those who come in winter when the smog is at its worst, can't wait to get out. Set midway between the Pacific and the Andes at an altitude of 543m, it's a city of almost six million people that suffers all the indignities of any modern megalopolis – gridlock, pollution, poverty, overcrowding and crime. But the relatively small central core remains an impressive colonial town of grand thoroughfares and plazas, where the pace of life is less frenetic than in most Latin American capitals. Nearby, 19th-century residential areas are newly trendy, with thriving restaurant and café scenes. And with its Mediterranean climate, Santiago is pleasantly warm when most tourists visit, in the southern summer.

History

The conquistador **Pedro de Valdivia** founded the city of Santiago de la Nueva Extremadura on 12 February 1541, laying out the usual Spanish plaza and grid of streets to the west of Cerro Santa Lucía. Relations with the indigenous population soon soured and the town was burned down then rebuilt and fortified. There were also frequent earthquakes and floods, and development was stymied by colonial trade restrictions; only in the later 18th century did the city really begin to take off, with fine buildings in the Italian Neoclassical style. Development accelerated after independence as national institutions were established, and the

Safety in Santiago

Santiago is a very safe city, especially by Latin American standards, but tourists may be targeted by pickpockets and other petty criminals. Never leave baggage unattended, and keep an eye on your bags even in upmarket cafés. It's advisable to leave your passport in a hotel safe and just carry a photocopy of the details page. Muggings have been reported at scenic viewpoints such as Cerro San Cristobal, Cerro Santa Lucía and Cerro Manquehue, and these areas are best avoided in the evening, although security has been tightened.

The safest areas are the affluent *comunas* (boroughs) to the east of the centre such as Providencia, Vitacura and Las Condes, which have private security guards as well as police. *Comunas* that are probably best avoided are El Bosque (not to be confused with El Bosque Norte, an avenue in upmarket Las Condes), La Cisterna, La Granja, La Pintana, Lo Espejo, Puente Alto and San Joaquín (especially the druggy La Legüa neighbourhood) and San Ramón.

The southern entrance to the Cerro Santa Lucía (AR)

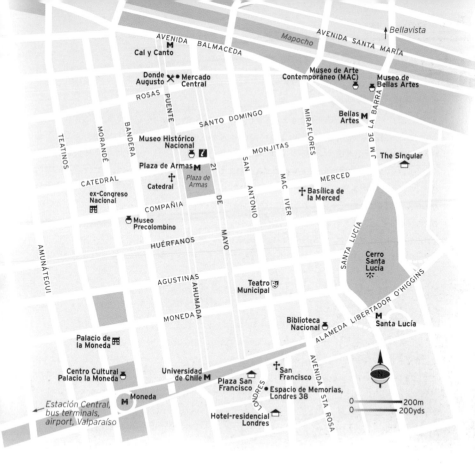

new richly built themselves showy mansions. From the 1850s French architectural influence was dominant; it was only in the 20th century that Chilean architects came to the fore.

Benjamín Vicuña Mackenna was only Intendant of Santiago from 1872 to 1875, but he left an ambitious programme for his successors to complete, including a ring road and improved police, water and tram services, and the beautification of Cerro Santa Lucía. There were still dreadful social problems, with foul slums known as *conventillos* in which only half the children survived to adulthood. There were no sewers until 1903, and drinking water supply was still inadequate as late as 1920.

In the 1920s Santiago began to sprawl as **industrialisation** gathered pace, and its population grew from 400,000 in 1910 to a million in 1940; now it's pushing six million. Its infrastructure has developed to match its growth, with a particularly efficient metro system and airport, plus a booming financial district, to the east of the historic centre, with rows of glass-fronted skyscrapers.

Practicalities

Santiago is the country's main entry point and transport hub. The **international airport** (known as Arturo Merino Benítez, Pudahuel or SCL ⓦ www.aeropuertosantiago.cl), 20km west, is busy but efficient, with a fine modern terminal (disability-friendly and mostly non-smoking). Arrival is swift and easy, taking half an hour from plane to street. There are ATMs, 24-hour money exchange, 24-hour baggage storage and car rental on offer, and it's an easy half-hour ride into the city. Tour operators should provide **transfers**, but otherwise **shuttles** to hotels are offered by TransVIP, Delfos and Turistik, and there's the frequent CentroPuerto **bus** service to Los Héroes, plus of course **taxis**.

The city's axis is the east–west **Alameda** (Avenida O'Higgins), the Valparaíso highway, which continues east to Providencia and Las Condes. The main **museums** and other **tourist sights** are in the historic centre, with newer attractions – including major **wine-making estates** – in the suburbs. Just outside the centre, 19th-century residential districts are being rediscovered and revived, notably bohemian **Bellavista**, across the river to the north of the

Accommodation

Exclusive
Aubrey ⓦ www.theaubrey.com
The Singular Santiago ⓦ www.thesingular.ida.cl/hoteles/the-singular-santiago

Upmarket
NH Ciudad de Santiago ⓦ www.nh-hotels.com
Plaza San Francisco ⓦ www.plazasanfrancisco.cl
Radisson Plaza Santiago ⓦ www.radisson.cl

Moderate
Hotel Conde Ansúrez ⓦ www.ansurez.cl
Hotel Montebianco ⓦ www.hotelmontebianco.cl
Hotel Neruda Express ⓦ www.hotelneruda.cl

Budget
Hostal Río Amazonas ⓦ www.hostalrioamazonas.cl
Hotel-Residencial Londres ⓦ www.londres.cl
La Casa Roja ⓦ www.lacasaroja.cl

historic centre. Just east, Providencia offers the best balance of liveability and working environment, while beyond it are the modern business districts (known as 'Sanhattan') which could almost be anywhere in North America. Further east, up against the Andean foothills, are the affluent *barrios altos* or high suburbs. Happily, you do not have to travel far in any direction to find fresh air; in particular, the coast is just 100km west, while the ski resorts immediately to the east offer a total contrast all year round.

The city's transport hub is around the **Estación Central** (with the Metro station of the same name), offering a fairly limited **train service southwards** only. On the western side of the station is the San Borja **bus terminal**, with the Alameda and Santiago terminals three blocks west, at the Universidad de Santiago Metro station. Public transport is good, especially the **Metro** (Ⓦ www. metrosantiago.cl); **buses**, however, require a prepaid smart card, which rules them out for many tourists. **Hop-on hop-off tours** are provided by Turistik (Ⓦ www.turistik.cl), who also run excursions to nearby wineries.

Most **exchange offices** are in the historic centre, on Agustinas between Ahumada and Bandera, with others on Pedro de Valdivia north of Avenida Providencia; the main chain is AFEX.

Eating out

Santiago now boasts a wonderful and largely unsung variety of restaurants and cuisines. There are some excellent Peruvian and Mexican places, as well as plenty of seafood and *parrilla* grills and other Chilean and international restaurants. The most expensive places are in the eastern suburbs, but there's excellent food and good prices all over.

Aqui Está Coco (perhaps the best fish restaurant in Santiago) La Concepión 236 Ⓦ www.aquiestacoco.cl

Astrid y Gastón (elegant French-inspired Peruvian cuisine) Antonio Bellet 201 Ⓦ www.astridygaston.com

Donde Augusto (in the Central Market, a popular and lively fish restaurant) Ⓦ www.dondeaugusto.cl

Europeo (the best French restaurant in town) Av Alonso de Córdova 2417 Ⓦ www.europeo.cl

La Casa en el Aire (an arty café) Ⓦ www.lacasaenelaire.cl

Liguria (longstanding and popular Italian restaurant) Ⓦ www.liguria.cl

Osadia (home to Chile's most inventive and charismatic chef) Av Nueva Costanera 3677 Ⓦ www.osadiarestoran.cl

Central Santiago highlights

Many visitors simply transit through Santiago, but the city's historic centre is well worth a day of your time, especially if you're interested in the big national museums.

Cerro Santa Lucía

This – **St Lucía Hill** – is the best starting point, both because the city was actually founded at its foot, and because of the views it offers. Terraces, paths and viewpoints were laid out between 1872 and 1874, and it was then decorated with statues, trees and flowers to produce an elegant venue for fashionable citizens to promenade. There's a free lift on its west side; it's not wise to be here at dusk or later.

Biblioteca Nacional

⊘ 09.00-20.00 Mon-Fri, 09.00-14.00 Sat, mid-Dec to early Mar 09.00-17.50 Mon-Fri only

At the southwestern corner of Cerro Santa Lucía, the **National Library** is a grand Neoclassical pile built between 1914 and 1824. There's usually an interesting exhibition in the central hall, often on some historical personage.

Parque Forestal

Until the river was canalised in 1891, the **Forest Park** was a rubbish dump where dogs, pigs and whores went about their business; however, in 1910 it opened as a riverside park, and is now characterised by rows of mature plane trees with gravel paths, statues and fountains. It's also the setting for the National Museum of Fine Arts, detailed below.

Museo de Bellas Artes

Parque Forestal ⓦ www.mnba.cl ⊘ 10.00-18.50 Tue-Sun ⊜ free Sun

Opened for Chile's centenary in 1910, the **National Museum of Fine Arts** is a grand *fin de siècle* building with a spectacular main hall with a huge glass roof and lovely Art Nouveau ironwork. In the hall there are lots of 20th-century sculptures, a field in which Chileans, and Chilean women in particular, have excelled.

The main collection of Chilean painting starts with portraits by José Gil de Castro y Morales, a Peruvian who painted all the leading figures of newly independent Chile between 1814 and 1822. He was followed by various minor British artists and the Frenchman Raymond Monvoisin. Chilean artists finally began to make an impact in the late 19th century;

The Palacio de Bellas Artes provides a stunning venue for the National Museum of Fine Art and also the Museum of Contemporary Art. (PMA)

and they were mostly trained in Paris. There are three big canvases by the surrealist Roberto Matta (1911–2002), the greatest Chilean artist.

At the western end of the Museo de Bellas Artes, the **Museo de Arte Contemporáneo** (MAC, Museum of Contemporary Art; ⓦ www.mac. uchile.cl ⊘ Tue–Sat 11.00–19.00, Sun and holidays 11.00–18.00) hosts a changing programme of contemporary art. The MAC also has a branch at Matucana 464, Quinta Normal, open the same hours.

Mercado Central

Built of cast-iron parts fabricated in Britain and assembled in Chile for the National Exposition of 1872, this has been the city's premier **seafood market** ever since. An amazing variety of fish and crustaceans is laid out, glistening on beds of ice, and like all Chilean markets it also has

The Mercado Central is famed for its displays of fish and crustaceans and for its fine fish restaurants. (OL)

some of the best and cheapest restaurants in town. Just across the river are other characterful markets, for vegetables and flowers in particular.

Mapocho Station

This former rail terminus, built between 1905 and 1912, closed in 1987 and reopened in 1991 as one of the city's main cultural venues. Its vast main hall is a wonderful space for big noisy events but a bit dead-or-alive otherwise; there are also smaller upstairs rooms for exhibitions and performances, plus cafés and craft shops.

Plaza de Armas and Santiago Cathedral

Santiago's **historic central square** is a bustling and largely traffic-free space with the Central Post Office, National History Museum and City Hall (all fine 19th-century edifices) on its north side, and imposing arcades housing shops, restaurants and offices on the east and south sides. On the west is Chile's **grandest church**. Built by two German Jesuits between 1748 and 1775, its façade was soon remodelled in Neoclassical style, with two towers added by 1906. Its interior is undeniably impressive, with a long gloomy nave in which the gilded altars stand out, notably the marble high altar set with lapis lazuli.

Museo Histórico Nacional

Plaza de Armas 951 Ⓦ www.museohistoriconacional.cl ⊘ 10.00–17.30 Tue-Sun ⌂ free Sun and holidays

The Neoclassical Palacio de la Real Audiencia (1804–7) now houses the excellent **National History Museum**, which starts its account with an underwhelming room on the indigenous people of Chile and dated displays on the Spanish Discovery and Conquest. As you proceed right around the courtyard the displays get more informative, with good coverage of the colony's expansion and then retreat under Mapuche pressure, and the establishment of new towns in the 18th century. Upstairs, there's coverage of the work of the last colonial governor, Ambrosio O'Higgins, and of his son Bernardo – who created independent Chile's first two constitutions and the Alameda of Santiago – and of the next strongman, Diego Portales. Displays cover the 19th century's various civil wars as well as conflicts with Peru and Bolivia, and Chile's steady economic development, with the growth of railways from the 1850s and the nitrates industry in the 1860s. Meanwhile, displays on the 20th century cover the trades union activism which arose and the subsequent massacres, notably in 1907 in Iquique.

The 20th-century galleries begin with the presidency of Arturo Alessandri, who sought reforms to avoid revolution and established liberal democracy in place of the authoritarian conservative ascendancy. The consequences of the 1939 earthquake are well covered, with further industrialisation and the mushrooming of Santiago. There's a rather dry reliance on graphs and statistics for coverage of the Allende period, although social aspects are dealt with as well as the purely economic and political. The museum ends with the remaining half of Allende's glasses, discovered in the wreckage of La Moneda after the 1973 coup.

Museo de Arte Precolombino

Bandera 361 ⓦ www.precolombino.cl ⊘ closed for restoration until the end of 2013, but normally open 10.00–18.00 Tue-Sun ☞ free Sun and for children and students

A block from the Plaza de Armas, the former Real Aduana (Royal Customs House) is now the **Museum of Precolombian Art**, housing the most impressively displayed collection in Chile, and one of the most valuable, too. The collection of artefacts produced in the Americas before the arrival of Europeans comprises over 3,000 pieces covering a period of over 5,000 years. Little of it, however, is directly concerned with Chile, as it concentrates on the more advanced cultures further north. The quality of the ceramics and stone carvings is stunning, as is their variety; the discussion of varying burial techniques is particularly illuminating. The Andean area, covering much of Peru and Bolivia, is characterised by superb textiles up to 3,000 years old and preserved by the extreme dryness of the altiplano.

There are informative captions in Spanish and shorter ones in English; it's also one of the more disability-friendly museums in Chile, although the lift is tiny.

Plaza de la Constitución

The open space on the north side of the government palace, La Moneda, has been remodelled as a **beautiful esplanade**. It is surrounded by **statues** of presidents (including Allende, to the disgust of unrepentant right-wingers), and other significant figures such as Diego Portales. On its west side stands the former **Hotel Carrera**, the grandest hotel in town from 1940 to 2004 – it's said that when Fidel Castro visited Allende, the CIA planned to assassinate him with a sniper in the Carrera.

The south façade of La Moneda is less impressive than the north, and **Plaza de la Libertad** is also smaller and less attractive than the Plaza de la Constitución. In addition to being blighted by the hectic traffic fighting its way along the Alameda; it was remodelled in 1995 (and renamed Plaza del Cuidadanía, although the name hasn't caught on). Both squares are flanked by the drab office blocks of the Barrio Civico, built between 1932 and 1938 to house government ministries and other official bodies such as the National Theatre. The main survivor from earlier times is the Santiago regional Intendencia, immediately east of the palace at the corner of Morandé and Moneda, which was built between 1914 and 1916 as newspaper offices.

Palacio de la Moneda

Alameda and Morandé (Metro La Moneda) Ⓔ visitas@presidencia.cl Ⓦ www.gob.cl/english/la-moneda/ven-a-conocer-la-moneda ✎ free tours in English are available Mon–Fri, book at least ten days ahead, and bring your passport

The masterpiece of the Italian architect Joaquín Toesca, who established the Neoclassical style in Chile, this **palace** was built between 1784 and

Changing the guard ceremony at the presidential palace, La Moneda (VT/S)

1805 as the royal mint. It was the presidential residence from 1848 until 1958, and then the seat of government; it was bombed and burned down during the military coup of 11 September 1973 (see page 14), and rebuilt in 1981. There's a changing of the guard ceremony at 10.00 on even-dated days, on its north side (Plaza de la Constitución).

The excellent **Centro Cultural Palacio de la Moneda** (Moneda Arts Centre; ⓦ www.ccplm.cl ⊘ 09.30–19.30 daily ⦸ free Mon–Fri till 12.00) is under the lawn on the palace's south side.

Quinta Normal

Metro Quinta Normal ⊘ summer 08.00-20.30 Tue-Sun, winter 08.00-19.00
Founded in 1830 as a **botanic garden** to test which foreign species could successfully be introduced to Chile, this is perhaps the most attractive park in Santiago. It is also home to various museums, notably the **Museo Nacional de Historia Natural** (National Museum of Natural

Santiago's *barrios*

Santiago has some very atmospheric *barrios* or neighbourhoods, mostly areas that became run-down when the middle classes moved to the eastern suburbs and were then rediscovered by students and artists, before becoming desirable again.

Bellavista

For most visitors, northern Santiago, across the Mapocho River, is synonymous with the Barrio Bellavista, a bohemian area taken over in the last couple of decades by trendy restaurants and bars; however, there is more to see and it's worth visiting in daytime too. This was an area of farms and market gardens known as La Chimba, and only really began to be built up in the 1920s.

Pío Nono (meaning Pope Pius IX) is the main drag of the nightlife scene, as well as sidewalk craft sales at weekends. The liveliest and most creative

restaurants in town are here; it's an ever-changing scene and many restaurants may have closed and been re-invented by the time you read this. There are better and more established places on the parallel streets, Ernesto Pinto Lagarrigue to the west and Constitución to the east.

The hottest clubs are in Bellavista, the only area where it's possible to move easily from place to place, and where you'll find the only gay clubs, as well as most of the best *salsotecas*.

Barrio Brasil

The heart of Barrio Brasil, just west of the historic centre, is the attractive **Plaza Brasil**, with fine specimens of native trees. The *barrio* was developed in the 1920s and was fairly affluent until the middle classes moved to the *barrios altos* and then the Via Norte-Sur severed it from the centre of the city. In the last two decades various private universities have moved into the area, refurbishing buildings and bringing money and youthful vigour to the area; the Metro and a new footbridge across the Via Norte-Sur at Huérfanos have also linked the *barrio* to the centre again. The plaza is ringed by cafés, as well as the **Galpón Victor Jara**, a venue for young musicians and political activists. Just west of the plaza on Compañía, the **Templo de la Preciosa Sangre** is a big salmon and cream basilica with palms in front and is rather more attractive than the better-known **Basilica del Salvador**, at Huérfanos 1781 (esquina Almirante Barroso).

Barrio París-Londres

This small area just across the Alameda from the historic core is somewhat reminiscent of the Latin Quarter of Paris. Consisting of just two cobbled streets, Calle Londres and Calle París, it was developed in the 1920s in the former orchard of the San Francisco monastery. Many of the buildings have been refurbished and some now house characterful budget hotels.

Barrio Concha y Toro

On the north side of the Alameda between Cumming, Brasil and Erasmo Escala, this tiny area, now pedestrianised, was developed in the 1920s and 30s. Buildings designed by many of the leading architects of the time have Neogothic, Neoclassical, Neocolonial and even Bauhaus features, but all share a historical-eclectic aesthetic.

Painted wall in Barrio Bellavista, Santiago (DAB/A)

In addition to the Wall of Memory at the Cementerio General, there's a photo display of the disappeared at the Museum of Memory and Human Rights. (VPP)

History; Ⓦ www.mnhn.cl ☉ all year 10.00–17.30 Tue–Sat, 11.00–17.30 Sun and public holidays ☞ free Sun and public holidays) and the open-air **Museo Ferroviario** (Railway Museum; Ⓦ www.museoferroviario.cl ☉ summer 11.00–19.00 Tue–Fri and 11.00–18.50 Sat–Sun, winter 10.00–17.00 Tue–Fri and 11.00–17.50 Sat–Sun), the biggest and best of its type in Latin America, with 16 steam locomotives.

On the east side of the Quinta, the **Museo de la Memoria y los Derechos Humanos** (Museum of Memory and Human Rights; Matucana 501 Ⓦ www.museodelamemoria.cl ☉ 10.00–20.00 Tue–Sun ☞ free), in a dramatic modern building exemplifying transparency, has powerful displays on the 1973 coup and the return to democracy, as well as human rights more generally and contemporary art displays.

Immediately south of the Quinta, the **Museo Artequín** (Av Portales 3530 Ⓦ www.artequin.cl ☉ 09.00–17.00 Mon–Fri, 11.00–18.00 Sat–Sun and holiday) occupies one of the most striking buildings in Santiago. This was the Chilean pavilion at the Great Universal Exhibition of 1889 in Paris, built of cast iron and glass by French architect Henri Picq, then dismantled and shipped to Chile; in 1992 it was handed over to

the municipality of Santiago, which opened the Artequín, an educational display about the great art of the Western world.

La Chascona

Márquez de la Plata 0192, Bellavista Ⓦ www.fundacionneruda.org
☺ Mar-Dec 10.00-18.00 Tue-Sun, Jan-Feb 10.00-19.00 Tue-Sun

The great poet Pablo Neruda built this house from 1953 for his third wife, Matilde Urrutia, and named it 'The Tangle-haired Woman' for her. In an improbable location abutting the foot of Cerro San Cristóbal, the house is in three parts stepped up the hillside, all filled with an eccentric collection of knick-knacks. Like his other houses in Valparaíso and Isla Negra, it's run by the Fundación Pablo Neruda, and it's worth seeing all three if possible.

Cementerio General

☺ summer 08.00-18.00 daily, winter 08.30-17.30

Almost everyone of importance in Chilean life has been buried in this **cemetery**, a mile north of the city's markets (although O'Higgins, Neruda and Mistral have been moved elsewhere; and Pinochet was not buried here for fear his tomb would be vandalised). There's a **Wall of Memory** commemorating over 4,000 of the Disappeared (see pages 15 and 17), as well as the oversized tombs of Salvador Allende and Pinochet's advisor Jaime Guzmán, assassinated in 1991. It's fascinating to wander through the maze of huge Neoclassical, Gothic, Moorish and Egyptian family mausoleums, watching cats, dogs and the strangely cheery workers go about their business.

Savour Santiago and the Central Valley

JOURNEY LATIN AMERICA

Don't hurry too quickly from Santiago: it is full of well-kept secrets such as the grand old neighbourhoods of Paris y Londres, Concha y Toro, Barrio Brazil and Lastarria. The fertile region surrounding the capital is dotted with wineries, many with upmarket accommodation. Even as a day trip, these vineyards offer a great rural contrast within easy reach of the city – some as close as 30 minutes from Santiago by car. Finally, don't miss a visit to the bohemian port of Valparaíso.

Four wineries in and around Santiago

Beyond excursions to Valparaíso (*Chapter 6*; see pages 120–7) and Andean ski resorts such as Farellones, La Parva and Valle Nevado (page 107), the most popular outings from Santiago are to **wineries**, some of which are actually within the city itself. In addition to the wine, you'll see gracious houses in parks laid out in the 19th century by French landscapers.

Concha y Toro

Virginia Subercaseaux 210, Pirque ⓦ www.conchaytoro.com

The country's biggest winemaker runs an intensive tourist operation at its historic estate, 27km south of Santiago; they offer eight one-hour tours a day in English (ⓣ 2 476 5269 or 853 0042). You'll see the exterior of the house (1875) and visit the park (which has a lake, sheep and very tall *Araucarias*) and cellars, including the famous Casillero del Diablo (Devil's Store), before a tasting of three wines.

Viña Cousiño Macul

Av Quilín 7100, Peñalolen ⓦ www.cousinomacul.cl

The oldest and most famous of Chile's vineyards runs English-language tours (ⓣ 2 351 4135 or 351 4166 ⓔ ventas@cousinomacul.cl) lasting 45 minutes, which include a tasting of two wines; you'll see the winery and cellar (1872) before being released into the shop.

Viña Undurraga

Camino a Melipilla, Km34 ⓦ www.undurraga.cl

This was one of Chile's first wine exporters, although it's now less innovative than others. Founded in 1885, it has vineyards here and also in the Maipo, Colchagua, San Antonio and Maule regions. Tours (ⓣ 2 372 2850 or 372 2865 ⓔ visit@undurraga.cl) last 75 minutes and visit the park, winery and cellars before a tasting of three wines.

Parque Metropolitano

Plaza Caupolicán, Bellavista ⓦ www.parquemet.cl

This is a large **park** housing various attractions such as a Japanese garden, zoo, cultural centre, wine bar and the Mapulemu Botanic Garden. Its highlight, however, is the peak of Cerro San Cristóbal, reached by a **funicular** (ⓦ www.funicular.cl ⊘ 13.00–20.00 Mon, 10.00–20.00 Tue–Sun) from Plaza Caupolicán (with a stop at the

Wine barrels at the Cousiño Macul winery (CB)

Viña Santa Rita

Camino Padre Hurtado 0695, Alto Jahuel ⓦ www.santarita.cl

The leading Maipo Valley winery, on a colonial hacienda 45 minutes south of Santiago, this is famed for the cellars where Bernardo O'Higgins and 120 of his men hid after the disastrous battle of Rancagua in 1814 (hence the name of one of their main lines, 120). Tours (ⓣ 2 362 2590 or 362 2594 ⓔ reservastour@santarita.cl) include a tasting of two wines and are free if you spend a minimum of P12,500 on lunch at the fine Doña Paula restaurant (ⓣ 12.15 and 14.00 Tue–Sun). There's also the excellent Andean Museum, with five rooms of Mapuche and Rapa Nui artefacts, textiles, ceramics from northern Chile and jewellery from what are now Peru and Colombia.

zoo). On the 860m summit, a sanctuary was constructed in 1903 to mark the 50th anniversary of the doctrine of the Immaculate Conception; the 14m iron and bronze statue of the Virgin was brought in parts from Paris and erected in 1908, and the faithful made all-day pilgrimages to leave offerings. Between 1922 and 1925 the funicular was built with funds from the Italian government, to help the pilgrims on their way.

Palacio Cousiño

Dieciocho 438 (Metro Toesca) ⓦ www.palaciocousino.co.cl ⊘ 09.30-13.30 and 14.30-17.00 Tue-Fri, 09.30-13.30 Sat-Sun and holidays

This is the grandest of the city's Belle Époque aristocratic mansions open to the public, built between 1870 and 1878 by Paul Lathoud for the Cousiño family. It was given to the city in 1940 and served as a guesthouse for official visitors until 1977. Indira Gandhi, General de Gaulle and Golda Meir stayed here, but a fire damaged the upper floor in 1968 just before Queen Elizabeth II was due to stay. One bedroom still has the original furniture but the others are not exact copies. Note the half-tonne electric chandelier of Bohemian crystal in the entrance atrium (lowered for cleaning four times a year) central heating vents with the family monogram, and the black marble banisters and huge mirror on the stairs, together with paintings of the Cousiño family in Santiago and Paris; there are also paintings by Raymond Monvoisin. In the dining room don't miss the majolica plates set into the ceiling, the 5m velvet curtains, and the French furniture and seats of Spanish leather. On the south side of the palace, in the Plaza Las Heras, there are superb mature trees including Moreton Bay fig trees, Bhutan pines, an Australian bottle tree, sweet chestnuts and palms.

Villa Grimaldi

Av José Arrieta 8401, Peñalolén (Metro PlazaEgaña, then bus 513 or D09) ⓦ www.villagrimaldi.cl ⊘ 10.00-18.00 daily, tours 10.30, 12.00 and 15.00 Tue-Fri

Just to the south of La Reina is one of the city's most disturbing sights, a **colonial villa** in which about 4,000 political detainees were tortured and 226 were killed between 1973 and 1978. At the end of the dictatorship it was sold to a general who demolished it, and the site was finally bought by a non-profit group to become the Parque por la Paz or 'Peace Park'. It is slowly being rebuilt, but at present it is a pleasant garden with mature trees, and a swimming pool where prisoners were hidden under a tarpaulin when human rights organisations visited. At the end of the site is a memorial bearing the names of those killed here.

You might also visit the ***espacio de memorias*** at Londres 38 in central Santiago (ⓦ www.londres38.cl ⊘ 10.00-18.00 Tue-Fri, guided visits midday and 16.00 Tue-Fri, by appointment Sat-Sun ℰ free); this was used as a torture centre between 1973 and 1974, and is now a bare house, a space for memories indeed.

Museo Nacional Aeronáutico y del Espacio

Av Pedro Aguirre Cerda 5000, Los Cerrillos Ⓦ www.museoaeronautico.gob.cl
◷ 10.00–17.30 Tue-Sun 𝄢 free

Founded in 1944, the **National Museum of Aeronautics and Space**
moved to this modern building in 1992; it's owned by the air force, but
there's no military presence or overt recruiting. In front of the museum
are various historic planes (including the Chilean-built T-35 Pillán
trainer); inside are replicas of the Wright Flyer (1903), the Bleriot XI
used for the first public flight by a Chilean in 1912, several World War I
planes, and a World War II Spitfire. Genuine preserved craft include a
P47 Thunderbolt, a B26 Douglas Invader, a Douglas DC6 and a Bell 47
helicopter, all types of plane used by the Chilean Air Force after World
War II. There are also cases of memorabilia and quite a lot of historical
information, although you'll need decent Spanish to benefit from this.

6 Central Chile

Chile's central coast is dominated by the twin cities of Valparaíso and Viña del Mar. Valparaíso is a port and a lively touristic and artistic centre, whereas Viña del Mar is a holiday resort best known for its beaches and its song festival. In this small area of Mediterranean climate and vegetation, it is tempting to draw parallels with California: Valparaíso is Chile's San Francisco – a city in a stunning natural setting with a rough bohemian ethos, while Viña is more like Los Angeles, with its beaches and entertainment industry. To the north and south of the cities is a rocky coastline with many beautiful coves and beaches that are also very popular holiday resorts.

Chile's premier white wine-growing area, the Casablanca Valley, is just inland on the main highway to Santiago, while north of Santiago, La Campana National Park is an oasis of native flora that offers good hiking and views. To the east, Chile's most prestigious ski resort, Portillo, makes an excellent stopover in the midst of the high Andes on the highway to Mendoza in Argentina.

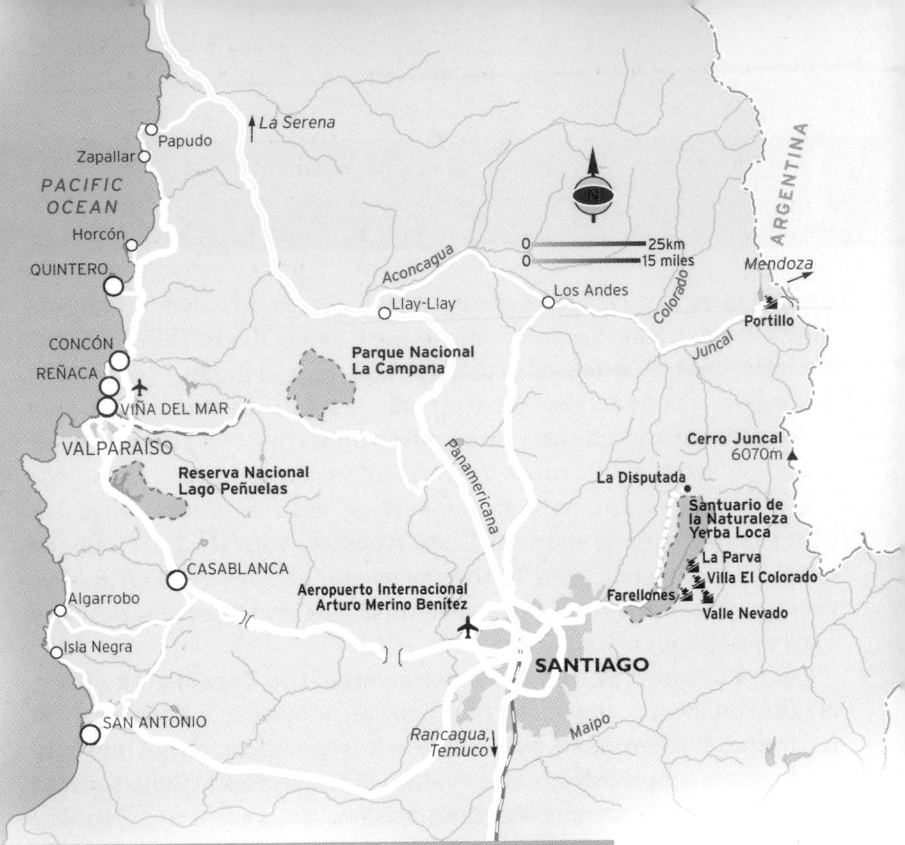
La Serena
Papudo
Zapallar
PACIFIC OCEAN
Horcón
QUINTERO
CONCÓN
REÑACA
VIÑA DEL MAR
VALPARAÍSO
Reserva Nacional Lago Peñuelas
Parque Nacional La Campana
Aconcagua
Llay-Llay
Los Andes
0 25km
0 15 miles
Colorado
ARGENTINA
Mendoza
Portillo
Juncal
Panamericana
Cerro Juncal 6070m
La Disputada
Santuario de la Naturaleza Yerba Loca
La Parva
Villa El Colorado
Farellones
Valle Nevado
CASABLANCA
Algarrobo
Aeropuerto Internacional Arturo Merino Benítez
Isla Negra
SANTIAGO
SAN ANTONIO
Rancagua, Temuco
Maipo

Valparaíso and around

Valparaíso's appeal is somewhat due to its crazy geography: it is built partly on reclaimed land and partly on steep hills reached by the Victorian elevators (*ascensores*) that are now the city's trademark feature (see page 124). There's also the blend of blue-collar and bohemian residents that makes it so lively and creative. Valparaíso has always had its unique charm, but for a long time it was pretty rough round the edges and really only for less delicate types; nowadays it is resurgent, with lots of urban renewal projects, taking pride in its industrial past whilst becoming accessible and tourist-friendly.

History

Under Spanish rule, Valparaíso was Chile's main port but it only really developed after independence, when a colony of British merchants established itself here and trade boomed. The foreigners settled on the hills right behind the port and business centre, while Chileans lived mainly on the hills further west. In 1906 the city was levelled by a huge earthquake (8.2 on the Moment Magnitude scale), then the Panama

Canal's opening in 1914 and the development of artificial substitutes for Chile's nitrates hit the port hard. Consequently, the city in which future presidents Allende and Pinochet grew up was a run-down place with many social problems. The export boom of the last two decades has revived it, and it has rediscovered its heritage, inspired first by a few left-field artists, then by a broader community of enthusiasts and promoters. Valpo was placed on UNESCO's World Heritage List in 2003, and work continues to save the elevators, restore run-down areas, and open up the waterfront. The 2010 earthquake, while not causing massive damage here, has left several museums and other sights closed.

Valparaíso highlights

The 'Plan' or lower town consists of narrow busy streets lined with the grand buildings of former British banks; at Condell 1546 the Palacio Lyon (1881) now houses the **Museo de Historia Natural** (Museum of Natural History; ⊙ 10.00–13.00 and 14.00–18.00 Tue–Sat, 10.00–14.00 Sun and public holidays). Recently reopened following the 2010 earthquake, the museum is home to an excellent collection focused on marine life and ecology, as well as dioramas of pre-Hispanic cultures. In the basement, the **Galería de Arte Municipal** (Municipal Art Gallery; ⊙ Tue–Sun 10.00–19.00) houses temporary art shows.

View of Valparaíso from Cerro Artillería (DAS)

Practicalities

The main gateway to central Chile – the area around Santiago – is **Santiago's international airport** (known as Arturo Merino Benítez, Pudahuel or SCL Ⓦ www.aeropuertosantiago.cl). It is just northwest of the capital and is close to the main highway that runs from Santiago to Valparaíso and Viña del Mar. On an organised tour you will usually be met here, and all the major **car rental** agencies have offices at the airport.

From the capital it takes about 1 $\frac{1}{2}$ hours to reach Valparaíso or Viña (slightly less from the airport) on a good highway (Ruta 68) that passes through the Casablanca wine country. The best bases from which to explore central Chile are Santiago (see *Chapter 5*, page 102) and Valparaíso; Viña has some decent hotels and restaurants, but fewer other attractions.

In recent years many boutique hotels and fine restaurants have opened in Valparaíso in beautifully restored old buildings, and weekenders from Santiago and international tourists have flocked there. There are also some fine restaurants in the Casablanca Valley wineries which shouldn't be overlooked (see pages 123 and 129–31).

Accommodation

Exclusive
Acontraluz (Valparaíso) Ⓦ www.hotelacontraluz.cl
Grand Hotel Gervasoni (Valparaíso) Ⓦ www.hotelgervasoni.com
Hotel del Mar (Viña del Mar) Ⓦ www.enjoy.cl/enjoy-vina-del-mar

Upmarket
Casa Higueras (Valparaíso) Ⓦ www.casahigueras.cl
Harrington B&B (Valparaíso) Ⓦ www.harrington.cl
Hotel O'Higgins (Viña del Mar) Ⓦ www.panamericanahoteles.cl/eng/ohiggins.html

Moderate
B&B Casa del Sol (Viña del Mar) Ⓦ www.bbcasadelsol.com
Brighton B&B (Valparaíso) Ⓦ www.brighton.cl
Hotel Puerta de Alcalá (Valparaíso) Ⓦ www.hotelpuertadealcala.cl

Budget
Hostal Casa Aventura (Valparaíso) Ⓦ www.casaventura.cl

Viña is Chile's answer to Los Angeles, with its glitzy casinos and beaches. (NH/S)

Valparaíso and Viña have all the amenities you'd expect in a major tourist centre: **information offices**, **internet** facilities, and **exchange** and transport services; there are also **ATMs** at the airport and in all smaller resorts.

Roads in the region are generally excellent, but to reach some of the smaller outlying resorts and sights you'll have to travel some way inland and then back out to the coast. Valparaíso and Viña are linked by a new **metro**, but **local buses** are cheaper and provide the only direct links with the inland parts of Valparaíso; these can also be reached from the lower city by **shared taxis**. Within Valparaíso there are also **private taxis**, and **one trolleybus line**, from the old Aduana to Avenida Argentina. These vintage vehicles originally operated in the USA and Switzerland half a century ago; they receive little of the attention lavished on the *ascensores*, but also deserve preservation.

Hotel Asturias (Viña del Mar) ⓦ www.hotelasturias.cl
Hotel Capric (Viña del Mar) ① 2 978 295
Luna Sonrisa (Valparaíso) ⓦ www.lunasonrisa.cl
The Yellow House (Valparaíso) ⓦ www.theyellowhouse.cl

Eating out

Café Turri (Valparaíso; a superb fish-based menu and the best view) Cerro Concepción 147 ⓦ www.turri.cl
Café Vinilo (Valparaíso; stylish modern cuisine, funky setting) Almirante Montt 448 ⓦ www.cafevinilo.cl
Cap Ducal (Viña del Mar; well-established seafront fish restaurant, shaped like an ocean liner) Av Marina 51 ⓦ www.capducal.cl
Delicias del Mar (Viña del Mar; relatively upmarket seafood restaurant) San Martín 459 ⓦ www.deliciasdelmar.com
Epif (Valparaíso; best vegetarian food in the city) Grossi 268 ⓦ www.epif.cl
Le Filou de Montpellier (Valparaíso; long-established, authentic French restaurant) Almirante Montt 382 ⓦ www.lefiloudemontpellier.cl
Macerado (Casablanca; excellent option in the wine country) Av Portales 1685 ⓦ www.macerado.cl

Stairways to Heaven – the *ascensores*

Valparaíso's most distinctive feature is perhaps its *ascensores* or elevators, built over a century ago to link the flat harbourside district with the residential hills. There were once over 30, carrying 12 million passengers a year. More recently they became very rundown, with many abandoned and the rest expected to go the same way; in 1996 the World Monuments Fund listed them among the world's 100 most threatened monuments, raising first publicity and then funds for repairs, and in 1998 the government listed them as national monuments.

Nevertheless almost all are now closed, but thankfully not those most needed by tourists. The oldest (and still the most profitable) is the **Ascensor Concepción** (or Turri), built in 1883, only a few years after braided steel cables became available; it rises 70m to the Paseo Gervasoni viewpoint on Cerro Concepción. Nearby, the **Ascensor Reina Victoria** (built in 1902) gives the city's best urban view. Also very popular is the **Ascensor Artillería** (1893), which takes visitors up to the Naval Museum. Others you may use are the **Ascensor El Peral** (1902) to Paseo Yugoeslavo, and **Ascensor Cordillera** (or Serrano, 1887) to Cerro Cordillera.

The Ascensor Artillería (SS)

Some are private and others are municipally owned and there are a variety of fares and working hours (roughly 07.00–23.00 daily), although none costs very much. There's been discussion for years of the government buying the private ones and restoring them, and of restaurant developments to bring more foot traffic, but so far nothing has happened.

Strictly speaking they are all funicular railways except for the **Ascensor Polanco** (1916; reached by a 150m tunnel from Calle Simpson), which is a genuine elevator. It can take just eight passengers and there are only two others like it in the world – in Lisbon and in Stockholm.

The 'Plan' ends at the wide **Plaza Sotomayor**, centred on the **Monument to the Heroes of Iquique** where the remains of Prat and others killed in the naval Battle of Iquique in 1879 reside. Beyond is the **Muelle Prat**, the tourist sector of the docks, where boat trips start and cruise ships dock. North of Plaza Sotomayor is the oldest part of the city, **Barrio Puerto**, where you'll see the fine cast-iron **Mercado Puerto** (1924) and the **Matriz Church** (1837), a plain Neoclassical structure housing a 17th-century Spanish carving of Christ. From here Cochrane runs for another couple of blocks to the Aduana (Customs house; 1855), from where the

Monument to the Heroes of the Battle of Iquique, Plaza Sotomayor, Valparaíso (SS)

Ascensor Artillería rises to the **Museo Marítimo Nacional** (Naval Museum; ☉ 10.00–17.30 Tue–Sun and public holidays).

Just south of the Matriz Church, an alley leads up to **Cerro Cordillera**. Alternatively, you can walk halfway down Serrano and take the Ascensor Cordillera, from the top of which Merlet leads to the **Museo Lord Cochrane** (Lord Cochrane Museum; ☉ 10.00–18.00 Tue–Sun ✍ free). This single-storey house was built in 1841 on part of what was the Castillo San José and although the museum is of little interest there's a fine view of the city from its terrace.

Back near Plaza Sotomayor, the Ascensor El Peral (or the nearby steps, or a shared taxi up Almirante Montt) brings you to **Paseo Yugoeslavo** – an attractive hillside promenade on Cerro Alegre that was once the centre of the British commercial colony. Facing the *ascensor* is the **Museo de Bellas Artes** (Museum of Fine Art; ☉ 10.00–18.00 Tue–Sun ✍ free) in the stunning Palacio Baburizza (1916); the collection includes atmospheric paintings of 19th-century Valparaíso and works by minor European artists. Miramar and Lautaro Rosas lead through an area of multi-coloured **19th-century houses**, many now art galleries and restaurants; then the steep Calle Templeman leads to **Cerro Concepción**, an attractive area that was the heart of the city's German community. Before reaching their **Lutheran church** (1897) you'll pass the **Anglican Church of St Paul** (1858) at Pilcomayo 566.

At the northwestern end of Templeman are **Paseo Gervasoni** (another fine viewpoint) and the Ascensor Concepción (or Turri), which goes down to the 'Plan'. At Paseo Gervasoni 448 the **Casa Mirador Lukas** (⊘ 11.00–18.00 Tue–Sun) houses a small exhibition of the works of the cartoonist Lukas (active 1958–88). Going back to the Anglican church and turning right, you can follow Almirante Montt down to Plaza Aníbal Pinto, then follow Condell past the Natural History Museum to **Plaza Victoria**, the most spacious of the city's squares, with a dull cathedral (built in the mid 20th century) on the far side.

Just south is the **Museo a Cielo Abierto** (Open Air Museum), a circuit of steps and passageways decorated with murals by well-known Chilean artists. The brickwork is in bad condition and so the paint tends to flake and fade, even though it is touched up by students; there's also a lot of graffiti. This leads up to **Cerro Bellavista**, with its colourful and eccentric houses. It's another 500m or so uphill to **La Sebastiana**, **Pablo Neruda's Valparaíso home** at Ferrari 692 (⊘ Christmas–end Feb 10.30–18.50 Tue–Sun, Mar–Christmas 10.00–18.00 Tue–Fri, 10.30–18.00 Sat–Sun and holidays). You'll be given an audioguide or information sheet and can wander at your own pace, which makes the visit more enjoyable than at Neruda's other two houses: La Chascona in Santiago (see *Chapter 5*, page 113) and Isla Negra (see pages 128–9), south along the coast.

Pablo Neruda's Valparaíso home, La Sebastiana (AFPN)

This house is slightly less eccentric but contains an impressively eclectic collection of bits and pieces.

Heading westwards on Avenida Alemania and then down Cumming, you'll pass the **Carcel** (the former jail, now a cultural centre) and reach the cemeteries on Cerro Panteón. The most interesting is the **Cementerio de Disidentes** (⊘ 09.00–13.00, 15.00–17.00 Mon–Sat, 09.00–13.00 Sun and holidays), its gravestones bearing mainly British and German names.

At the eastern end of the city, the **Barón Clocktower** (1877) is virtually hidden under a flyover at the junction of Avenida Argentina and the Costanera. A pedestrian route is signposted to the **Muelle Barón**, a jetty which gives fine views of the port, as well as of pelicans and sea lions.

year 2019

THE RITZ-CARLTON®

2/19

Sawzlyg

Abraham
Tina Susan

12/19 Dinner

Lauren Pete Karen
Jeff
Hannah
Katherine

12/20 Breakfast

Maggie
Brian
Leo
Jacqueline
Gentil
Catherine

Mandy (SF)
(Mandy's Mom)

(EA)

Impressions of Valparaíso

Many writers have tried to capture Valparaíso's unique appearance: **Che Guevara** wrote of 'its strange corrugated iron architecture, arranged on a series of tiers linked by winding flights of steps and funiculars ... its mad-house museum beauty heightened by the contrast of different-coloured houses mingling with the leaden blue of the bay.' Chilean author **Antonio Skármeta** wrote: 'They say that Valparaíso was built following the steps of a drunken sailor following his beloved through the hills. It is the only city in the world that everyone finds harmonious although it has no symmetry.'

But the bard of Valparaíso is **Pablo Neruda**, who hid here while letting it be supposed that he had fled abroad and later returned to make his home at La Sebastiana (see opposite). He describes how 'the hills of Valparaíso decided to dislodge their inhabitants, to let go of the houses on top, to let them dangle from cliffs that are red with clay, yellow with gold thimble flowers, and a fleeting green with wild vegetation'. He continues, 'But houses and people clung to the heights, writhing, digging in, worrying, their hearts set on staying up there, hanging on, tooth and nail, to each cliff. The port is a tug-of-war between the sea and nature, untamed on the cordilleras.'

Valparaíso

RAINBOW TOURS

Now a World Heritage Site, Valparaíso's colourful houses are perched on a steep hillside overlooking the Pacific Ocean. Somewhat ignored by Chileans, the narrow streets, restored 19th-century houses and boutique hotels give the town bohemian charm. Take the funicular up the hill from the city centre and book a walking tour with a professional guide. With its year-round temperate Mediterranean climate, Valparaíso is a perfect break from the busy capital.

South of Valparaíso

From Santiago, Ruta 78 (the Ruta del Sol) leads southwest to the country's leading port, San Antonio, and the string of coastal resorts to its north. This has been christened the Litoral de las Poetas or 'Coast of the Poets', due above all to the house of the larger-than-life Pablo Neruda at Isla Negra (see below) but also because of connections with Nicanor Parra (in Las Cruces), Vicente Huidobro and the little-known Adolfo Couve (both in Cartagena).

Algarrobo, 76km from Valparaíso, is the last of the resorts along this stretch of coast and is an attractive spot popular with families and sailing enthusiasts hosting regular regattas in summer. It's notable mainly for the world's largest swimming pool (almost a kilometre in length) in the billion-dollar **San Alfonso del Mar** resort immediately to the north.

There are various small lagoons and wetlands along the coast that are home to water birds such as swans, ducks, herons and coots.

Isla Negra

Isla Negra (which is neither black nor an island) is about 30km southwest from the Santiago–Valparaíso highway at Casablanca, and 25km north of San Antonio (via Cartagena). It is known for **Pablo Neruda's house** (ⓦ www.fundacionneruda.org ⊘ 10.00–18.00 Tue–Sun, Jan–Feb open until 20.00), which is busy and cramped so can only be visited in small groups that follow on each other's heels. If you want an English-language tour, you should book in advance by calling the number above.

Neruda bought Isla Negra in 1938 and remodelled it between 1940 and 1942 and 1958; he moved to La Sebastiana in Valparaíso (see page 126) after 1961. Like his other houses, Isla Negra is full of bric-a-brac, with more of a maritime theme here where he played at being a sea-captain (his 'nauti-bits', perhaps). The house is crowded with figureheads, model ships, nautical prints and all sorts of trinkets; you leave by an external staircase and go into the south wing by a corridor lined with masks and carvings from around the world. Neruda's study contains a figurehead, a huge telescope, preserved butterflies, maps, masks, musical instruments and a fantastic fireplace; the exit hall contains a full-sized papier-mâché horse, and leads to a toilet that was for the use of men only due to its collection of Victorian porn. Finally, there's a room where Neruda's planned exhibition of sea-shells has recently been installed, together with a giant clam and a narwhal tusk.

After the tour you're released into the garden – just above the grave of Neruda and his third wife Matilde Urrutia – with its fantastic views of the rocky coast. There is also a bookshop and a good restaurant here.

Pablo Neruda's private bar in his house at Isla Negra (AL)

The Casablanca wineries

Since the early 1980s the Casablanca Valley has developed as Chile's first cool-climate wine-growing region (similar to California's Sonoma Valley). It's known for white wines, notably Sauvignon Blanc and Chardonnay, but also produces some excellent Syrah, with some Pinot Noir and Merlot grown, too. Some wineries also produce red wine with grapes trucked in from the Maule Valley and elsewhere. Many of the wineries are big and kitschy, set on hills overlooking Ruta 68, the *autopista* between Santiago and Valparaíso. This location means

Wine and poetry

travel **Art**

This two-day excursion introduces visitors first to the wine-making tradition of beautiful Casablanca Valley, and then to the magic of Nobel laureate Pablo Neruda's poetry at his house (now a museum) in the coastal village of Isla Negra. Casablanca Valley, not far from Santiago, is home to several world-class wineries – a perfect complement to Isla Negra, where Neruda wrote some of his most memorable works and where he lies buried.

they get a lot of visitors, including tour groups and excursions from cruise liners. The Casablanca Ruta del Vino is now inactive, so visitors can call the wineries direct or contact Wine Tours Chile (Ⓦ www.winetourschile.com).

Starting from the east, **Viña Veramonte** (Ⓦ www.veramonte.cl) is by the toll plaza at the exit from the Zapata tunnel; known for Sauvignon Blanc, they also make big reds. The largest contiguous vineyard in Chile, they offer tours of their state-of-the-art winery, cellars and museum (reservations Ⓣ 32 232 9924 Ⓔ salaventas@veramonte.cl) ending with a generous tasting and a visit to the shop (Ⓞ 09.00–17.30 Mon–Fri, 09.00–14.30 Sat, and Sun Dec–Mar), which sells local cheese as well as wine. Nearby is **Viña Quintay** (Ⓦ www.quintay.com), which opened in 2009 and is now starting to welcome tourists. They produce a fine Sauvignon Blanc.

Viña Indómita (Ⓦ www.indomita.cl) has one of Chile's most over-the-top winery buildings, but it does house a fine restaurant with great views (Ⓞ lunch daily, dinner Oct–Apr Fri–Sat). Viña Indómita produces Chardonnay and Sauvignon Blanc, as well as reds with Cabernet Sauvignon, Carmenère, Pinot Noir and Merlot grapes grown in the Maipo Valley. The winery is open for 75-minute tours and tastings from 10.00 to 18.00 daily with the tour cost redeemable against lunch at the restaurant).

Just east of Casablanca, **Viña Mar** (Ⓦ www.vinamar.cl) is known for whites, including sparkling wines, but is increasingly producing reds, too. The winery is now modelled on Viña's Palacio Vergara.

North of the highway, **Viñedos Orgánicos Emiliana** (Ⓦ www.emiliana.cl) offer informative tours (Ⓣ 9 9327 4019/ 2 353 9151 Ⓔ wineshop@emiliana.cl) of their vineyard (organic and biodynamic for over a decade) and cellar, with tastings and picnic lunches available. There are also various farm animals that will entertain the children. The **shop** is open April to November 10.00–17.00 daily, December to March 10.00–18.00 daily. Further north is the most tourist-friendly of the Casablanca wineries, **Viñedo Estancia El Cuadro** (Ⓦ www. elcuadro.cl), where a tour of five to six hours is offered (Ⓣ 2 519 7503 Ⓔ info@elcuadro.cl). The price includes a carriage ride through the vineyards, a folklore show, a winery tour, lunch and unlimited tastings.

South of Casablanca near Lagunillas in the San Antonio Valley, **Viña Matetic** (Ⓦ www.mateticvineyards.com) has a third of its area planted with Syrah, as well as Sauvignon Blanc, Chardonnay and Pinot Noir. It offers hour-long tours of its organic vineyards, winery and cellars (Ⓣ 2 595 2661 Ⓔ tours@matetic.com) and the entry fee covers two to four tastings. It also has a smart new guesthouse and the Equilibrio restaurant (Ⓣ 9 8920 20660 Ⓔ equilibrio@mateticvineyards.com Ⓞ 12.30–15.30 Tue–Sun).

Viña Morandé (Ⓦ www.morande.cl), just outside the town of Casablanca, doesn't offer tours even though it's one of the pioneer Casablanca wineries (operating since 1982). It does, however, boast the fine House of Morandé restaurant (Ⓣ 32 275 4700/1 Ⓔ houseofmorande @morande.cl Ⓞ 11.00–17.00 Tue–Sun).

The state-of-the-art winery of Viña Veramonte (GASH)

Viña del Mar and around

Just 15 minutes from bustling Valparaíso, the broad avenues of Viña del Mar and its sandy beaches offer a clear contrast. Laid out as a model town in 1874, Viña's boom years came in the 1930s, when its balls, race-meetings and casino were legendary. Since the 1980s large numbers of Argentines have also come to enjoy Viña's 3.5km of beaches.

Viña del Mar highlights

To the south of the Estero Marga Marga, a largely dry river used for car parking, is the main shopping and business area; to the north is a grid of housing, hotels, bars and restaurants. At the south end of Puente Libertad, **Plaza Vergara** is a fitting centrepiece to the city, with mature trees, statues and the Neoclassical **Teatro Municipal** (Municipal Theatre; 1930) on its east side. To the south across the busy highway (Viana/Alvárez) is the main entrance to the **Quinta Vergara** (⊙ 07.00–19.00 daily, closes 16.00 on concert days ॐ free), a park where 15,000 people gather nightly in February for Viña's Festival Internacional de la Canción (International Song Festival), Chile's biggest festival of light and pop music, televised across the continent. Among superb trees from across Asia and Australasia is the neo-Venetian **Palacio Vergara**, built between 1906 and 1910 and now crumbling. The main highway runs west to meet the coast by the **Reloj de Flores** ('Clock of Flowers'), not far south of the **Castillo Wulff**. Built in 1906 for a coal and nitrate magnate, the castle now houses temporary art shows (⊙ 10.00–13.30, 15.00–17.30 Tue–Sun ॐ free); you can cross a bridge with a scratched glass floor to a tower on a rock island. It's overlooked by the **presidential summer palace** (built in 1930); immediately to the east of the summer palace in the upmarket residential district of Cerro Castillo is the **Castillo Brunet**, now owned by the police.

Castillo Wulff houses temporary art shows in Viña del Mar. (CB)

Chile Wine and Gourmet Tour

SouthAmerica.travel

Imagine basking in the sunshine of Viña del Mar and Valparaíso, the beach destinations near Santiago de Chile. Dine on fresh salmon in view of the snow-capped Andes. Stroll along world-class vineyards and sip Carmenère and Cabernet Sauvignon. Head south to visit the Lakes District towns including Puerto Varas and also Chiloé Island. Here, time stands still, and volcanoes, lakes and fresh air dominate the landscape. It's Chile. It's paradise.

On the north side of the river the **beaches** begin at the **Casino Municipal** (Av San Martín 199 ⓦ www.casino.cl), opened in 1930 this is Chile's biggest and glitziest casino and is a mixture of Greek, Roman and Assyrian styles. Eight blocks inland, the Neoclassical **Palacio Carrasco** stands in a small park, beyond Rodin's sculpture *La Defensa*. Built for a nitrate magnate in 1912, Palacio Carrasco is now the city's cultural centre and library (☉ 09.00–19.00 Mon–Fri, 09.00–14.00 Sat). It currently houses the best collection of European art in Chile, mostly bought in Europe between 1868 and 1872 and displayed in the Palacio Vergara until the 2010 earthquake. Works include those by Chilean masters such as Alberto Valenzuela Llanos, Pedro Lira Rencorcet, Alfredo Valenzuela Puelma, Juan Francisco González and the Grupo Montparnasse, sent to Europe on a mass government scholarship in 1928 (see *Chapter 1*, page 22). There are also paintings by Nasmyth, Rubens, Poussin, Sorolla y Bastida and perhaps ten Italian Renaissance masters, although some are of dubious authenticity.

Just around the corner in the same park, at 4 Norte 784, the **Museo Fonck** (☉ 10.00–18.00 Mon–Fri, 10.00–14.00 Sat–Sun and holidays) stands behind an Easter Island *moai*, one of just seven not on the island. There's a superb display covering Rapa Nui (Easter Island) here, with three rooms of carvings, utensils and ornaments. Other exhibits cover the peoples of Chile's far south, including Mapuche as well as other Chilean cultures (with items up to 10,000 years old). Upstairs are displays of natural history (including a fossilised whale's jawbone and some butterflies) and minerals such as lapis lazuli.

In another small park a couple of blocks further east, at Quillota 214, the **Palacio Rioja** (1907) now houses a music conservatory which puts on free concerts in summer; you can also visit the ground floor, with all its original Belle Époque furnishings in place (☉ 10.00–13.30, 15.00–17.30 Tue–Sun).

The city's remaining major sight is 6km east in El Salto, where the **Jardín Botánico Nacional** (☉ Apr–Sep 10.00–18.30 daily, Oct–Mar 10.00–19.30 daily ☞ more expensive on Sun) was created from 1918. It's home to 800 species, including cacti, Chilean palms and the *toromiro* tree, now extinct in the wild on its its native Easter Island.

North of Viña del Mar

North of Viña, the coast is largely developed for tourism as far as Concón, at the mouth of the Río Aconcagua. Beyond here it is wilder and emptier but there are some interesting small resorts (increasingly known for their charming boutique hotels) before the coast road finally swings inland to join Ruta 5, the Panamericana.

First stop, 6km north of Viña, is **Reñaca**, an upmarket enclave with pricey apartments ranged along its hilltops in blocks like Maya pyramids or Tamil temples. This is also the nightclubbing centre of Chile, at least for a couple of months in summer. The road, blasted along the rocky coast in 1917, continues north to **Concón**, 17km from Viña. The first part of town, Caleta Higuerillas, is a small fishing port surrounded by boardwalks and excellent seafood restaurants, with modern developments to the north. Beyond the Río Aconcagua, the coast road passes the 11km **Ritoque Beach**, known for surfing and beach-fishing, before a side-road runs into **Quintero**, 43km from Viña del Mar. This is a fishing cove that has featured off and on in Chilean history since 1536, when Alonso de Quintero passed by with a shipload of supplies for Diego de Almagro's expedition. On the sheltered east side of a rocky headland, the fishing port is now full of yachts as well as fishing boats, and there are seafood restaurants and stalls selling *empanadas de mariscos* (shellfish pasties).

Another side road leads to **Horcón** (10km north), a tiny fishing cove that's popular with Santiago's hippies and has a semi-legal nudist beach 5km to the south. It's a good place to buy handmade jewellery, beads, leatherwork and ceramics. A very laid-back locale, the big excitement of the day is watching horses pull the fishing boats up the beach before enjoying the sunset. The seafood is excellent, notably the cheese *empanadas* with *camarón*, *ostión* or *jaiba* (shrimp, scallop or crab) that were invented here. Finally, 21km to the north, beyond the luxury resort of Marbella and the beautiful beaches of **Maitencillo**, another side road leads to the exclusive resorts of Zapallar and Papudo. Most of **Zapallar**'s homes (built after the 1906 earthquake and owned by Santiago's richest families) form a harmonious jumble surrounding the

Which Chilean destination would you recommend most?

That's a tough question: Chile offers such a diverse range of destinations! There's the amazing Atacama Desert in the north; the Mediterranean-like central region with Santiago, Valparaíso, and the wine valleys; the lush temperate rainforests to the south; and the endless labyrinth of fjords and glaciers of wild, pristine Patagonia. Each region has a specific flora and fauna and its own rich cultural heritage. I recommend travelling from north to south!

That sounds quite adventurous; is Chile suitable only for travellers looking to 'rough it'?

Not at all! Chile has a well-developed tourist infrastructure, with mid-range and luxury accommodation available in even the most remote areas. Visitors can explore the rugged outdoors by day, and return to a delicious dinner and a warm bed in the evening. And, of course, our bilingual guides and travel professionals are on hand to ensure a hassle-free trip.

Photo © Patagonia Camp

Most people come to Chile to experience the outdoors. Is Santiago also worth a stay?

Definitely! Santiago's a thriving, vibrant metropolis with first-class restaurants and dazzling nightlife, outstanding museums and cultural sites, colourful neighbourhoods of artists and craftsmen, and plenty of shopping opportunities. And don't forget the wine valleys just south of the city. Whether you're visiting Chile for one week or three, a few days in Santiago are a must.

Chilean-German tour operator travelArt has offices in Santiago, Puerto Varas and Punta Arenas. They offer high-quality tailor-made tours throughout Chile, including cultural excursions, active travel, wine tours, wellness holidays, cruises and much more. We spoke with Judith Nagel, Product & Contracting Manager.

ⓣ +56 (0)2 2378 3440 ⓔ info@travelart.com
ⓦ www.travelart.com & www.facebook.com/english.travelArt.Chile

A familiar sight for the residents of Horcón as horses pull the fishing boats from the sea at the end of the working day. (ETL)

bay, with a fishing cove and a child-friendly beach. A moist microclimate allows exuberant vegetation to flourish, and there's also plenty of marine life here, much of it available for consumption by the fish dock.

Papudo, 81km from Viña del Mar, is the northernmost of central Chile's resorts, a minor port from which footpaths lead along a rocky headland to attractive viewpoints.

East of Viña del Mar
La Campana National Park

Just off the Panamerican Highway north of Santiago, the peak of Cerro La Campana (1,880m) is easily visible to the southwest. It's the centre-point of La Campana National Park, now a UNESCO Biosphere Reserve and one of the few areas where the native flora of central Chile survives. It makes an ideal day-trip from Santiago or the coast and, with 1,400m of steep ascent, it's also an excellent way to prepare for more arduous treks and climbs in the Andes, although it won't be much help with acclimatisation.

Most of the park is covered by the sclerophyllous (hard-broadleaf evergreen) forest of the central coastal cordillera; this is surprisingly dense and varied, comprising over a dozen species of small tree. However, the park is best known for its last substantial stands of Chilean wine-palm (*Jubaea chilensis*), 60,000 of which survive in the northern Ocoa sector. The **Ocoa sector** can be reached simply by turning off the Panamerican Highway at Km100 and following the road south up the Rabuco Valley for a dozen kilometres.

To reach the **summit**, you need to enter the park from the southwest just as Darwin did when he climbed the mountain in 1834. From the park gate it's just over 4km on the Sendero Andinista to the summit, but it can take four hours and you're not allowed to start after midday.

Portillo

Portillo ski resort (2885m) is 152km from Santiago at the top of the 29 bends that lead up to the Los Libertadores border and the crossing into Argentina. Skiing supposedly began here during the construction of the Transandean Railway (opened in 1910); in the 1930s rudimentary ski lifts were installed and the present hotel dates from 1946. Portillo is still one of the most prestigious ski resorts in South America, holding the world skiing speed record. The **Hotel Portillo** (Ⓦ www.skiportillo.com) was refurbished in the early 1990s but still feels more like a clubhouse than a ski hotel. The season opens in June or early July; in August and September the hotel is full, with the US and Austrian teams in residence as a rule, but there are still virtually no queues for lifts.

In summer, like all ski resorts, it looks pretty awful, but there is some **good hiking**, and the restaurant is open even if the hotel is closed.

Other ski resorts near Santiago

Santiago's main axis, the Alameda, runs eastwards and follows the Río Mapocho into the Andes, with some great hiking possibilities where the Sendero de Chile runs along the crests of the precordillera. The ski season lasts from mid-June until early October and all the resorts are an easy day trip from Santiago, although it takes 1½ hours to reach Valle Nevado.

A series of tight switchbacks climb to **Farellones** (2,470m; 32km from Santiago), the oldest of the Mapocho Valley ski stations. It has a few nursery slopes (and relatively low-quality ski rental) and is now a residential base for the resorts higher up the hill, especially **Villa El Colorado** (2,430m; Ⓦ www.elcolorado.cl), just 2km further by road and rather less as the skier flies. This is Chile's most popular ski area, with the best *après-ski*, and is pretty busy at weekends. The road continues for 5km to **La Parva** (2,650m; Ⓦ www.laparva.cl), a smart enclave of private apartments where the Santiago élite gathers.

Turning right at the entry to Farellones, it's 14km to **Valle Nevado** (3,025m; Ⓦ www.vallenevado.com), the highest and most modern of the resorts, and the most popular with northern-hemisphere ski companies. It looks much like Les Arcs or any modern French ski resort, with apartment blocks with ski-jump roofs, and French and Italian restaurants – no surprise, as it was built by a French company in the 1980s. Offering a combined ticket with La Parva, it has the largest ski area in the southern hemisphere, and the best skiing and snowboarding in this area, especially on weekdays. Heli-skiing and heli-boarding are available, but real experts should head for Portillo.

7 Northern Chile

Northern Chile, especially the far north or Norte Grande, is all about the desert – the oldest and driest in the world, and one that's also rich in archaeological remains. Inca and pre-Inca fortifications survive thanks to the very dry climate of the Atacama Desert, and mummified corpses are still being found. Although it virtually never rains, snow does fall on the Andes, providing water for oasis villages that have been inhabited for thousands of years by Aymara and other indigenous peoples. Further north, where Chile borders Peru and Bolivia, the altiplano is a high plateau that's rich in wildlife.

The Norte Chico or Little North, nearer Santiago, is more habitable although still very dry, with the remains of Chile's early mining industry, massive hilltop astronomical observatories, and the historic but still very lively beach resort of La Serena. In rainy years wild flowers burst forth from seemingly barren ground in a stunning phenomenon known as the *desierto florido*, but this is too unpredictable to plan a tour around.

Norte Chico

The Norte Chico is much less arid than the Norte Grande, but it still looks like a desert to the untrained eye; year-round rivers bringing water from the Andes allow farming in the valleys. You'll also find here many remains of pre-Hispanic cultures and of early mining enterprises. Nearer Santiago the climate is 'Mediterranean', although still pretty scrubby; on the coast there are some delightful sandy coves and pockets of remarkably luxuriant vegetation, watered by the sea mist.

The Norte Chico's principal tourist destination is La Serena, adjacent to the port of Coquimbo; the historic mining city of Copiapó dominates the north of the region, but this tends to be overflown by most tourists, together with smaller towns along the Panamerican Highway, such as Vallenar, Caldera and Chañaral. There are beaches and national parks along the coast near La Serena; tours will usually include an excursion inland to the Elqui Valley, known both for its production of *pisco* (grape brandy) and for its 'hippy' residents who have made this a centre of New Age spiritual tourism. There are also public astronomical observatories not far from La Serena – the real scientific exploration takes place on remote mountain tops further north, but this is the centre of Chile's fast-growing astronomic tourism business.

La Serena

La Serena, 474km north of Santiago on the Panamericana, is one of Chile's oldest cities but is also a very happening resort. There are fine

Juvenile pelican at Coquimbo harbour (N/NRA)

colonial and Neocolonial buildings, notable churches, some interesting museums, and enjoyable excursions nearby too. In fact, the beach area a couple of kilometres west of the city centre, is easily overlooked by those short of time.

History

The city was founded in 1544 and re-established after native attacks; it was a staging post for supply ships from Peru and then the administrative centre for much of northern Chile. Silver was found just north of La Serena in 1825, and Chile's first copper rolling mill was established here in 1851, with a railway following in 1865.

Gabriel González Videla, born in La Serena in 1898, was President of Chile from 1946 to 1952 and was responsible for the Plan Serena, which remodelled the city centre between 1948 and 1952. The city was already rich in colonial buildings, but the initiative introduced a consistent Neocolonial style of architecture that still characterises La Serena today. In the 1980s tourism really took off here, with beach-lovers coming from Argentina as well as Santiago. Recently there has been a considerable influx of students to the city, fuelling the nightlife year-round.

La Serena highlights

There are 30 churches in La Serena – details of some are given below – as various religious orders established bases here for members travelling to the Viceroy's seat in Lima; the city has been ravaged by pirates and by earthquakes (especially in 1796 and 1975), but many buildings have survived.

Practicalities

La Serena has excellent transport links, including a modern **airport** (in the suburbs just 5km east) with several flights a day to Santiago and the northern cities of Copiapó, Antofagasta and Iquique. From the bus terminal just south of the centre there are frequent services north and south and less frequent ones inland to Vicuña and the Elqui Valley; roads are of a good standard, even the few unpaved ones. As Chile's busiest beach resort, it has many hotels and restaurants of all standards as well as all other services.

Accommodation

Upmarket
Hotel Costa Real Ⓦ www.costareal.cl
Hotel Diego de Almagro Ⓦ www.dahoteles.com
Hotel La Serena Plaza Ⓦ www.hotelserenaplaza.cl

Moderate
Hotel Del Cid Ⓦ www.hoteldelcid.cl
Hotel Londres Ⓦ www.hotellondres.cl

Budget
Hostel El Punto Ⓦ www.hostalelpunto.cl

Most of the churches are of stone, giving them a more European feel than many in Chile. Since mining brought prosperity in the 19th century a number of foreign architects worked here, producing local versions of international styles. From 1830 to 1860 the Neoclassical style was dominant, before being succeeded by the so-called Clásico Serenense from 1850 to 1880. La Serena's trademark Neocolonial style developed from 1910, but it was the Plan Serena programme that caused many new public buildings and others in this style to appear all over the city. Perhaps the best examples of Plan Serena architecture are along **Pedro Pablo Muñoz** (not to be confused with Anfion Muñoz). **Francisco de Aguirre**, the main avenue just south of the colonial centre, was also remodelled at this time and a central reservation lined with trees and statues was put in.

The **Intendencia** or regional government, on the north side of the Plaza de Armas, was built in 1948 as a cornerstone of the Plan

The Sernatur tourist office is on the plaza at Matta 461 (① 51 225 138 ⊘ Mar-Dec 09.00-18.00 Mon-Fri, 10.00-14.00 Sat, Jan-Feb 09.00-20.00 daily). Most hotels offer Wi-Fi and there are various internet centres; ATMs are plentiful and exchange offices include Cambios Talinay at Prat 515 and Intercam at de la Barra 435.

You can also find food, accommodation, ATMs and other services in the region's smaller towns, but the range and standard will not be as high as in La Serena.

Residencial Suiza ⓦ www.turismolaserena.cl/residencial-suiza

Eating out

The seafront Avenida del Mar in La Serena is lined with lively bars and restaurants, but the best eating is in the city centre.

Café Colonial (café serving breakfast and sandwiches, best coffee in town) Balmaceda 475 ① 51 216 373
Donde El Guatón (excellent grill-house) Brasil 750 ① 51 211 519
El Cedro (Lebanese and Chilean dishes, pleasant patio) Prat 572 ① 51 221 427

Serena. On the eastern side of the plaza are the **City Hall** (1937), **Law Courts** (1938), **Archbishopric** (1938) and the Neoclassical **cathedral**, built between 1844 and 1856 by the French architect Jean (de) Herbage.

Facing the cathedral across the plaza, the **Casa González Videla** was built in eclectic style in 1890 on the site of Francisco de Aguirre's house, and was the president's home until 1977; it now houses the **Museo Histórico Regional Presidente Gabriel González Videla** (President Gabriel González Videla Museum of Regional History; ⊘ 10.00–18.00 Mon–Fri, 10.00–13.00 Sat and holidays). Part of the display here is a tribute to the president and his wife, and there's some good early 20th-century Chilean art. It's easy to miss the main hall where the museum's greatest treasure, a portrait by Gil de Castro of San Martín in 1818, can be found. Upstairs there's a decent display on regional history, with often excellent temporary exhibits.

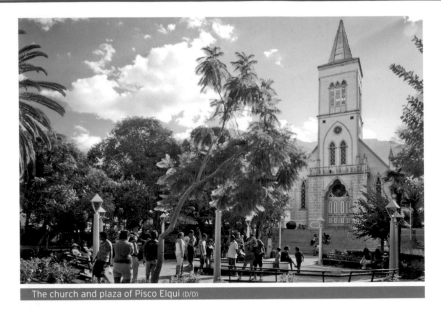

The church and plaza of Pisco Elqui (D/D)

On the plaza's south side, across Cordovez, is the **church of Santo Domingo** (1755–75), which has a simple Neo-Renaissance nave; the façade was added in the late 19th century, followed between 1906 and 1912 by the striking open-frame tower.

A block east of the plaza at Prat and Balmaceda, the **church of La Merced** was built in 1709, with a Neogothic façade and wooden tower added in 1881. Two blocks south is the **church of San Francisco**, the city's oldest, built sometime between 1585 and 1627 in Renaissance style; a Baroque façade was added later.

Two blocks east of the Merced and San Francisco, the **Museo Arqueológico** (Archaeological Museum; Ⓒ muarse@entelchile.net ⊘ 09.30–17.50 Tue–Fri, 10.00–13.00, 16.00–19.00 Sat, 10.00–13.00 Sun), built in 1954 by Mario Muñóz, incorporates a splendid doorway dating from 1820. Around an attractive little patio, exhibits cover the area's geology, the arrival of the first nomadic hunter-gatherers, and the development of settled agriculture and of the distinctive Diaguita ceramics, together with photographs of the city's more recent development. The museum's prize exhibit, however, is the 2.5m high *moai* or stone statue from Easter Island, which President González Videla 'arranged' to have donated to the city in 1952.

Behind the museum, on Benavente, is the **Liceo Gabriela Mistral** (1948), another key part of the Plan Serena. Just northwest, the **church of San Agustín** was built in 1672, rebuilt in 1755 and rebuilt again after the 1975 earthquake; it has a bare stone Neo-Romanesque nave and 18th-century woodwork.

West of the centre, between Pedro Pablo Muñoz and the Panamericana, the **Parque Pedro de Valdivia**, a grassy expanse punctuated by sports grounds and parked cars, also contains the largest **Japanese Garden** (☉ 10.00–20.00 Tue–Sun) in South America (26,000m²); a beautifully maintained oasis around a lake with two islands, linked together by Japanese bridges.

Avenida Francisco de Aguirre runs west to the **Faro** or lighthouse (actually built as a tourist viewpoint between 1951 and 1953). This marks the northern end of **Avenida del Mar**, a 6km strip of restaurants, bars and *cabañas* that in summer is a heaving mass of bronzing humanity.

Excursions from La Serena

Northern Chile is the world centre of **astronomical tourism**, due to its dry air and clear dark skies, and there are some excellent tourist observatories inland from La Serena (in addition to the huge scientific observatories). In the Elqui Valley, east of La Serena, the most convenient are **Cerro Mamalluca** (Ⓦ www.mamalluca.org) and **Cerro Mayu** (Ⓦ www.cerromayu.cl). The Elqui Valley is also known for its alternative therapies and organic foods, as well as the irrigated plantations growing fruit for export and for *pisco*. Mamalluca is near **Vicuña** (61km from La Serena), the valley's main town, where you can visit the museum dedicated to Nobel Prize-winning poet Gabriela Mistral; it's another 32km to Pisco Elqui, with its *pisco* distilleries and New Age cafés.

On the coast 120km south of La Serena, the **Bosque de Fray Jorge National Park** (☉ Dec–Mar 09.00–17.30 daily, Apr–Nov Thu–Sun and

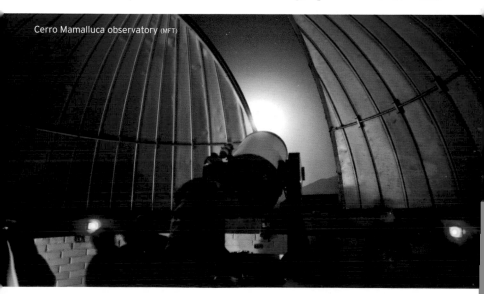

Cerro Mamalluca observatory (MFT)

public holidays) is a popular stop-off and an unexpected haven of greenness, thanks to heavy sea mists. You can hike through forest more familiar in southern Chile, with around 80 species of birds. On the way from La Serena to Fray Jorge you'll pass the lovely **sandy beaches** of Totoralillo and Las Tacas and the fishing coves of **Guanaqueras** and **Tongoy**, where you'll find fantastically fresh seafood.

Norte Grande

Although Chileans sometimes forget it, the Norte Grande (Great North) has been Chilean for barely 130 years, and one might be forgiven for asking why they bothered seizing the world's driest desert, together with some almost equally inhospitable altiplano, populated by Aymara people who have little in common with any other Chileans. The answer lies, of course, in the area's mineral wealth, and above all in nitrates, used as fertiliser and for making explosives until synthetic alternatives were developed in the early 20th century. As luck would have it, copper mining then took over to keep the region's economy thriving.

The Atacama is the world's oldest desert, together with the Namib Desert in southern Africa, and its driest. Sitting behind a low range of coastal hills, it is totally insulated from maritime influences and

View of Lago Miscanti in the Atacama Desert (I/S)

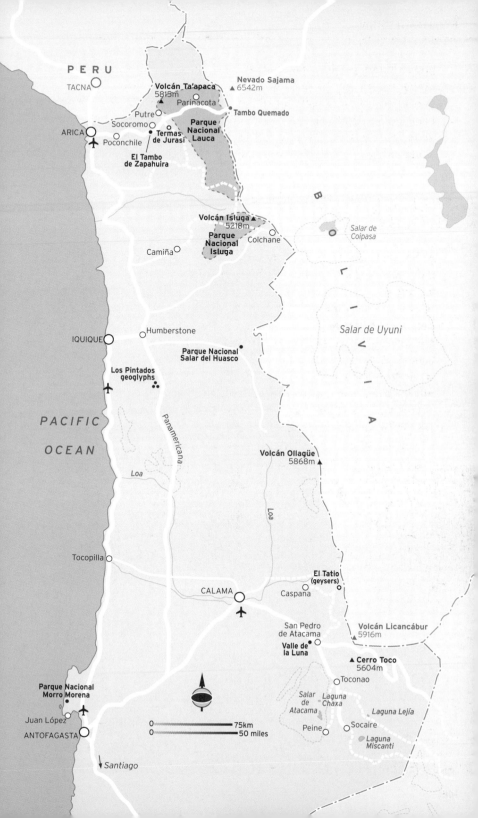

Practicalities

The **Panamerican Highway** mostly runs just inland of the coastal hills, with paved links to all major towns – it's a long lonely drive and if you're just going to San Pedro de Atacama it's far easier to **fly** direct from Santiago to Calama (1,230km) and transfer via a good highway. The major coastal cities are also well served by air and make good bases with reliable hotels and other services.

On the altiplano, the Lauca National Park is usually reached by road from

Accommodation

Antofagasta
Upmarket
Enjoy ⓦ www.ingles.enjoy.cl
Panamericana Hotel Antofagasta ⓦ www.hotelantofagasta.cl

Moderate
Hotel Colón ⓦ www.hotelcolon.cl
Hotel Parina ⓣ 55 223 354

Budget
Hotel Dakota ⓣ 55 251 749
Residencial El Cobre ⓣ 55 225 162

San Pedro de Atacama
Exclusive
Alto Atacama Desert Lodge ⓦ www.altoatacama.com
explora ⓦ www.explora.com
Tierra Atacama ⓦ www.tierraatacama.com

Upmarket
Altiplanico ⓦ www.altiplanico.cl
Awasi ⓦ www.awasi.com
La Aldea ⓦ www.hotelaldea.cl

Moderate
Hostel Katarpe ⓦ www.sanpedroatacama.com/ingles/hs-catarpe.htm
Tambillo ⓦ www.hoteltambillo.cl

Arica – a huge climb from sea level to 4,400m, so altitude sickness can be a real problem – but it can also be reached more gradually from the south, on much rougher roads. There's adequate accommodation in Putre, but none elsewhere on the altiplano – to the south in particular you should be prepared to camp. There is no public transport on the southern part of the altiplano, and tours operate out of Arica rather than Iquique. There's also no ATM anywhere on the altiplano (US dollars are accepted in places, at a poor rate) and limited shops; medical facilities are also virtually non-existent.

Budget
Hostal Mama Tierra ① 55 851 418
Residencial Sonchek Calama ① 55 851 112

Iquique
Upmarket
Hotel Artuto Prat Ⓦ www.hotelartutoprat.cl
Hotel Gavina Ⓦ www.gavina.cl
Terrado Suites Ⓦ www.terrado.cl

Moderate
Hotel Cavancha Ⓦ www.hotelcavancha.cl
Hotel Riorsa ① 57 420 153/423 823

Budget
Hotel Carlos Condell ① 57 313 028 Ⓔ hotel-carlos-condell@entelchil
Hostel La Casona 1920 Ⓦ www.casonahostel.com

Arica
Upmarket
Hotel El Paso Park Ⓦ www.hotelelpaso.cl
Panamericana Hotel Arica Ⓦ www.panamericanahoteles.cl/eng/arica.html

Moderate
Hotel Bahía Chinchorro Ⓦ www.bahiahotel.cl
Hotel Gavina Express Ⓦ www.gavinaexpress.cl

Budget
Hostal Sunny Days Ⓔ sunnydaysarica@hotmail.com
Hotel Las Palmas II ① 57 232 994

Rock pinnacles overlooking the Salar de Tara, Los Flamencos National Reserve (NH/S)

has hardly changed in millions of years; its coastal fringe has been inhabited for only about 10,000 years, with permanent settlements and agriculture established inland around 3000BC. A few transversal valleys carry snowmelt water from the Andes; these provided a toehold for early human habitation, in conjunction with the thriving marine life of the Humboldt Current. Inland from the desert is the precordillera or the foothills of the Andes, at 1,200–3,500m, leading to the altiplano or highlands, a plateau created from the ash thrown out by the spectacular volcanoes that rise to 6,330m. It's high and cold, but marshy grasslands are home to camelids and a wide variety of birds, notably flamingos.

Nowadays the Norte Grande is dominated by the coastal cities of Antofagasta, Iquique and Arica, all major ports but also of historic interest and with attractive beaches. However, its touristic centre is San Pedro de Atacama, an oasis in the high desert. There's a wide range of hotels and restaurants here, together with excursions to salt pans, geysers, volcanoes and Inca forts.

Antofagasta and around

Antofagasta, 1,361km north of Santiago, is the industrial capital of northern Chile, but it also has a lively holiday trade. It owes its existence to its suitability as a port, firstly for the export of nitrates (a natural fertiliser, discovered in 1865 less than 20km inland), then for silver (from 1870) and now for copper. The originally Bolivian city was occupied by Chile in 1879, at the start of the War of the Pacific, and never looked back; it's now a lively city of around 300,000 people and Chile's fifth largest.

Its busy downtown area has some attractive nitrate-era buildings, and more open and modern zones stretch north and south along the *costanera*. The centre of the city is **Plaza Colón**, centred on the strangely miniaturised **Clock Tower**. It was erected in 1912 by the British community to celebrate the centenary of Chilean independence and its chimes sound like Big Ben. On its southeastern side, the Neogothic **cathedral** (1906–17) contrasts with the **Municipal Theatre** to its left, a very raw piece of brutalist concrete. Half a block south at Latorre 2535, the gaudy new **Casa de Cultura** (once the city hall) faces an even grander **fire station**, both built at the start of the 20th century.

A block north of the plaza, the FCAB **railway offices** (1888) blend Neoclassical style with practicality; to the rear are a British-built steam tank engine, a steam crane and some carriages. There's no public admission but it is possible to visit the small museum (at Bolívar 255) by reserving 48 hours ahead (℗ 55 206 590 Ⓔ jlyons@fcab.cl ⅋ free). Across the road at the corner of Bolívar and Washington, the new **Centro Cultural Estación** (⊘ 09.00–19.00 Mon–Fri, 10.30–20.30 Sat–Sun ⅋ free) hosts temporary exhibitions in a restored historic building.

Where Bolívar reaches Balmaceda (the *costanera*), the **Museo Regional** (Regional Museum; ⊘ 09.00–17.00 Tue–Fri, 11.00–14.00 Sat, Sun and holidays ⅋ free Sun and holidays) is in the former customs house, a modular building erected in Valparaíso in 1867 and brought here in 1888. On the ground floor are exhibits on geology, ecology, archaeology and the Spanish conquest; upstairs (via exterior stairs) exhibits cover more recent history.

Across the road are two more fine examples of nitrate-era Neoclassical architecture (both built in 1910), the former **maritime passenger terminal** and the former **Gobernación Marítima** (Maritime Administration), linked by a covered walkway.

A few hundred metres north, at the **Terminal Pescadero** or fishing terminal, the attraction is the **wildlife**, with sea lions, turkey vultures, cormorants, pelicans and several species of herons and gulls waiting to snap up fish waste thrown into the harbour. This is also the place to take **boat trips** into the bay.

Eating out in Antofagasta

Club de la Unión (traditional fixed-price menus) Prat 474 ℗ 055 268 371
El Arriero (grill-house, with quirky uniforms and pianists) Condell 2644 ℗ 55 264 371
Picadillo (lively seafront restaurant, international menu) Av Grecio 1000; Ⓦ www.picadillo.cl

The nitrate pampa

Between Antofagasta, Calama and Iquique you won't miss the relics of the nitrate-mining boom, Chile's first industrial revolution when vast fortunes were made in an area which was not even Chilean territory at first. Find here areas of what seem like peat diggings or ploughed land, ruins of adobe buildings, and small, desolate cemeteries. Some of the ghost towns are remarkably well preserved thanks to the dry desert, and are increasingly visited by tours.

Rougly midway between Antofagasta and Calama, **Baquedano** was once a major rail junction, where the FCAB (the Antofagasta to Bolivia Railway) crossed the state-owned Longino from Santiago to Iquique. Both lines still carry small amounts of freight, and nowadays trains are diesel-hauled, but 5m-gauge steam locomotives (the oldest a Henschel 2-6-0, built in 1911) and a few carriages are still kept in the depot roundhouse and can be seen, with care. Despite the Museo Ferroviario sign, there is no museum as such, although there are plans for one.

Not too far north on the Panamericana is the nitrate *oficina* (processing plant) of **Chacabuco**, which operated only from 1924 to 1938 and was used as a concentration camp by the Pinochet regime in the 1970s; restoration has been under way since 1992, with German aid, and it's now perhaps the best preserved of the *oficinas* (⊘ 09.00–18.00 daily). In the theatre you can see Art Nouveau murals and photographic displays, as well as a view of the whole town and plant. You can also see the church, market, workers' housing and the immense liquefaction plant where the gas is condensed into a liquid.

Just off the Panamericana near the junction to Tocopilla, **María Elena** is one of the very few nitrate mines still working (it wasn't even founded until 1926, after the discovery of synthetic nitrates). There's a fully fledged municipality here, with 10,000 inhabitants, and the Barrio Cívico (including two schools, a theatre, *pulpería* (general store) and public baths) is now a national monument. The **Museo Arqueológico e Histórico** (Archaeological and Historical Museum; ⊘ 09.00–13.00, 16.00–19.00 Mon–Sat, 10.00–13.00, 17.00–20.00 Sun), on the west side of the plaza, covers pre-Hispanic archaeology and the nitrates period.

Pedro de Valdivia is south from María Elena and here the *oficina* (founded in 1931) uses the new Guggenheim process, as at María Elena. For a while the two *oficinas* accounted for half of Chile's nitrate production, but Pedro de Valdivia closed in 1996, its population moving to María Elena. Again, there's a plaza surrounded by grand buildings such as a theatre, hospital, school and church, all now national monuments but stripped bare nevertheless.

Much further north, on the Panamericana about an hour from Iquique, the *oficinas* **Humberstone and Santa Laura**, both disused since 1960, are among the very few nitrates plants surviving in anything like their original state. Despite being listed as national monuments in 1970, they remained subject to vandalism, theft and the depredations of time and weather until 2002 when an industrial museum was established at Humberstone. Even now, Santa Laura still has only token protection.

Humberstone is a full-sized ghost town, and few visitors make it as far as the remnants of the actual industrial sector; at Santa Laura there's little trace of residential buildings, but the massive crusher and liquefaction plant still stand, rattling in the desert wind. **Humberstone** (⊘ 09.00–18.30 daily) was founded in 1862 and renamed in 1934 in honour of James (or Santiago) Humberstone, the British manager who introduced a modified version of the 'Shanks system' for extracting nitrates from the raw caliche. Virtually nothing has been done to the

site (other than installing toilets in a container behind the gatehouse) and you may be amazed by the amount of graffiti. The plaza is surrounded by imposing buildings, including the *pulpería*, the school and market, a hotel and the theatre, which still has its original stage and seating. To the north of the hotel you'll find the town's swimming pool, a surprisingly large tank of cast-iron plates, with diving boards still in place.

Just to the west, **Santa Laura** is not as grand as Humberstone but you can still see the huge liquefaction plant, as well as the infirmary, market and tiny plaza. There's a museum in the manager's house, with the usual bottles, gramophones and faded photos.

The abandoned Humberstone nitrates *oficina*, near Iquique (MO)

La Portada, near Antofagasta (AL/S)

South of the centre and the port are the **ruins of Huanchaca**, a massive smelting works built between 1888 and 1892 to process Bolivian silver ore. Only a few walls remain, below which a new museum is being built by the Universidad Católica del Norte, to cover geology, anthropology and astronomy. Just north in the UCN campus, their present **museum** (⊘ 09.00–12.00, 15.00–18.00 Mon–Fri ✆ free) focuses on the region's mineral wealth.

The headland closing off Antofagasta bay curves around to the north to reach the small beach resort of Juan López, 32km from Antofagasta; you'll pass **La Portada**, the rock arch seen on every Antofagasta tourist leaflet. Nearby is the **Morro Moreno National Park**, where sea mists allow a rare variety of cacti and other plants to survive in the desert.

San Pedro de Atacama and around

The undisputed tourist centre of the Atacama, 103km southeast of Calama by a good paved road, San Pedro de Atacama was once only visited by backpackers who stayed in the many cheap hostels lining its

Eating out in San Pedro

Café Adobe (fine cuisine, open fire on the patio) Caracoles 211 ⓦ www.cafeadobe.cl

Café Tierra Todo Natural (great homemade wholefood and vegetarian snacks) Caracoles 271 ⓦ www.tierratodonatural.cl

La Casona (imaginative menu using quinoa, llama meat and other local foodstuffs) Caracoles ⓦ www.lacasonadeatacama.cl

When to visit

At 2,440m, the sun shines about nine days in ten, with an average maximum temperature of 24°C in January and a minimum of 5°C. In July, the average maximum is 21°C and the minimum -1°C; there can be light frosts in San Pedro, but at altitude it's much colder with temperatures of -10° to -15°C before dawn at El Tatio. There's very little artificial illumination, so star-gazing is great here.

dusty streets. In the last decade there's been something of a revolution, with half-a-dozen very exclusive hotels opening.

San Pedro de Atacama is a small dusty town of unpaved roads and single-storey adobe houses, and is mostly dedicated to the pursuit of the tourist dollar. The centre is dominated by travellers' hangouts, tour companies and the excellent **Museo LePaige**, which explains Atacaman archaeology and anthropology (see below, page 156). However, like many oases, there's more to San Pedro than meets the eye; the tourist zone is only two blocks by five, while 15 *ayllus* or traditional communities are hidden away among the trees and irrigation channels stretching south for a dozen kilometres.

Due to the dry climate, **archaeology** lies thick on the ground in this area; the earliest site dates from 11,600 years ago, when cave-dwelling

The few dusty streets that form the core of San Pedro de Atacama come to life in the evening. (AF)

San Pedro de Atacama

We love the quirky little oasis town of San Pedro de Atacama, from where you can take day trips to see adobe-built, indigenous villages, the salt flats with bright pink flamingos and the El Tatio Geysers. Watch the sunset over the Valle de la Luna (Valley of the Moon), stargaze in the clear, cloudless skies and soak in a thermal bath. It's well worth splashing out on a three-night package at one of the luxury boutique hotels, complete with pool and spa.

hunters arrived from the altiplano. There's evidence of camelid domestication about 4,800 years ago; the San Pedro culture formed 3,000 years ago, succeeded by the more sophisticated Classic Atacameño (or Kunza) culture 2,000 years ago. This reached its peak in the 12th century, ending with the arrival of the Incas around 1450. Naturally the oasis was on the Incas' main road, and the Spaniards established a mission in 1557. During the nitrates boom, San Pedro was a halt for cattle being driven from Argentina to provide fresh beef for the nitrate *oficinas*, but once bypassed by the railways it became a backwater until it was discovered by global tourism.

San Pedro de Atacama highlights

On the east side of the plaza (next to the tourist office) is the town's oldest building, the **Casa de Pedro de Valdivia** (or Casa Incaica). This adobe house was supposedly built by Francisco de Aguirre for de Valdivia's arrival in 1540 and now it houses temporary exhibitions. Across the plaza, the **church of San Pedro**, built in 1744, has very rustic vaulting of cactus wood slats and algarrobo beams with leather binding; the bell tower is relatively recent replacement.

Immediately northeast of the plaza, the modern **Padre LePaige Archaeological Museum** (⊘ 09.00–18.00 Mon–Fri, 10.00–18.00 Sat–Sun and holidays) has a superb collection of relics of the area's ancient cultures. Father Gustave LePaige was a Belgian Jesuit who lived in San Pedro from 1955, dedicating himself to local archaeology. You'll see monochrome ceramics; the red-and-black ceramics of the Classic Atacameño culture; the Inca ceramics with images of the sun; and there are also mummies and a few colonial Spanish items such as a church bell. Make a circuit of the main pavilion and then head down the left-hand arm to see the Treasury of beaten gold bands dating from AD500-900. The museum shop sells reproductions of exhibits and other craft works.

Excursions within easy reach of San Pedro

San Pedro is the base for visiting desert destinations such as the Valle de la Luna and the ruins of Tulor, as well as pre-Hispanic *pukarás* and geoglyphs and the geysers at El Tatio.

At 2,500m, San Pedro is a good spot for acclimatisation and day trips to altitude, and there are plenty of volcanoes to tackle when you're ready. Agencies offer a standard menu of trips, most competing at bargain-basement prices. Hotels and hostels are likely to work with an agency which will pick you up at the door (very useful for those 04.00 departures to Tatio). If you're staying at a hotel with its own excursion programme it's all much easier (and departure for Tatio may be an hour later).

The obligatory excursion is to the **Valle de la Luna (Valley of the Moon)**, 15km southwest of town; wind-blown sand has produced weirdly shaped rock formations reminiscent of The Arches and similar parks in the western USA. They would soon be washed away if it ever rained here. It's fantastic at sunset, when the rocks turn red, gold and amber, but it then gets pretty chilly. You can get here under your own

The Valle de la Luna is the most popular excursion from San Pedro de Atacama. (A/S)

Andean volcanoes seen from the Inca fort of Quitor. (MáCM)

steam, on foot or by mountain bike (easily rented in San Pedro). The more interesting excursions approach from the far side so you can hike for an hour or two in the silence of this desolate landscape rather than with the hordes following the road from San Pedro (there can be up to 300 people here for sunset, although of course most come in minibuses).

Leaving town by the same road and heading southwest through the *ayllu* of Coyo, you'll reach the ruins of **Tulor**, a 10km bike ride each way. This settlement was occupied between 800BC and AD500; the distinctive circular houses were preserved by being buried in the sand until LePaige discovered them in the 1950s. They were only excavated in 1982, with a boardwalk built alongside as well as two replicas across the road.

An easy excursion, by foot or bike or organised tour, is to Quitor and Catarpe, just north of San Pedro. It's about half an hour's walk to the ticket office below the **pukará de Quitor** (⊙ Jan–Mar 07.30–19.45, Apr–Dec 08.30–18.30), which can be seen as you come up the valley. Built in the 12th century, this fort was reinforced by the Incas; Spanish forces were driven off in 1536, but in 1540 it was overrun by Francisco de Aguirre. Now there are over 200 rather over-restored structures in an area of 3ha; it's worth continuing to the ridge for the view.

Continuing up the left bank, the road gets worse; on foot it takes about 45 minutes to a sign for **Catarpe**. Go to the right to the mouth of a gully and then up to the left/north to see the battered remains of the Inca administrative centre, a defensible hilltop site with just a few traces of walls remaining. It's possible to hike across to the Tatio road, but without a guide it's best to return the way you came (9km each way).

The other obligatory excursion, well beyond hiking range (97km from San Pedro), is to **El Tatio**, the world's highest substantial **geyser field** at 4,321m (the road there reaches 4,500m). Underground water meets the magma feeding the area's volcanoes and the resulting steam forces its way up through rock fissures producing 40 geysers in an area of 3km by 700m; the steam is 85°C, and when it meets the sub-freezing dawn temperatures spectacular columns of steam up to 6m high are formed (sounding like massed kettles boiling). There's some rusty pipework from an abandoned geothermal energy scheme, and a swimming pool; you should see vicuña, llama and ñandú, as well as cacti.

The road has been improved recently, especially between San Pedro and Puritama, and you could probably find your way there by car; however, almost everyone takes a tour, leaving San Pedro well before dawn. Some return to San Pedro, perhaps with a stop at the Puritama hot springs, but others make a loop back via Caspana, Ayquina and Calama airport.

Salar de Atacama and surrounds

To the south of San Pedro lies the Salar de Atacama, **Chile's largest saltpan**; to its east lie some tiny settlements that are well worth visiting, on and near the road to the little-used Paso Sico crossing to Argentina. At 2,300m above sea-level, the Salar has a rough broken-up surface, nothing like the billiard table-like surface of Bolivia's Salar de Uyuni; nevertheless it's an intriguing and attractive landscape in its own right. The **Reserva Nacional Los Flamencos**, in seven separate parts, protects saltpans, lagoons and desert where drought-resistant plants struggle to survive. Mammals include foxes, vicuña and southern mountain cavy, and birds include rhea, tinamou, all three Chilean species of flamingo,

Lagunas Altiplanicas and Salar de Atacama

The elevation and extreme desert environment of the Atacama can be challenging for unaccustomed visitors, but this tour makes it trouble-free. From San Pedro, it visits the vast Atacama Salt Flat and the altiplano lagoons, with pink flamingos, highland villages, and the snowy peaks of fitfully sleeping volcanoes as some of the highlights. The dry conditions are ideal for astronomical observations: we recommend a look at the stars through a telescope at night.

coots, Andean gulls, condors, and Gay's seed-snipe. The most visited sector, on the outskirts of San Pedro, protects the famous Valle de la Luna; the biggest is around the Salar de Tara; but perhaps the most interesting is the Soncor sector, 60km south of San Pedro around Laguna Chaxa. To get here, you'll pass through the Tambillo sector, protecting a tamarugo wood, and the village of **Toconao**, known for carvings in volcanic liparite. Its church was built in 1744 and its separate bell tower, the finest in the area, in about 1750.

Laguna Chaxa is the best site for seeing flamingos in this area; another 42km south, the road ends at the church of Peine (also c1750), but you should walk on to the ruins of **Peine Viejo**, a group of circular Atacameño houses dating from before the 12th century. There are the remains of an Inca *tambo* (relay post) here, and a late 16th-century chapel that was one of Chile's first three National Monuments, declared in 1951. You can also walk south to a rock overhang with pictographs, the oldest dating from 2000–3000BC.

Nowadays Peine makes its living from lithium mining (the Salar de Atacama contains 40% of the world's reserves, as well as potassium and borax); an unpaved road heads west over the saltpan to the mine and after 230km reaches Baquedano on the Panamerican Highway.

From Toconao, you can take the Paso Sico road to **Socaire**, another oasis village with pre-Hispanic terraced fields, and the stunning **Laguna Miscanti** (4,350m), its deep-blue waters surrounded by desert and volcanoes; there are more flamingos here, and ñandúes and ducks. From Toconao there's another sidetrip to **Laguna Lejía** (4,190m), which is well known for birds, notably the horned coot.

The massive **Volcán Licancábur** rises to 5,916m immediately east of town; it's possible to get to the top (where there's an Inca shrine) by mountain bike or by hiking, with guides who may even carry oxygen. The Paso Jama road continues east, passing north of **Cerro Toco**

(5,604m), the easiest and most popular of the area's peaks, which is used by those acclimatising for higher volcanoes such as Sairécabur (6,100m) or Apagado (5,700m), just north of Licancábur.

Many new **radio-telescopes** are being built by consortia of northern-hemisphere universities at an altitude of 5,000m, 60km from San Pedro. The world's largest, ALMA (the Atacama Large Millimeter Array), opened in 2011 and has 64 dishes 12m in diameter.

Iquique and around

The industrial motor of the Norte Grande, Iquique (1,850km north of Santiago) is also the most attractive of the northern port cities, with a good beach, great seafood and a distinctive Neoclassical style of architecture developed in the early 20th century. From 1828, nitrates were exported through the city (then in Peru), and in 1879 following the naval Battle of Iquique – a glorious defeat that created Chile's greatest military hero, Arturo Prat – the city was seized by Chile, starting the nitrate boom which lasted until 1920. During this period there developed the 'Georgian' Neoclassical style of architecture seen at its best on **Calle Baquedano**, where houses have two-storey balconies and an upper floor that is almost completely open under a (usually rusty) tin roof, to catch a cooling breeze. After the decline of the nitrate industry, Iquique became the world's leading exporter of fishmeal.

The city's hub is **Plaza Prat**, surrounded by attractive buildings, notably the Croatian and Spanish clubs, and the **Municipal Theatre**, built as an opera house between 1889 and 1890. From here the pedestrianised Calle Baquedano runs south to the beach and is lined with a fine selection of homes built between 1880 and 1920, mainly of imported Oregon pine from the USA. The former Law Courts (1892) at Baquedano 951 house the **Museo Regional** (Regional Museum; ☉ 08.30–16.00 Mon–Fri, 10.30–13.00 Sat ☞ free), with displays on wildlife, indigenous archaeology and life, and the *oficinas de salitre* (nitrate plants).

Plaza Arturo Prat, Iquique (SS)

Eating out in Iquique

Boulevard (café with authentic French cuisine, notably the seafood) Baquedano 790 ⊕ 57 413 695
Club Español (traditional fixed-price menus, fabulous setting) Plaza Prat 584 ⊕ 57 423 284
El Sombrero (city's finest seafood restaurant, with Peruvian and Mediterranean touches) Los Rieles 704 ⊕ 57 435 050

At the corner of Baquedano and O'Higgins, is the **Palacio Astoreca** which was built in 1904 as a mansion for a nitrate magnate; it's now the university's cultural centre and well worth a look inside whether or not there's an interesting show on (⊘ 10.00–13.00, 16.00–19.30 Tue–Fri, 10.00–13.30 Sat, 11.00–14.00 Sun ⊛ free). Three blocks south at the corner of Baquedano and Riquelme, the **Museo Histórico Militar** (Museum of Military History; ⊘ 10.00–13.15 Mon–Fri ⊛ free) really gives too much detail of the army's role in the War of the Pacific, from the Chilean viewpoint.

Northwest of Plaza Prat is a **cathedral** built in 1885 in Italian Neoclassical style, it has an attractive star-spangled blue ceiling. Just west of here on Esmeralda, the former Aduana or Customs House (1871) houses the **Museo Naval** (Naval Museum; ⊘ 09.00–12.30, 15.00–18.00 Tue–Sat, 09.30–13.00 Sun ⊛ free); the Chilean survivors of the Battle of Iquique were briefly held here, and the museum is a memorial to Prat and the heroes of Iquique. Around the corner to the west is a fine interior courtyard with a local history display.

There's good **wildlife** viewing in the fishing harbour, immediately west, where sea lions and pelicans jostle for fish scraps. From the covered **Muelle de Pasajeros** (passenger pier; 1901), boats will take you around the harbour or – for a longer trip – to the site of the Battle of Iquique.

Just north, across the road from the bus terminal, the **Museo Corbeta Esmeralda** (tours only, book a day ahead ⊕ 57 530 812 ⓔ reservas@ museoesmeralda.cl except Sun when it's first come, first served ⊘ 10.00–13.00, 14.00–18.00 Tue–Sun,) is a splendid replica of the ship (built in Britain in 1855) sunk in the Battle of Iquique.

For many people the focal point of Iquique is the beach, or rather the two main beaches of **Playa Cavancha** and **Playa Brava**, south of the centre on either side of the rocky Peninsula de Cavancha. The sheltered Playa Cavancha is more popular, with swimming and surfing year-round; the aptly named Playa Brava or 'Wild Beach' to the south is better for sunbathing than swimming.

Sights near Iquique

Just before the junction of Ruta 16 with the Panamericana, 46km inland from Iquique, you can visit the ghost town of **Humberstone** and the preserved nitrate processing plant of the **Oficina Santa Laura** (see box, page 153). On Saturday mornings, the Transatacama tourist train (☏ 2 620 9620 ⓦ www.transatacama.com) runs from Iquique (outside the bus terminal) to Santa Laura and Humberstone, and on to the **Pintados geoglyphs** (☉ 10.30–17.30 daily). The Pintados geoglyphs, next to the Panamerican Highway 96km southeast of Iquique, are perhaps the most impressive array of rock art in Chile.

Arica

Founded in 1565, Arica was the port for the fabulous Potosí silver mines in what is now Bolivia; these days it's increasingly popular with Bolivians for beach holidays and surfing. Part of Peru until 1880, it still has something of a Peruvian feel, with Arequipeña beer, subtropical fruit and Quechua textiles for sale. It's known as 'the city of eternal spring' for its balmy climate and has the warmest water for bathing in Chile; sometimes it has no rain for years on end, but it can be misty.

The city is not especially attractive but has a few interesting buildings, including a couple prefabricated in France to designs by Gustave Eiffel. The **cathedral**, on Plaza Colón, was designed by Eiffel in 1875, 13 years before he became famous for building a tower in Paris; it was intended for a Peruvian town, but Arica's church was destroyed by an earthquake

The Pintados geoglyphs line a route taken by ancient llama caravans to the sea. (AK)

The former Aduana or Customs House in Arica was designed by Gustave Eiffel. (AYZ/S)

in 1868, and the new church was sent here instead.

To the west of the cathedral is the tourist office and the **Aduana** or customs house. Also by Eiffel (1874), the Customs House is now a cultural centre (☉ 09.00–21.00 ✍ free) and displays interesting historical photos as well as hosting temporary shows. Just to the north, a squat steam locomotive sits in front of the terminus of the railway to La Paz, and to the west across the busy highway is the port entrance; you can walk in to the **Terminal Pesquero**, or fishing port, to watch the night herons, turkey vultures, cormorants, pelicans, gulls and sea lions waiting for scraps of fish guts. You can also take **boat trips** from here.

Behind the cathedral, Colón leads south to **Casa Bolognesi**, headquarters of the Peruvian commander Francisco Bolognesi who was killed in 1880. It is where the Peruvian consulate now puts on occasional exhibitions. Carry on up to the **Museo de Sitio Colón 10** (10 Colón St Museum; ☉ 10.00–18.00 Tue–Sun), built over some ancient Chinchorro graves and displaying some of the mummies which were buried there between 4,200 and 3,800 years ago, and continue to the top of El Morro, where a fort (captured by Chile in 1880) houses the **Museo Histórico y de Armas** (Museum of History and Weapons; ☉ 09.00–22.00 daily). This museum tells a slightly one-sided story of the War of the Pacific.

Avenida Comandante San Martín leads south from the port to the city's main beaches, **El Laucho** and then **La Lisera**. To the north of

Eating out in Arica

Casino La Bomba (one of the best of Chile's typical fire-station canteens) Colón 357 ① 58 255 626

El Arriero (good mid-range grill-house in pedestrianised zone) 21 de Mayo 385 ① 58 232 636

Maracuyá (the best seafood restaurant, by the ocean) San Martín 321 ⓦ www.restaurantmaracuya.cl

town are more beaches and then the wetlands of the **Lluta River**, where thousands of migratory birds feed.

Avenida Diego Portales leads up to the **Azapa Valley**. This oasis is worth a visit, above all for the University of Tarapacá's superb **Museo Arqueológico** (Archaeological Museum; ⓦ www.uta.cl/masma ⊙ Mar–Dec 10.00–18.00, Jan–Feb 09.00–20.00). With the very helpful handouts in English, French or German you'll follow developments from the very first settlers gathering seafood on the coast, through the ceramics of the Arica culture and the Chinchorro mummies (the oldest in the world), to contemporary Aymara culture on the altiplano. There's also a fine selection of geoglyphs or patterns of stones, dating from 1000 to 1400, on the southern hillsides of the Azapa Valley, which can be glimpsed from the main road on the north side of the valley, or visited more closely by bike, taxi or car, following the Circuito Arqueológico signs.

To the altiplano

From Arica the good paved highway to La Paz leads to Putre, the best option for spending a night to acclimatise to altitude. This has long been a trade route between the highlands and the sea, so it's no surprise to see geoglyphs, probably created in pre-Hispanic times to act as waymarks for llama caravans. About 23km from the Panamericana is the Inca settlement of **Molle Pampa**, and just beyond (at 540m) the village of **Poconchile**, known for its plain little Andean church, built in 1605 and rebuilt in the 19th century. The highway continues up the Lluta Valley and then climbs on to a high bare plateau in a couple of massive hairpins known as the **Cuesta del Aguila**, before passing through a zone of scattered candelabra cacti, up to 5m tall, which look like nothing so much as a bad hair day.

The road dips briefly to pass the **Pukará de Copaquilla** (3,250m); built in the 12th century, it was restored in 1979 and there's now a roadside viewpoint from which you can see the fortifications above a 150m-deep gorge. Next comes the **Tambo de Zapahuira**, with ancient walls on both sides; it seems that this wasn't so much a *tambo* (relay post) as a trading post, and there are also *chullpas* or tombs visible 150m to the south.

Just after you see the first snowy peak ahead, a paved road turns left to **Socoroma** (2,900m), an isolated little village with a church built in 1560 amid pre-Hispanic terraces.

Putre

At 3,525m above sea level, Putre was founded in 1580 by the Spanish who moved here to escape malaria in Arica. It's now a simple town of

When to visit

The best season for birding and botanising is from March to May, after the rainy season (when mornings are usually sunny); from mid-May to the end of June nights are at their coldest, about -5°C in Putre and -20°C on the altiplano. July to December are the best months for trekking and adventure tourism, and flamingo chicks are visible in July and August. From October to December you may see *polluelos* or ñandú chicks tended by their fathers.

about a thousand people plus the members of an army regiment; it's a good place to break your journey to acclimatise to altitude, and there are some worthwhile hikes in the area, especially if you're interested in birds or cave paintings. It's also possible to embark on more serious ornithological tours, and hikes up the stunning **Volcán Ta'apaca** (or Nevados de Putre; 5,815m), overlooking the town to the north.

The main street is Baquedano, with a few *hospedajes* and restaurants; the plaza is two blocks to the north, dominated by the **church**. This dates from 1670 but was thoroughly rebuilt in 1871 when the present façade and choir were added; the altarpiece dates from 1895. It's kept closed, but you can ask at the *casa parroquial*, to the right, to visit. The town's houses are simple but many have fine **stone doorways**, most bearing dates in the late 19th century.

It's also worth mentioning the **Termas de Jurasi**, recently refurbished hot springs that are 3km down a dirt road on the right just after Km130 on the La Paz Highway (3km east of the Putre junction). These are covered open-air pools 50–53°C, and there's a caretaker who does a fine job of keeping everything clean.

On the altiplano

Parque Nacional Lauca

From Putre the highway climbs on to the altiplano, entering the **Lauca National Park** after 10km (at 4,400m); the ranger post (☉ 09.00–12.30, 13.00–17.30 Mon–Fri) is another 9km on (at Km146), just beyond the hot springs of Las Cuevas, where there's a concrete pool of water at 31°C. The park straddles the paved highway from Arica to Bolivia and covers 1,378km² of puna between 3,200m and 6,342m. The park was a massive 5,200km² in area until 1983 when – despite having been declared a UNESCO World Biosphere Reserve just two years earlier – huge areas were excised from it and reconstituted as the Reserva Nacional Las Vicuñas and Monumento Natural Salar de Surire, in order to allow mining.

It receives just 280mm of precipitation per year (as rain in summer and snow in winter), and average temperatures range from 20°C to –10°C at night. There are some woods of *queñoa* (*Polylepis rugulosa*) below 3,800m, but above this altitude there are only wet and dry *praderas* (grasslands) and *bofedals* (damp, marshy areas), with cushion plants (*llareta*; *Laretia compacta*) that seem, well, cushiony, but in fact are very solid; under the green exterior there's very dense wood that is used for fuel by the Aymara.

Visiting the park and wildlife highlights

There are few **mammals** found here, other than the four camelid species, pumas, vizcachas, the taruca or northern huemul, and the red fox. The only reptiles are Liolaemus lizards and a non-venomous snake; there are also a couple of frogs. There's a greater variety of **birds** (at least 130 species), especially at the lakes: most notably giant coots, various ducks, the black-crowned night-heron, and all three Chilean species of **flamingo** (see box, overleaf). The Andean avocet also feeds on fly larvae in salt lakes. On dry land you may find the puna rhea, puna plover, puna tinamou, diademed sandpiper plover, raptors such as condor and black-chested buzzard eagle, and plenty of passerines (perching birds).

Apart from the flamingos, the park's great success story has been the recovery of the **vicuña** population (depleted by poaching for their wool) from about 1,000 to 16,000. Currently the most threatened species is the puna rhea, due to egg poaching.

Five minutes' walk from the ranger post it's easy to see vicuña and vizcacha as there is a *chacu* or rock funnel and corral used in pre-Hispanic times to round up vicuña.

The highway crosses a watershed to the **Bofedal de Parinacota**, a wide marshy area, source of the Río Lauca and the best grazing in the park for camelids; there's also plenty of birdlife on its lagoons, notably giant coots. It lies at the foot of Los Payachatas, the twin dormant volcanoes Parinacota (6,330m) and Pomerape (6,232m).

At Km162 the road reaches **Chucuyo** (4,300m), little more than half-a-dozen houses-cum-shops and three truckers' restaurants; local women

Puna plover
(JL)

Parinacota church (I/D)

sell alpaca wool goods here, which are excellent value. This is also a good location for **birding**. Another 5km on, a road leads left/north for 5km to the larger village of **Parinacota** (4,392m), well worth visiting for its 17th-century church, rebuilt in 1789. Built of stone and whitewashed, the church is thatched with bunchgrass, with a separate squat bell tower at one corner. Its interior was painted in the 17th century by a Cuzco artist; there's also a bizarre collection of the skulls of former priests, ancient books, and a table chained to the wall that supposedly used to walk through the village at night. Catholicism in the altiplano certainly retains many pre-Christian elements.

The village houses are usually shut up, with the population living in Putre, Arica and elsewhere and gathering only for *fiestas* on, for instance, 30 August and 8 September, when llamas are sacrificed to *pachamama* or Mother Earth, alongside more conventional Catholic rites. Conaf's chalet-style *guardería* is the best source of information on the national park and adjoining reserves (☉ 09.00–12.30, 13.00–17.30 Mon–Fri).

The most exciting excursion here is the **ascent of Cerro Guane Guane** (5,097m), which is relatively easy for anyone reasonably fit and acclimatised, taking about six hours return. There's also a 9.5km hike from the village to the **Mirador Lagunas** on the La Paz Highway, passing the Lagunas de Cotacotani, a *bofedal* dotted with lagoons. Continuing along the highway, it's another 5km to a *mirador* (viewpoint) over Lago Chungará (4,512m), a lake surrounded by snowy volcanic peaks, notably Volcán Parinacota to the north and Volcán Guallatiri (6,061m) 25km to the south, the area's only active volcano, with fumaroles that are usually steaming. **Lago Chungará** was formed when a lava flow blocked the headwaters of the Río Lauca; now its water seeps through the volcanic rock to the Lagunas de Cotacotani, and then to the Bofedal de Parinacota and into the Río Lauca. The lake is home to Andean geese, gulls and ducks, all three Chilean species of flamingo, and 8,000-odd giant coots, which build floating nests of reeds.

It's 7km further to the Chilean border post and another 7km to the actual frontier and Bolivian border post at Tambo Quemado (4,660m). This is the site of a **market** on alternate Fridays when the Aymara from both sides of the border meet and trade, with the Chileans keen to buy coca leaves (for *maté de coca* tea) among other things.

Flamingos

The rarest and largest of Chile's three flamingo species (up to 1.2m in height) is the Andean flamingo (*parina grande*; *Phoenicoparrus andinus*), which (in captivity) lives for up to 25 years; the James' flamingo (*parina chica*; *P. jamesi*) was thought extinct until 1957, but there are now known to be around 3,500 in this region. The Chilean flamingo (*flamenco rojo*; *Phoenicopterus chilensis*)

Andean flamingos (LK/S)

ranges from the puna to the Torres del Paine; the others are only in this area. They feed on small molluscs and crustacea such as brine shrimps, algae and diatoms (which stain the lakes red); the three species have differently sized filters in their beaks so that they don't compete for the same food. The total Chilean population of flamingos was about 73,000 in 1986 and fell to 13,000 in 1994; it's recovered to 17,500, but they are still vulnerable.

Around Parque Nacional Lauca

To the **north** of the Lauca National Park there lies a sizeable but little-known area of altiplano squeezed up between Peru and Bolivia. From Parinacota a rough dirt road continues north through a larger *bofedal*, also well populated by camelids, and after 28km reaches **Caquena**. This is another village that's virtually abandoned except at *fiesta* time and has a 16th-century church that was rebuilt in 1891. Passing through **Cosapilla**, with its 17th-century church, the road reaches Visviri (4,069m), 86km from Parinacota. The main site of interest to visitors, a 12km hike to the southwest, is the **Pukará de Visviri**, a fort that was built between 1100 and 1400.

Immediately to the **south** of Lauca is the **Reserva Nacional Las Vicuñas**, covering 2,091km² at between 4,300 and 5,600m; this is rather wilder, with roads open only from March to November, and even then best tackled in a 4x4 – some local operators will arrange this.

From here the rough road continues south for another 48km to the **Monumento Natural Salar de Surire**, a saltpan of 113km² at 4,245m. It's named after the rhea (*suri* is the Aymara word for the rhea or ñandú, the flightless South American ostrich), but you can also see vicuña,

the three Chilean species of flamingo, hairy armadillo and vizcacha, a colony of which is right by the *guardería*.

Continuing south and swinging to the east around the *salar*, it's 17km to the **Termas de Polloquere** hot springs where there's very basic accommodation and camping.

Parque Nacional Isluga

The **Isluga National Park** covers 1,747km² of estepa de altura (high-altitude steppe), dominated by volcanoes such as the smoking peak of Volcán Isluga (5,218m). Receiving less than 350mm of rain per year, the terrain is largely covered by a scrub of queñoa, with *llareta* cushion plants and marshy *bofedals*. Isluga is far less visited than Lauca, so it's quieter but with fewer facilities. Signs by rivers and springs warn of naturally occurring arsenic in the water in this area.

The park can be reached from Lauca to the north, by a very minor road from Camiña, or by the highway from Iquique to Bolivia via the Colchane border crossing. From Colchane it's 6km northwest to the village of **Isluga**, which like Parinacota, consists of houses which are opened up only at *fiesta*-time, while its Aymara population spends most of its time at remote settlements with the llamas and alpacas. The whitewashed 17th-century church here was restored in 1998, but is only used once a year, on 21 December – the Feast of St Thomas the Apostle. You'll pass the park entrance here, and in 10km reach the village of Enquelga (3,850m), site of the park administration (☉ 08.30–13.00, 14.00–17.30 Mon–Fri).

Continuing to the west, roads pass either side of **Laguna Arabilla**; the southern one is better as a rule, and takes a longer route through the park, turning sharp right at Latarana, after meeting the road from Puchuldiza and Chusmiza. Just west of Latarana, on the minor road to Camiña, is **Laguna Parinacoya** (or Parinacota), where you can see birds and camelids. To the north, the roads meet and head north towards the Salar de Surire; just before leaving the park there are some more *aguas calientes* or hot pools a couple of kilometres to the east. It's 89km by the longer road from Enquelga to the Guardería Surire.

Chile has so many different climates and regions; what's the best way to see them all?

It's better to explore a couple of regions in depth rather than try to see it all. I recommend that visitors to Chile also visit Argentina so you can explore deserts, Mediterranean climates and Patagonia on both sides of the Andes. In the north, the Atacama and Salinas Grandes demonstrate the immense beauty of the altiplano. In the centre of Chile, the mild climate is great for a visit to Santiago's wine region, and don't miss its Argentine counterpart: Mendoza. Chile and Argentina pair well, and give you a more diverse taste of South America.

What tours do you recommend for exploring Patagonia and glaciers?

Spend at least a day visiting Torres del Paine. We offer various itineraries and cruises that include this national park. Another great way to see Patagonia in Chile is to take a cruise of the ice fields. And Patagonia doesn't stop at the border: in Argentina, you'll see the Perito Moreno Glacier near El Calafate, the largest advancing glacier in the world, plus penguins and whales!

What is a unique must-see sight for a first-time traveller to Chile?

The Atacama Desert is a unique add-on to any Chile itinerary. Spend one evening witnessing the sunset, and you will know what I mean. The desert has no clouds, and so there are always beautiful sunsets. Every evening, the sky, mountains and desert glow red and light up with amazing colours.

SouthAmerica.travel is the expert in 4* and 5* South America tours. Licensed and bonded in the US, they have been sharing their passion for South American travel since 1999. They have offices in Seattle, Buenos Aires, Lima, Rio de Janeiro and Stuttgart. We spoke to the CEO, Juergen Keller.

① +44 (0)20 3026 0287 (UK), +1 800 747 4540 (US)
Ⓔ chile@SouthAmerica.travel Ⓦ www.SouthAmerica.travel

8 Santiago to the Lakes District

South of Santiago, the Central Valley is Chile's heartland, heavily settled since colonial times and producing large quantities of fruit and wine. Between the Andes and the coastal cordillera, it's marked by a series of rivers flowing west to the Pacific, with no watersheds between them. To the south is Araucanía, the Mapuche heartland, now dominated by the forestry industry; in the Andean foothills to the east lie a succession of superb national parks, with great hiking on the slopes of massive volcanoes. Further south is Chile's Lakes District, where dairy cattle provide the foreground to photos of further volcanoes looming over gorgeous lakes. There are few ocean beaches here, but the lakes are busy in summer and there are all kinds of adventure sports available, above all in Pucón.

South of Santiago

Densely populated since colonial times, the Central Valley is a prosperous agricultural area, with a row of attractive towns that offer good hotels and restaurants and some historic attractions. To the east, there are some stunning but relatively little-known national parks and reserves in the Andean foothills that are well worth visiting.

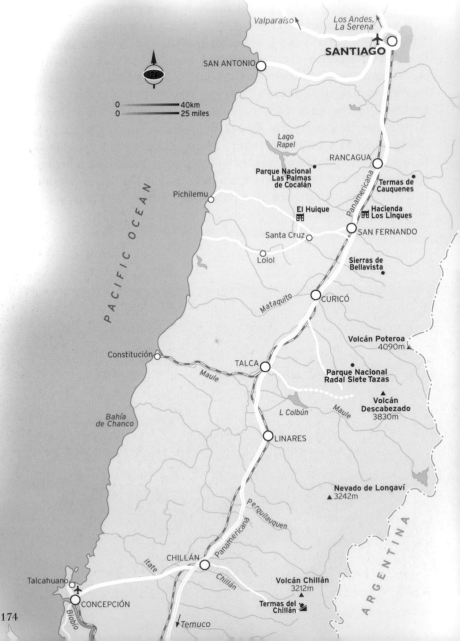

Santa Cruz and the wine roads

Chile's wine-producing area is creeping north and south, with new vineyards doing well in the Elqui and Limarí valleys near La Serena, and the Biobío and Malleco valleys south of Concepción; but its heartland is to the south of Santiago. Above all (as far as tourism is concerned), the Colchagua Valley, centred on the attractive little town of Santa Cruz, is famed for its red wines (notably Carmenère) and its visitor-friendly wineries, many of which have now opened boutique hotels. This was the first of Chile's wine areas to create a wine route or Ruta del Vino (Ⓦ www.rutadelvino.cl), in 1996, co-ordinating visits, independently or in organised groups, to eight major wineries. This was followed by other wine routes in Casablanca and the Curicó and Maule valleys.

Hacienda Los Lingues

Just a few kilometres north of San Fernando (4km east from Km124.5 of Ruta 5; Ⓦ www.loslingues.cl), the Hacienda Los Lingues is a **colonial estate** and mansion that's now perhaps the most exclusive hotel in Chile. Owned by the same family since 1599, the house was built in the 17th and early 18th centuries, with the wings added a century later in the same style. The beautifully preserved house is full of antiques, with lovely gardens, a chapel, a working farm and stables where pure Chilean Aculeo horses are bred. Overnight stays are pricey, but day

Eating out in Colchagua

In central Santa Cruz, your best option is the **Los Varietales** restaurant at the Hotel Santa Cruz Plaza (see page 178). There are a couple of fine restaurants on the northern edge of Santa Cruz, including La Casita de Barreales and Vino Bello, and several others on vineyards in the area; tables should be reserved in advance.

El Candil (grill that also serves tapas and good wines) Ⓦ www.elcandil decolchagua.cl
La Casita de Barreales (fine Peruvian food, closed Mon) Ⓣ 72 824 468
Rayuela Wine & Grill (grilled foods and the Pairings menu offering dishes matched with specific wines) Ⓦ www.viumanent.cl/wine-tourism/restaurant
Viña Casa Silva Chile and international food in a country-style restaurant) Ⓦ www.casasilva.cl
Vino Bello (Italian-Californian food wonderfully matched with local wines) Ⓦ www.vinobello.cl

Practicalities

Santiago and Concepción are Chile's two biggest cities, and the area between them is the most populous part of the country, with a succession of major towns linked by **Ruta 5** (the Panamerican Highway) and (as far as Chillán) by passenger **trains**, too. Concepción has an **airport**, and in the north of the region, Santa Cruz and the Colchagua wineries are easily reached from Santiago airport.

The **Panamericana** is a modern dual-carriageway the length of this region, with good links to all its cities; heading towards the Andes and the many stunning national parks, roads may be unpaved but they are well maintained and usually open except in the most extreme weather (or volcanic eruptions).

The **Maule wine route** has an office in central Talca (Av Circunvalación Oriente 1055 ① 8 157 9951 ⓦ www.valledelmaule.cl ⊘ 09.00–18.00 Mon–Fri), from where visits to a dozen vineyards can be arranged.

Towns such as **Rancagua**, **San Fernando** and **Linares** have all the essential services and at least adequate mid-range hotels and restaurants.

Santa Cruz was until recently a sleepy country town, and although it's now a centre for wine tourism there's only one decent hotel and restaurant in

visits are possible and include lunch, swimming and a demonstration rodeo. It's far easier, however, to visit El Huique (see page 183).

Santa Cruz and the Colchagua Valley

Leaving the Panamericana at San Fernando, it's under an hour southwest on the so-called Carretera del Vino (Wine Highway – actually leading to Chile's surfing capital of Pichilemu) to Santa Cruz, the heart of the Colchagua Valley. This is the key area for wine tourism in Chile (along with Casablanca and the big wineries on the southern edge of Santiago, see pages 129–31 and 114–15 respectively). The town itself is dominated by one man, former arms dealer Carlos Cardoen, who has set up a splendid museum, a casino, the town's finest hotel (the Santa Cruz Plaza), and the valley's only vineyard that's unashamedly set up for tourism rather than just tolerating it as a side activity (Viña Santa Cruz, see pages 182–3).

The heart of Santa Cruz is its tree-studded **plaza**, where the clock tower housing a carillon and the tourist information centre stands in the southwest corner. Also on the southern side of the plaza is a rather unusual church (1879), almost altiplánico with its rough white exterior and fort-like protrusions. It was largely destroyed in the 2010

the town itself, with many fine alternatives on the vineyards. It has a **tourist information centre** on the main plaza but it may be better to ask at the **Ruta del Vino office** for information about the area (① 72 823 199 ⓦ www.rutadelvino.cl ⊘ 09.00–18.00 Mon–Fri, 10.00–18.00 Sat–Sun). The office can book tours, with or without your own transport; English-, French- and German-speaking guides are available. Note that you can also turn up independently at many wineries.

Curicó has one of Chile's finest plazas but little in the way of facilities beyond ATMs and one good hotel. The best restaurants are in this hotel and at the Miguel Torres vineyard (see pages 183–4), just a couple of kilometres south. Mapuyampay Hotel Gastronómico, about 30km northeast of Curicó, is a gastronomic haven, run by a Belgian cookery writer. **Talca**, where there's still plenty of evidence of the massive 2010 earthquake, is larger and a bit more industrial than the agricultural towns to north and south and has some decent hotels and restaurants. Talca and **Concepción** are student towns and have some lively **bars** and **pubs**. Concepción has all the services you might need, including a few excellent restaurants. For those wishing to visit the ski resorts and the national parks in the cordillera to the east, **Chillán** is an excellent base.

For accommodation options, see overleaf.

earthquake and is being rebuilt in concrete.

The **Museo de Colchagua**, one of Chile's best museums, is just across a bridge from the plaza at Avenida Errázuriz 145 (ⓦ www.museocolchagua.cl; ⊘ 10.00–18.00 Tue–Sun). After a ten-minute video, exhibits start with geology, including fine fossils and the skeleton of a giant sloth, and archaeology, including a Chinchorro mummy. The amazing collection of pre-Hispanic artefacts from the length of the Andes include gold and silver, ceramics, textiles (as well as wonderful pieces with feathers), plus shrunken heads from the Amazon and two Inca *quipus*

The Museo de Colchagua, Santa Cruz (Tit/D)

Accommodation

Exclusive
Hotel Casa Silva (San Fernando) Ⓦ www.casasilva.cl
Hotel Santa Cruz Plaza (Santa Cruz) Ⓦ www.hotelsantacruzplaza.cl

Upmarket
Gran Hotel Isabel Riquelme (Chillán) Ⓦ www.hotelisabelriquelme.cl
Gran Hotel Termas de Chillán (Termas de Chillán) Ⓦ www.termaschillan.cl
Hotel Diego de Almagro (Concepción) Ⓦ www.tinyurl.com/DAconcepcion
Hotel El Araucano (Concepción) Ⓦ www.tinyurl.com/elaraucano
Hotel Las Terrazas (Chillán) Ⓦ www.lasterrazas.cl
Hotel Marcos Gamero (Talca) Ⓦ www.marcosgamero.cl
Hotel Nevados de Chillán (Termas de Chillán) Ⓦ www.nevadosdechillan.com
Hotel Terraviña (Santa Cruz) Ⓦ www.terravina.cl
Hotel Vendimia (Santa Cruz) Ⓦ www.hotelvendimia.com
Las Majadas Guest House (Camino el Huique) Ⓦ www.bisquertt.cl/majadas.php
Mapuyampay Hotel Gastronómico (Curicó) Ⓦ www.mapuyampay.cl
Posada de Colchagua (Isla de Yaquil) Ⓦ www.posadacolchagua.cl
Residence Lapostolle (Clos Apalta vineyard) Ⓦ www.en.lapostolle.com

Moderate
Casa Chueca (Talca) Ⓦ www.trekkingchile.com/casa-chueca

or message strings. There are collections of conquistador weapons; colonial and Mapuche silverwork; relics of the War of the Pacific and the pacification (ie: conquest) of Araucanía; printing presses and the like; a *huaso* room with brands, spurs and huge wooden stirrups; and some horse-carriages. Fittingly for an arms-dealer, there are plenty more weapons, from samurai swords to a Krupp field gun, as well as German pistols and Goering's hunting knife. Outside are traction engines and other agricultural machines, and a whole railway station, with a steam locomotive that worked the Pichilemu line until 1965. Two new rooms are on Darwin and the amazing rescue of the 33 miners from the San José mine in 2010.

Carlos Cardoen is also behind the **Tren del Vino** project, which reopened 57km of the Pichilemu railway line, from San Fernando to Peralillo, but has been out of action since the 2010 earthquake. Passengers travelled one way by steam train and returned by bus after lunch, winery visits and lots of entertainment.

Hostal del Puente (Talca) ⓦ www.hostaldelpuente.cl
Hotel Comercio (Curicó) ⓦ www.hotelescurico.cl
Hotel Cordillera (Chillán) Arauco 619 ⓣ 42 215 211
Hotel Cruz del Sur (Concepción) ⓦ www.hotelcruzdelsur.cl
Hotel Javier Carrera (Chillán) ⓦ www.hoteljavieracarrera.cl
Hotel Manquehue (Concepción) ⓦ www.hotelmanquehue.cl
Hotel Palmas Express (Curicó) Membrillar 728 ⓣ 75 320 066
Hotel Raices (Curicó) ⓦ www.hotelraices.cl
MI Lodge (Termas de Chillán) ⓦ www.milodge.com

Budget
Hostal Canadá (Chillán) Libertad 269 ⓣ 42 234 515 ⓔ hostelcanada@hotmail.com
Hostal Libertad (Chillán) Libertad 244 ⓣ 42 221 263
Hostal SerAna (Talca) ⓦ www.hostalserana.cl
Hotel Casa de Campo (Santa Cruz) ⓦ www.hotelcasadecampo.cl
Hotel San Sebastián (Concepción) ⓦ www.hotelsansebastian.cl
Residencial Colonial (Curicó) Manuel Rodriguez 461 ⓣ 75 314 103
ⓔ resicolonial@terra.cl
Residencial Ensueño (Curicó) Manuel Rodríguez 442 ⓣ 75 221 788
Residencial Metro (Concepción) Barros Arana 464 ⓣ 41 225 305

Eating out options are listed under the relevant towns and cities below.

Visiting the Colchagua wineries
Hacienda VIK
Millahue, San Vicente de Tagua Tagua ⓦ www.vik.cl
Scientific studies all over South America led Norwegian businessman
Alexander Vik to establish his vineyard here, with the simple aim
of producing the continent's best wine. A high-tech winery is still
under construction, but the first vintage, made in 2009 and released
in 2012, does promise to be superb. It's largely Cabernet Sauvignon
and Carmenère, with plenty of ripe cherry and plum and a wonderful
balance of acidity and tannin.

Casa Silva
Just off Ruta 5, north of San Fernando ⓦ www.casasilva.cl
The oldest winery in Colchagua, Casa Silva was founded around a
hundred years ago and has a 19th-century manor house and one of the
oldest barrel rooms in Colchagua. The tour covers the estate's history in

detail, including the massive damage wreaked by the 2010 earthquake; there's also a collection of classic cars. Tastings are held in the visitor centre/shop, where you can also buy wines by the glass. You'll see why their Carmenère is renowned, with its richly concentrated fruitiness and herbaceous character.

Viña Santa Helena
Just off Ruta 5, north of San Fernando Ⓦ www.santahelena.cl
Although Viña Santa Helena is one of Chile's main wine exporters it is not as prestigious as some in this area. Tours are available in English, German and Spanish, with pre-booking required on Saturdays. They must be booked 12 hours in advance and there must be a minimum of four people for them to run.

Viña Viu Manent
Cunaco, just east of Santa Cruz Ⓦ www.viumanent.cl
Family-owned since 1935, this winery is known for its superb Malbec and Viognier. You can tour the vineyards by horse carriage, or even on horseback if you prefer, before seeing the winery and cellar and finishing with a tasting.

Neyen
Camino Apalta Km11 Ⓦ www.neyen.cl
Vines have been planted here since 1890 but they only began making their own wines (Carmenère, Cabernet Sauvignon and Syrah) in a modern winery in 2003. In addition to standard tours they also offer evening tours, plus hiking and horseriding.

Visitors tour the Viu Manent vineyard by horse carriage. (VVM)

Viña Casa Lapostolle

Just northeast of Santa Cruz Ⓦ www.lapostolle.com

This French-owned winery uses a French 'flying winemaker' to produce now iconic wines such as Clos Apalta, using natural yeasts, largely organic vineyards and a gravity-fed winery. There are tours daily.

Viña Montes

Just northeast of Santa Cruz Ⓦ www.monteswines.com

One of Chile's most famous wineries, founded in the late 1980s by Aurelio Montes. He uses Feng Shui and Gregorian chant in the barrel room, as well as more conventional techniques, to produce the ultra-premium Montes Alpha 'M', Montes Folly and Purple Angel, in addition to more affordable wines. Tours visit the vineyard in an open truck and then see the modern winery, before a tasting.

Viña Santa Laura

Aka Laura Hartwig; Camino Barreales, 1km north of Santa Cruz Ⓦ www.laurahartwig.cl

Santa Laura is walking distance from central Santa Cruz on Camino Barreales. A boutique winery of just 80ha which produces only reserve wines (Cabernet Sauvignon, Chardonnay and Merlot, separately and blended). Tours are offered throughout the year.

Viña Mont Gras

Camino Isla de Yáquil s/n, Palmilla Ⓦ www.montgras.cl ⊘ May–Oct Mon–Sat, Nov–Apr daily

Viña Mont Gras was only founded in 1992 and produces fine wines (including Carmenère) mainly for export. They now own vineyards in several other areas of Chile. There are tours year round.

Estampa

Palmilla Ⓦ www.estampa.com ⊘ May–Oct Tue–Sat, Nov–Apr daily

A new winery, making commercial blends with grapes brought from both coastal and inland vineyards. Tours are offered but it's also possible to come just for a tasting.

Viña Bisquertt

15km northwest of Santa Cruz Ⓦ www.bisquertt.cl

Situated in a charming park amid a display of old wine presses, this winery grows red and white wine grapes at various locations along the Colchagua Valley, aiming to express the terroirs as fully as possible. Tours are available daily.

Viña Santa Cruz

Fundo El Peral, 27km southwest of Santa Cruz Ⓦ www.vinasantacruz.cl

The only winery really focused on tourism, with a small wine museum, hiking, horseriding and a horse carriage, plus a 35.5cm astronomical telescope, one of the world's largest collections of meteorites and a car museum (housing Cardoen's huge collection). They also plan to open a Wine Museum in Santa Cruz in 2013. A cable car takes visitors to the Cerro Chamán cultural zone where the buildings are designed to reflect the cultures displayed within – Mapuche, Aymara and Rapanui are all represented. The winery specialises in Carmenère, along with Cabernet Sauvignon, Malbec and Syrah; they're growing white grapes nearer the sea. Their wines are full and open, but with an Old World style underpinning of acid and tannin. Tours take place daily.

El Huique

Following the highway northwest past Palmilla, it's 14km from Santa Cruz to a junction signposted to El Huique, 3km north. El Huique (☉ 11.00–17.30 Tue–Sun) is one of the **best-preserved haciendas** in Chile, due to its only having had five owners since it was built in 1829. Juan José Echeñique left it to his daughter Gertrudis (wife of President Federico Errázuriz Echaurren), and it was donated to the army in 1975. The main house, full of antique furniture and photographs, stands on three sides of a beautiful patio, filled with palm trees and climbing jasmine. Nearby is the chapel with a tower that was built in the 1850s but then collapsed in the 2010 earthquake. Around the house are other patios and outbuildings, giving a good idea of how haciendas like this maintained an almost entirely self-sufficient lifestyle.

Lolol

The picturesque **village** of Lolol, 41km west of Santa Cruz (and just beyond Viña Santa Cruz) was badly hit by the 2010 earthquake, and rebuilding has been slow because so many of the damaged houses were historic single-storey adobes. The church (one of Chile's oldest) was also badly damaged. Next to the town hall, the **Museo Artesanía Chilena** (Museum of Chilean Crafts; ☉ 10.00–19.00 Tue–Sun) opened in 2009 and is well worth a visit.

Curicó wine route

The town of **Curicó**, 50km south of San Fernando on Ruta 5 and the railway, is the centre of the Curicó wine area. It was badly hit by the 2010 (and 1985) earthquakes, but remains a quiet and relaxing place to stop. Less well known as a wine-making area than Colchagua, it's also cheaper and more welcoming. The focus has been more on bulk than on quality, and it's still not very innovative, with some of Chile's biggest wine-makers (Concha y Toro, Montes, Errázuriz and Santa Rita) growing grapes here but not producing anything special. The crucial exception is **Miguel Torres** (Longitudinal Sur km195, 5km south of Curicó; Ⓦ www.migueltorres.com), who came from Catalonia and revolutionised

Eating out in Talca

Club Unión Social (affordable fixed menus) 3 Oriente 1040 ⓣ 71 221 586
Rubén Tapia (upmarket traditional food of the area) 2 Oriente 1339
ⓦ www.rubentapia.cl

Chile's wine industry in the 1980s. He is experimenting with Riesling, Gewurztraminer, Mourvèdre and other unusual (for Chile) grapes, and has also led the way in wine tourism. His winery, just south of Curicó, is the only one in the area that can be visited without booking (⊘ Oct–May 10.00–19.00, Jun–Sep 10.00–17.00 daily, hourly, one-hour tours including two samples). There's an excellent restaurant, and you can buy wine by the glass. Tours of all the other wineries must be arranged through the Ruta del Vino office in Curicó (ⓦ www.rutadelvinocurico.cl). They are: **Viña AltaCima** (ⓦ www.altacima.cl); Echeverría (ⓦ www.echewine.com); Mario Edwards (ⓦ www.rutadelvinocurico.cl/nuestras-vinas/vina-mario-edwards); Millamán (ⓦ www.millaman.cl); and San Pedro (ⓦ www.sanpedro.cl). Curicó is also notable for its Fairtrade wine, with a number of small producers supplying the Origin Wine's Fairhills project (ⓦ www.fairhills.co.za).

Maule Valley

Chile's largest wine-growing area, the Maule Valley is known for light fruity reds (especially Cabernet Sauvignon, Merlot and Carmenère), largely managed for quantity not quality. It's now also known for Carignan, from vines planted over 60 years ago. This was mostly abandoned but is now being revived, with dry-farming techniques to

keep the tannins in check. Similarly, the País grape, introduced to Chile by the conquistadores, is being rediscovered.

The two most interesting wineries for tourists are Balduzzi, just 300m from Ruta 5 in San Javier, and Gillmore, halfway from San Javier to Constitución. **Balduzzi** (Av Balmaceda 1189, San Javier; ⑳ www.balduzziwines.com ⊘ 09.00–18.00 Mon–Sat) offers a basic tour that lasts just 45 minutes but includes four samples; the premium tour lasts an hour and includes nine samples. **Gillmore Winery** (Tabontinaja, Camino a Constitución Km20; ⑳ www.gillmore.cl ⊘ Aug–May 09.00–18.00 Mon–Sat) is nearer the coast and produces fresh yet complex red wines. This winery is also packed with things for tourists to do, including a menagerie, bike trails, wine spa and guesthouses.

Concepción and surrounds
Concepción

Concepción is situated 519km south of Santiago at the mouth of the Río Biobío and is Chile's second largest city and a major industrial and educational centre.

Concepción was founded in what is now Penco, 12km northwest, and soon became the administrative and ecclesiastic centre of southern Chile; earthquakes in 1730 and 1751 led to the city being moved to its present site (although the city's people and its sports teams are still referred to as *penquistas*). Nevertheless, the city was hit by earthquakes in 1939, 1960 and 2010.

On the west side of the central **Plaza Independencia**, the **cathedral** was built between 1940 and 1950 in a Romanesque–Byzantine style, with mosaics by Alejandro Rubio Dalmati (1913–2009; who also worked on

The mural *Presencia de América Latina* (Presence of Latin America) in the Casa del Arte in Concepción was painted by the Mexican artist Jorge González Camarena in the aftermath of the 1960 earthquake that levelled much of the city. (JGC)

Eating out in Concepción

Pasta de la Nona (excellent Italian) Pedro de Valdivia 521 ⓣ 41 279 3999
Le Château (finest French restaurant in the region) Colo-Colo 340 ⓣ 41 229 977
Verde que te quiere verde (one of southern Chile's best veggie restaurants) Colo Colo 174 ⓣ 41 225 0291

Chillán's cathedral). Three blocks northeast the **Tribunales de Justicia** (Law Courts) are a semi-circular building on concrete columns. From here the diagonal Pedro Aguirre Cerda runs due east to the **Universidad de Concepción's Casa del Arte** (House of Art; ⊘ 10.00–18.00 Tue–Fri, 11.00–17.00 Sat, 11.00–14.00 Sun ⊗ free) on Plaza Perú; in the foyer is the brilliant mural *Presencia de América Latina* by Jorge González Camarena (1965), inspired in part by Neruda's *Canto General*. There are temporary art shows, and upstairs a permanent collection that starts with colonial art, including two paintings by Gil de Castro. There are later paintings by Rugendas, Monvoisin and Pedro Lira; a romantic landscape by Antonio Smith (1832–77); a nude by Alfredo Valenzuela Puelma; two striking works by José Tomás Errázuriz (1856–1927); and a big Fauve landscape by Alberto Valenzuela Llanos.

There's an interesting frieze above the arch of the Medical Faculty (1946) to the east of the Casa del Arte; passing through the arch, you can walk through the university campus. The campanile, built in 1942, was inspired by Berkeley's and is now the university's symbol.

Heading southwest from the university for ten blocks, the **Galería de Historia** (History Gallery; ⊘ 15.00–18.30 Mon, 10.00–13.30, 15.00–18.30 Tue–Fri, 10.00–14.00, 15.00–19.00 Sat–Sun ⊗ free) is a set of 15 amusing dioramas of events in the city's history, along with a few Mapuche arrowheads and the like.

Six blocks southwest of the plaza, the old railway station, opened in 1943, is a fine piece of Modernism that now houses the regional government; in the former ticket hall (open daily), a mural (1943–45) by Gregorio de la Fuente depicts scenes of local history from an idyllic past through conflict to a glorious industrial future.

Well northeast of the centre, near the bus terminals, the **Museo de Historia Natural** (Museum of Natural History; ⊘ 10.00–13.30, 14.30–17.30 Tue–Fri, 15.00–17.30 Sat–Sun and holidays) is on Plaza Acevedo, now a Parque Jurásico with full-size models of dinosaurs. It was founded in 1902 by British naturalist Edwin Charles Reed and has displays of fossils, stuffed animals and Mapuche artefacts; it also covers local archaeology and the coal industry.

Talcahuano

The port of Talcahuano sits on the sheltered Bahía de Concepción, 15km north of Concepción and is visited by some cruise ships. It is worth a visit for the beautifully preserved ship *Huáscar* (⊙ 09.30–12.00, 14.00–17.30 Tue–Sun), now a shrine to the heroes of the War of the Pacific. Foreign tourists must leave their passport at the gate of the naval base but cameras are allowed; a raft on a fixed rope is hauled by a couple of sailors across to the *Huáscar*, anchored a short distance away. Built for the Peruvian navy in 1865 at Lairds' shipyard in Birkenhead, England, the *Huáscar*'s moment of fame came in 1879 when the Chilean Lieutenant Arturo Prat died gloriously in an attempt to capture her off Iquique. More or less alone, she then held off a Chilean invasion until she was captured later in 1879 at the Battle of Angamos, and went into service in the Chilean navy. *Huáscar* was restored in 1951, with interesting displays below decks. You can also watch pelicans diving vertically into the sea for fish, rather than waiting for scraps as they do at fish docks.

Between Concepción and Talcahuano, the **Museo Hualpén** (⊙ 10.00 –13.00, 14.00–19.00 Tue–Sun ⅌ free) is in the mansion of Pedro del Río Zañartu (1840–1918), who left it, and the collections acquired in a lifetime's globe-trotting, to the city. It's an attractive but under-

Portraits of the heroes of the War of the Pacific on the *Huáscar* (TC)

maintained house, built in 1885, in an attractive park; the collections include Mapuche and Rapanui artefacts, an Egyptian mummy, and much more from Europe and Asia.

Chillán

A vibrant and prosperous city, 81km east of Concepción and 407km south of Santiago, Chillán was the birthplace of many world-class artistic figures, as well as the 'father of the nation', Bernardo O'Higgins. Founded as a fort in 1565, it was moved after 'Darwin's earthquake' in 1835 to its present site. In the 1850s a road was built to Tomé to allow wheat exports, and from 1877 it was on the main railway from Santiago to the south. The massive earthquake of 1939 killed 15,000 people here and demolished 90% of the city; although there's nothing left of colonial Chillán, some of the replacements are very striking indeed.

The superb new **cathedral**, completed in 1960, stands on the east side of the plaza, a parabolic arch supported by ten concrete ribs; the only windows are set into the ribs and the west end, and all face west, producing a stunning effect in late afternoon light. There's a good mosaic on the façade, by Alejandro Rubio Dalmati, and nearby the 36m cross-cum-campanile is a memorial to those killed in the earthquake.

The city's other major sight is the **Escuela Mexico** (Mexican School) at O'Higgins 250, on a smaller plaza northwest of the city centre; it too was built after the 1939 earthquake, with aid from the Mexican government. It was decorated by Mexico's second most famous muralist (after Diego Rivera), David Alfaro Siqueiros (1896–1974). Upstairs in the library, *Muerte al Invasor* ('Death to the Invader') reveals his communist and anti-colonialist ideals in allegories of Mexican and Chilean history.

Next door, on the corner of O'Higgins and Vega de Saldias, the **Museo Internacional de la Gráfica** (International Museum of Graphic Art; ☺ 08.00–13.00, 15.00–17.00 Mon–Fri, 08.00–13.00 Sat, 09.00–14.00 Sun ♨ free) hosts changing exhibitions of prints.

Two blocks directly west of the plaza, the **Museo Claudio Arrau León** (Claudio Arrau Interactive Music Museum; Arrau 558 ☺ 09.00–13.30,

---

Eating out in Chillán

Casino de Bomberos (fixed menus, fire-station canteen) El Roble and 18 de Septiembre ① 42 222 233
Club de Ñuble (mainly meaty dishes in French sauces, formal) 18 de Septiembre 224 ① 42 222 186

15.00–19.00 Tue–Fri, 10.00–13.00, 16.00–19.30 Sat, 10.00–14.00 Sun
& free) is the birthplace of one of the 20th-century's greatest pianists,
who left over 3,000 recordings, from piano roll to CD (in fact he recorded
the first commercial CD). The museum is small and patchy, with Arrau
memorabilia and teaching materials.

To the southeast of the central grid at Maipón and 5 de Abril, the
feria is one of the best and liveliest markets in Chile; it's open daily (but
busiest on Saturdays) and offers great people-watching.

Termas de Chillán

To the southeast of Chillán a paved road leads most of the way towards
the border, to the Termas de Chillán, where hot springs and top-class
skiing combine to produce a year-round tourism resort. From Km68 to
Km73, a sector known as the Valle Las Trancas is lined with *cabañas*,
campsites, restaurants, and private cabins. Lodges in Las Trancas
(see pages 178–9) offer activities including hiking, a ropes course
and climbing wall, as well as a swimming pool and hot tub and an
astronomical observatory.

Moving on, the road climbs 6km further to the ski slopes, on the
slopes of Volcán Chillán (3,122m). This is perhaps the best ski terrain
in Chile, with more snow than nearer Santiago, but heavier powder.
In summer this becomes a fantastic area for hiking. At the hot springs,
just below the treeline at 1,650m, hotels (see pages 178–9) have indoor
and outdoor thermal pools and steam baths. In summer there's golf and
mountain-biking here, in winter dogsleds and snowmobiles, as well as
a casino.

Dog-sledding in Termas de Chillán (D/A)

Araucanía and the Lakes District

Moving south from the Central Valley, the country becomes wilder and less populated, with tiny Mapuche villages scattered among forestry plantations and, further south, the country's prime holiday district set between lovely lakes and volcanoes. To the east, a row of national parks offers great hiking in the Andean foothills, as well as hot springs. This area was only settled by European colonists from the 1860s, but is now developed and prosperous.

The capital of Araucanía (region IX) is **Temuco**, which is not a particularly touristic city. The country's adventure sports capital, **Pucón**, 1½ hours to the southeast, with plenty of activities for day and night, and lots of largely cheap accommodation and restaurants. The region's only city on the Pacific seaboard is **Valdivia**, a worthwhile detour off the Panamericana, with excursions to historic fortifications and wetland reserves. Beyond this, the Lakes District proper is packed with tourist sights and resorts, and driving distances are much shorter here than in other parts of the country. **Osorno** is less attractive than Temuco, but also has good links to national parks along the Andean watershed, while **Puerto Montt** is a working port with a gritty warmth to it. The main bases for tours are Pucón and Puerto Varas, although there are many other options with excellent accommodation and stunning scenery.

Temuco

Busy Temuco (677km from Santiago) is the capital of Region IX (Araucanía); with a population approaching 250,000 it's by far Chile's largest city south of Concepción. It's well worth visiting the museum and the market, which both in their separate ways give you an insight into the lives of the Mapuche people, who mostly live outside Temuco but come here to trade.

Eating out in Temuco

Casa de Empanadas (great range of *empanadas*, and sushi now too) Ⓦ www.facebook.com/casa.empanadas

Club Aleman (chalet-style German-Chilean restaurant) Senador Estébanez 772 Ⓣ 45 240 034

El Fogón (lively locals' grill-house) Aldunate 288 Ⓣ 45 737 061

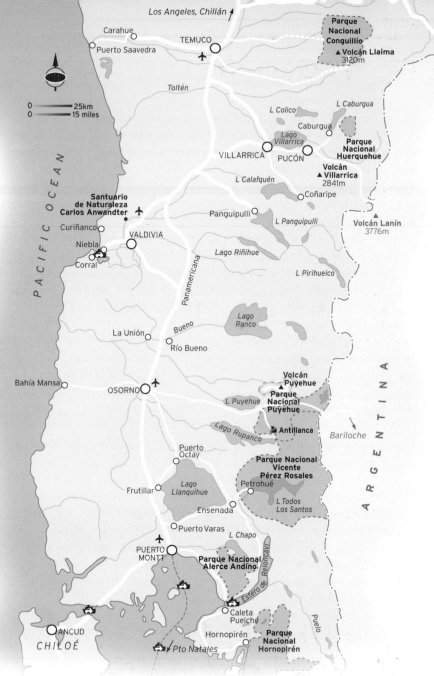

In 1552, Pedro de Valdivia founded the settlement of Ciudad Imperial 53km west of present-day Temuco. For a while southern Chile was ruled from here, but in 1599 the Mapuche drove the Spaniards out; they returned only in 1881 when Temuco was founded.

On the north side of the main **Plaza Aníbal Pinto** is the unattractive **cathedral** (1981–91); where most churches have a bell tower, this

Practicalities

Temuco has good **transport** links in all directions and Temuco and Osorno offer all the services you may require, such as **ATMs** and **exchange**, **internet** and **medical** facilities. A major **road** runs east from Osorno to the Puyehue National Park and the Argentine Lakes District.

There are **airports** at Temuco, Valdivia, Osorno and Puerto Montt (also serving Puerto Varas); all have flights to Santiago, and Puerto Montt also has flights south to Balmaceda and Punta Arenas.

The largest city between Temuco and Puerto Montt, Valdivia is a useful transport hub, although it is relatively far from the mountains.

Now thoroughly overshadowed by Pucón, Villarrica is a far quieter and more restful spot to stay the night, and has most of the usual facilities and services. Pucón has plenty of opportunities to buy **outdoor gear** and other

cathedral has an office tower, with a cross on it. Semi-buried beneath the plaza is the town's **art gallery** (⊙ 09.00–13.00, 14.00–20.00 Mon–Sat, 09.30–13.00 Sun, 09.00–14.00, 15.00–20.00 holidays ⅋ free), which hosts temporary shows. Don't miss the **Mercado Municipal** (⊙ Apr–Sep 08.00–18.00 Mon–Sat, Oct–Mar 08.00–20.00 Mon–Sat 08.00–15.00 Sun), two blocks north of the plaza. Opened in 1930, this is full of Mapuche life, with meat, vegetables and household utensils alongside crafts and tackier souvenirs, as well as some very cheap and cheerful eateries. You'll see Mapuche women in traditional dress and jewellery, even if it's largely put on for the tourists. Two blocks east is the **Casa de la Mujer Mapuche** (House of the Mapuche Woman; Diego Portales 1190 at Cruz), a craft co-operative showing and selling textiles, ceramics, basketry, stone- and silverwork, as well as music and publications. Alternatively, head east along Lautaro to the **Feria Libre**, a lively fruit and veg market just before the railway station.

Temuco's other sights are slightly out of the centre, starting with the **Museo Regional de la Araucanía** at Avenida Alemania 084 (Regional Museum of Araucanía; ⊙ 09.30–17.30 Mon–Fri, 11.00–17.00 Sat, 11.00–14.00 Sun ⅋ free on Sun). In a fine villa built in 1940, the museum focuses on the Mapuche culture, with pride of place going to the collection of silver jewellery which was historically made from Spanish coins to show off wealth while also being portable. There are also displays with old photographs of the arrival of the railway and of colonists from Europe, the city's growth and the effects of the 1960 earthquake.

travel essentials, and there are **internet/phone** centres there.

If you want **luxury accommodation**, your only choice is Puerto Varas, which also boasts some of the country's finest restaurants, as well as various **adventure sports outfitters**. Puerto Montt is perhaps not the prettiest town but it has plenty of **shops** and other services; there's also a good deal of decent accommodation.

Puerto Montt is a hub for all sorts of **shipping routes**; in addition to sailings to Chaitén and Puerto Chacabuco (see *Chapter 9*, page 230 for details), the bus-boat Cruce de Lagos and the ferry from Pargua to Chiloé, there's the weekly Navimag trip to Puerto Natales (see pages 244–5). There's also an increasing number of **cruiseships** calling at Puerto Montt; a proper cruise terminal is being developed, and the Empormontt terminal, used by Navimag and Naviera Austral is also due to be redeveloped. See overleaf for accommodation options.

Heading north from the plaza on Prat, after eight blocks you'll enter the **Monumento Nacional Cerro Ñielol** (◔ 08.00–19.00 daily), a densely forested hill that's preserved as the site of the signing of the 1881 treaty with the Mapuche. It's busy, despite its array of radio aerials, but can be unsafe after dusk. There's a good variety of native plants, notably the *copihue*, a red creeper that is the national plant.

About a kilometre north at Barros Arana 0565, the **Museo Nacional Ferroviario Pablo Neruda de Temuco** (Railway Museum; Ⓦ www.museoferroviariotemuco.cl ◔ 09.00–18.00 Tue–Fri, 10.00–18.00 Sat, Apr–Sep 11.00–17.00 Sun, Oct–Mar 10.00–18.00 Sun ◔ free until earthquake damage is repaired) was Chile's last depot for steam locomotives, a

National Railway Museum in Temuco (AUD/DH)

Accommodation

Exclusive

Hotel Antumalal (Pucón) ⓦ www.antumalal.com
Hotel Colonos del Sur (Puerto Varas) ⓦ www.colonosdelsur.cl
Hotel Cumbres Patagónicas (Puerto Varas) ⓦ www.cumbrespatagonicas.cl
Hotel Dreams Araucania (Temuco) ⓦ www.mundodreams.com/hotel/hotel-dreams-araucania
Hotel Dreams Valdivia (Valdivia) ⓦ www.mundodreams.com/ciudad/valdivia
Hotel Termas de Puyehue (Puyehue) ⓦ www.puyehue.cl

Upmarket

Alerce Mountain Lodge (Alerce Andino) ⓦ www.mountainlodge.cl
Diego de Almagro Puerto Montt (Puerto Montt) ⓦ www.tinyurl.com/DApuertomontt
Gran Hotel Pucón (Pucón) ⓦ www.enjoy.cl/enjoy-pucon
Holiday Inn Express (Puerto Montt) ⓦ www.hiexpress.com
Hotel & Apart Club Presidente Puerto Montt (Puerto Montt) ⓦ www.hotelespresidente.com/hotel_puerto_montt
Hotel Centinela (Puerto Octay) ⓦ www.hotelcentinela.cl
Hotel Colonos del Sur Mirador (Puerto Varas) ⓦ www.colonosdelsur.cl/mirador.htm
Hotel Don Eduardo (Temuco) ⓦ www.hoteldoneduardo.cl
Hotel Frau Holle (Frutillar) ⓦ www.frauholle-frutillar.cl
Hotel La Frontera (Temuco) ⓦ www.hotelfrontera.cl
Hotel García Hurtado de Mendoza (Osorno) ⓦ www.hotelgarciahurtado.cl
Hotel Lagos del Sur (Osorno) ⓦ www.hotelagosdelsur.cl
Hotel Naguilán (Valdivia) ⓦ www.hotelnaguilan.com
Hotel Puerta del Sur (Valdivia) ⓦ www.hotelpuertadelsur.com
Hotel Waeger (Osorno) ⓦ www.hotelwaeger.cl
Posada Puelo (Puelo) ⓦ www.posadapuelo.cl
Río Puelo Lodge (Puelo) ⓣ 65 232 921 ⓔ marcia@secretpatagonia.travel
Villarrica Park Lake Hotel (Villarrica) ⓦ www.pucon.com/parklake

Moderate

Aparthotel Río Cruces (Valdivia) ⓦ www.aparthotelriocruces.cl
Gran Hotel Osorno (Osorno) O'Higgins 615 ⓣ 64 232 171
ⓔ granhotelosorno@entelchile.net
Hostería de la Colina (Villarrica) ⓦ www.hosteriadelacolina.com
Hotel Continental (Temuco) A Varas 708 ⓣ 45 238 973

Hotel El Ciervo (Villarrica)
Ⓦ www.hotelelciervo.cl
Hotel Licarayén (Puerto Varas)
Ⓦ www.hotelicarayen.cl
Hotel Pumalal Express
(Osorno) Bulnes 630
Ⓣ 64 242 477 Ⓔ pumalal@
entelchile.net
Hotel Seminario (Puerto Montt)
Ⓦ www.hotelseminario.cl
Hotel Terrazas del Mar
(Puerto Montt) Ⓦ www.
hotelterrazasdelmar.cl

Puerto Montt city centre (SS)

Isla Las Bandurrias (Puelo) Ⓦ www.tinyurl.com/bandurrias
Kila-Leufú (Pucón) Ⓦ www.kilaleufu.cl
La Tetera (Pucón) Ⓦ www.tetera.cl
Mountainside Lodge (Cochamó) Ⓦ www.campoaventura.cl
Nuevo Hotel Turismo (Temuco) Ⓦ www.hotelturismotemuco.cl
Residencial Winkler (Frutillar) Av da Philippi 1155 Ⓣ 65 421 388
Riverside Lodge (Cochamó) Ⓦ www.campoaventura.cl

Budget

Casa Azul (Puerto Varas) Ⓦ www.casaazul.net
Casa Perla (Puerto Montt) Ⓦ www.casaperla.com
¡ecole! (Pucón) Ⓦ www.ecole.cl
Hostal Aires Buenos (Valdivia) Ⓦ www.airesbuenos.cl
Hostal Aldunate (Temuco) Aldunate 864 Ⓣ 45 642 438
Ⓔ hostalaldunate864@hotmail.com
Hostal-Cabañas Internacional (Valdivia) Ⓦ www.hostalinternacional.cl
Hostería Hue-Quimey (Villarrica) Ⓦ www.huequimey.cl
Hotel & Hostal Bilbao (Osorno) Ⓦ www.hotelbilbao.cl
Hotel Gamboa (Puerto Montt) 157 Pedro Montt Ⓣ 65 252 741
Hotel Sevilla (Temuco) Aldunate 153 Ⓣ 45 329 696
La Torre Suiza (Villarrica) Ⓦ www.torresuiza.com
Residencial Riga (Osorno) Amthauer 1058 Ⓣ 64 232 945
The Tree House (Pucón) Ⓦ www.treehousechile.cl
Zapato Amarillo (Puerto Octay) Ⓦ www.zapatoamarillo.cl

Eating out options are listed under the relevant towns and cities below.

dozen of which (built between 1915 and 1953) are still here; you can also see the presidential coach, built in Germany in 1923, and an articulated diesel express train. In the administration building there's detailed railway history, art, and a model railway.

Temuco also has a new zoo, the **Parque Zoológico Niri Vilcún** (☉ 10.00–19.00 Tue–Sun), 18km north at Km653 of Ruta 5. In an attractive park you can see native fauna such as puma, wild cats, llamas, foxes and pudú, as well as tropical birds and monkeys from other countries. It's fun for children, with play and picnic areas and a cafeteria.

Parque Nacional Conguillío

The **Conguillío National Park**, one of Chile's loveliest, lies to the east of Temuco, surrounding the spectacular 3,120m **Volcán Llaima**, whose lava flows have transformed what was a richly forested landscape and created a number of attractive lakes. The largest of these, **Lago Conguillío** (750ha), is connected by natural tunnels to the Río Truful-Truful. Llaima is one of Chile's two most active volcanoes, but the last big lava flows date from 1956 to 1977, since when (in 1971–2, 1979, 1984 and 1994) it has been spitting out toffee-like pyroclastics. This is the centrepiece of Chile's first Geoparque (⊛ www.geachile.com), aiming to show off and display the area's rich variety of geological features.

There's over 2m of precipitation a year here, producing a rich *coihue* forest, with *araucaria* above 1,400m, and lots of *quila* bamboo and *canelo* in the understorey. Wildlife includes pumas, *guiña* wildcats, pudú deer and skunks; there's also a wide range of birds, including waterfowl such as torrent ducks and geese, forest birds such as the Magellanic woodpecker, chucao, huet-huet and thorn-tailed rayadito, and the slender-billed parakeet, condor, red-backed hawk and Andean gull.

Visiting the park

From just beyond Melipueco, Km92 from Temuco, a poor road leads to the rear of the volcano, taking over two hours to drive to the park's administration building (just 30km north). From the Truful-Truful gate it's worth walking the 700m **Cañadon del Truful-Truful loop**, through colourful strata of volcanic ash with excellent views of the surprisingly large Truful-Truful Waterfall. The road continues through bare lava to Lago Conguillío, with fantastic views to the snowy Sierra Nevada. There is a café, a shop, and boat hire available.

Two **hiking** trails run parallel to the road from Playa Linda to Playa Curacautín, one along the beach to the north and the other to the south. You can continue on the Sendero Los Carpinteros to the Captrén gate, or loop south on the 1km Las Araucarias interpretative path. Perhaps the loveliest hike in the park is to the *miradores* (viewpoints) on the Sierra Nevada, an easy 10km in total.

It's possible to **climb** Volcán Llaima in a long day's outing from the Captrén gate using crampons and an ice-axe for the final icy section. The climb takes seven to eight hours, plus another four hours to return.

Villarrica and surrounds

The first half-dozen lakes of what is generally thought of as the Lakes District are actually in Araucanía (Region IX) and Los Ríos (Region XIV) rather than Los Lagos (Region X). Heading south from Temuco, it's 85km to the town of Villarrica, at the outlet of the Río Toltén from Lago

The Truful-Truful Falls in the Conguillío National Park (CJ-F)

Villarrica. It's another 25km to Pucón, Chile's adventure-sports capital, at the lake's southeastern corner, with the smaller lakes Caburgua and Colico to the north. It's a hilly area with national parks and reserves protecting lush Valdivian forest, and many hot springs.

The area has been populated for 13,000 years; in 1552 Pedro Valdivia established a fort in an area where the Spaniards were keen to pan gold from the streams. After the Mapuche uprising of 1599 it was besieged for three years before finally surrendering; the town was re-established in 1883, after two decades of 'pacification', and the surrounding area was colonised, with the Mapuche confined to *reducciones* or reservations. From 1914 tourists came here, arriving by train from 1933.

Villarrica

Immediately west of the tourist office at Pedro de Valdivia, the **Museo Arqueológico Municipal** (Municipal Museum of History and Archaeology; ⊘ Jan–Feb 09.00–13.00, 15.00–19.30 Mon–Sat, Mar–Dec 09.00–13.00, 18.00–22.00 Mon–Sat) is small but well worth the minimal fee. In the badly lit corridor there are interesting reproductions of colonial maps, but the main display is of Mapuche artefacts, notably bags made from cow udders and scrotums, and musical instruments such as the *kultrung* drum. On the west side of the museum the **Muestra Cultural Mapuche** is a crafts market surrounding a *ruca* or traditional thatched roundhouse; Mapuche food is also sold here. A festival is held here in the second week of February.

Just west of the cathedral at O'Higgins 501, a striking new building houses the Universidad Católica's local outpost; in the basement is the small but well-presented **Museo de Leandro Penchulef** (Ⓦ www. museoleandropenchulef.cl ⊘ 08.30–12.00, 14.30–18.00 Mon–Fri ⊛ free) housing Mapuche crafts, including two dugout canoes.

Pucón

From Villarrica a road, built in 1940, winds along the lakeside to Pucón. The Chilean army established a base here in 1883 and German

merchants soon settled. The town's first hotel, the Gudenschwager, opened in 1923, and Pucón became the centre of sport fishing in Chile, with tourists taking a steamer from Villarrica.

By 1969 the road was paved and in the last two decades the town has developed into Chile's **adventure sports** capital, with a plethora of companies competing to take you for white-water sports such as rafting, hydrospeed, canyoning and rappelling, as well as horseriding, hang-gliding and parachuting. There's the near-obligatory ascent of **Volcán Villarrica** (see box, page 201) to see the lava bubbling in the crater, plus in winter **skiing** on the volcano's slopes. There's also a glitzy casino and some fine restaurants and bars, attracting affluent Chileans as well as most foreigners visiting Chile; the fact that there's a pass to Argentina (with buses to Junín and San Martín de los Andes) doesn't hurt.

Pucón stands at the neck of a privately owned peninsula (where the most exclusive homes are), with **beaches** to both the north and west of the town. The new **Museo Mapuche Pucón** (Ⓦ www.museomapuche. cl ⊙ 11.00–13.00, 16.00–19.00 Tue–Sun) is a smallish basement room crammed with Mapuche silverwork, stone carving and ceramics plus a couple of baskets.

East of Pucón

The main international highway to Junín (Argentina) follows the Río Trancura, passing various hot springs before reaching **Curarrehue**, where it's worth stopping at the **Aldea Intercultural Trawupeyüm** ('Where we meet') at Héroes de la Concepción 25. This is a Mapuche cultural centre (⊙ 15 Dec–15 Mar 10.00–14.00, 15.00–21.00 daily, 16 Mar–14 Dec 11.00–14.00, 15.00–18.00 Thu–Sun), with a craft market and the Mapu Iyagi and Ruka Weney restaurants, serving authentic Mapuche food.

Eating out in Pucón

¡ecole! (superb vegetarian food) General Urrutia 592 Ⓦ www.ecole.cl
La Marmita (international food, including fondue and raclette, and seafood) Fresia 300 Ⓦ www.lamarmitapucon.cl
Senzo (pasta, risotto, steak, even sushi) Fresia 284 Ⓣ 45 449 005

At the Puesco frontier post (56km from Pucón) you'll find a ranger post and Environmental Education Centre, and a campsite and *hostería*. A little further up the road, hiking trails lead 15km east into the Quetrupillán sector of the Villarrica National Park and southeast to the west side of Volcán Lanín.

To the east of Volcán Villarrica, the rough road to Coñaripe crosses through the park's Quetrupillán sector; turning off the Camino Internacional 20km east of Pucón (following signs to the Termas de Palguín) this passes a series of waterfalls in magnificent lush forest. From the Quetrupillán *guardería* and campsite trails head north along the eastern flanks of Volcán Villarrica and back to the road.

The dozen *termas* or **hot springs** east of Pucón range in temperature from 30° to 45°C and from the very basic to the very luxurious. Visits can be arranged with tour companies in Pucón; the baths vary greatly, so try to pick the one that suits you. There are two on the east side of Volcán Villarrica: the **Termas de Palguín** (Ⓦ www.termasdepalguin. cl) is the oldest in the area, and has a decent hotel; day visitors must pay for entry and can eat in the restaurant. The **Termas Geométricas** (Ⓦ www.termasgeometricas.cl), further south, is one of the newest in the area in a cool, minimalist, almost Japanese style.

The Termas Geométricas, near Pucón (SS)

Climbing Volcán Villarrica

Volcán Villarrica (2,840m), squatting over Pucón, is the centrepiece of the **Parque Nacional Villarrica**, which covers 63,000ha between 600m and 3,776m in altitude and connects to Argentina's far larger Lanín National Park to protect a large swathe of native forest. It's one of Chile's two most active volcanoes, with ten eruptions in the 20th century. The last was in 1999, but the crater is always active, with lava visible and sulphurous fumes belching forth. The volcano can be climbed in eight hours, up and down, but you must take a guide unless you can show that you are experienced enough to tackle it alone.

Just beyond the park gate, 8km from the main road, you can head left for 4km to the **Cuevas Volcánicas**, in fact a lava tube, 500m of which are open to visitors (Ⓦ www.cuevasvolcanicas.cl ◷ 10.00–19.00 daily). It's well lit, and there are good geological displays.

At the **ski station**, 14km from Pucón, a lift takes hikers from 1,450m to 1,850m, near the summer snow-line. It takes about 3½ hours to the point at which crampons come off for the ten-minute scramble to the rim and an unforgettable view into the crater. The descent can be far too rapid if you're not careful; most people speed on their backsides down channels in the snow, and you'll need an ice-axe to control yourself properly.

Skiing started here in the 1930s, and a former logging lift was installed in the 1970s. There are now nine lifts and 20 pistes. Equipment can be rented here but is much cheaper hired from the tour companies on Avenida O'Higgins.

Turning left 27km east of Pucón on the Camino Internacional, it's about 5km to the **Termas de Menetué** (Ⓦ www.menetue.com), **Termas Trancura** (Ⓦ www.termastrancura.com), **Montevivo Parque Termal** (Ⓦ www.montevivo.cl) and **Termas de San Luis** (Ⓦ www.termasdesanluis.cl), all of which have modern facilities, with indoor and outdoor pools, spas, restaurant and hotel or *cabañas*. The most alternative is the **Termas de Panqui** (Ⓦ www.termas.cl/panqui.html), which calls itself a retreat centre. Turning off the international road just before Curarrehue, it's about 20km to the remote site where guests can stay in the Mapuche *rucas* or Sioux tipis that surround the hotel and its vegetarian restaurant. There are hot pools and mud baths, and massage, shiatsu and aromatherapy are also available.

To the northeast of Pucón, turning right off the Caburgua road towards Huife, there are another **five springs**, starting with the **Termas de Liucura** (Ⓔ termasdeliucura@gmail.com), where there's a cafeteria and camping. The **Peumayén Lodge & Termas Boutique** (Ⓦ www.termaspeumayen.cl) and the **Termas Quimey-Co** (Ⓦ www.termasquimeyco.com) are more upmarket, and the **Termas de Huife** (Ⓦ www.termashuife.cl) is the grandest in this area. It has three open-air pools (20–40°C), as well as an indoor spa with massages, and a good hotel and restaurant.

The **Termas Los Pozones** (Ⓦ www.termas.cl/pozones.html), 2km further, are very rustic, just bare pools dug by the river and lined with stones. There are no facilities apart from toilets and changing rooms, but many agencies run trips here in the evenings. The spring is open 24 hours a day, every day, but there's a three-hour maximum stay.

Caburgua and Huerquehue

From Pucón a paved road leads to the long thin **Lago Caburgua**; a road forks to the right up the Liucura Valley, passing the **Parque Ecológico Kodkod** (Ⓦ www.kodkod.net), which aims to combine sustainable tourism and wildlife conservation. This is also the entry to the **Santuario Cañi** (Ⓦ www.santuariocani.cl), the country's first private protected area; in the caldera of an extinct volcano, it's open for hiking and camping.

Lago Caburgua is a small resort with shops and desperately cold swimming. About 6km south are the **Ojos de Caburgua**, where water, leaving the lake through a dam of volcanic rock, bursts out in two dramatic waterfalls at a very popular picnic site.

To the left or west of Caburgua the **Playa Blanca** (White Beach) is so-called because of the shiny flakes of schist it's composed of; to the right is the **Playa Negra**.

Laguna Chica, Huerquehue National Park (I/FLPA)

The **Parque Nacional Huerquehue**, to the east of Lago Caburgua, offers the best **hiking** near Pucón, and is very popular for day-trips as well as longer stays. The temperate rainforest here has fewer creepers and epiphytes than on Volcán Villarrica, but is home to lots of fungi (many poisonous), and huge spiders and snails. There are also some lovely lakes.

Valdivia

Often bypassed by travellers heading down the Panamericana and focusing more on visiting the lakes and mountains to the east of the highway, Valdivia, 841km south of Santiago, is a historic city that's well worth a detour.

History

Jerónimo de Alderete took possession of the area in 1544, and in 1552 Pedro de Valdivia founded a city on the site of the indigenous village of Ainlil, renaming it after himself. The superb natural harbour became a staging post for ships between Lima and the Straits of Magellan, and an access point to the interior. By 1571 it had a population of around 2,000 colonists (plus about 4,000 Mapuche) and was Chile's second city. However, in 1599 it was destroyed in the general Mapuche uprising and abandoned along with all other Spanish settlements south of

Concepción. The Dutch arrived in 1643, but soon left in the face of Mapuche hostility. This stung the Spanish into re-occupying the site in 1645, establishing forts at Corral and Niebla, facing each other at the mouth of the estuary, and on Isla Mancera, in between. It remained an island of Spanish territory in a hostile hinterland, only beginning to expand after 1740.

The fortifications, hugely reinforced from the 1770s due to the threat of war with Britain, were nevertheless brilliantly captured in 1820 in a surprise attack by Lord Cochrane, one of the key events in Spain's expulsion from South America. From 1851 to 1875 large numbers of German emigrants arrived, establishing industries (making this the most prosperous city in Chile) and fanning out to farm the hinterland. However, in 1907 there was an earthquake and fire, with a worse quake in 1960, which caused the city and much of the surrounding area to drop 3m. After rebuilding, it now seems more like a small North American city rather than the typically Germanic place it used to be.

Valdivia highlights

Valdivia does have a plaza but there's more life on the **riverside** just west by the Mercado Fluvial, open-air stalls selling very fresh fish and shellfish. Sea lions (and birds) wait for scraps here but can no longer come ashore, where they occasionally used to bite people; rafts have been provided for them to sleep on. Across the road the **covered market** is less interesting; beyond it is the functional but effective

The waterfront and cathedral, Valdivia (J/S)

Eating out in Valdivia

Café Hausmann (traditional bar, famed for its steak tartare on toast) O'Higgins 394 ⓦ www.haussmann.cl

Café La Última Frontera (boho-student bar, serves real coffee, beers, sandwiches and veggie dishes) Pérez Rosales 787 ⓣ 63 235 363

cathedral, built between 1987 and 1996 to replace a temporary metal church that had stood here since the 1960 earthquake. To the south, the **waterfront** has been rebuilt since the 2010 earthquake; it's dominated by the **Faro Pendulo**, a 20m-high lighthouse supporting a Foucault's Pendulum. Moored alongside is the *O'Brien*, a British-built diesel-electric submarine, which was meant to become a museum until the funds ran out.

Just beyond, you'll pass the modern **Appeals Court** (at San Carlos), and leave the city centre on General Lagos, lined with the **villas** of Valdivia's 19th-century merchant élite. First comes the Casa Thater-Hoffman (1870) at No 733, now the **Centro Cultural El Austral** (☉ 10.00–13.00, 16.00–19.00 Tue–Sun ⅊ free); three rooms are furnished in late 19th-century style, while others display temporary art exhibitions. There's a row of four **historic buildings** across the road and then, across Yerbas Buenas, one of the two unimpressive *torreones* (1781), all that remain of the city's fortifications (the other is between the bus terminal and the Puente Calle Calle). There's a good group of historic buildings at the junction with Riquelme, including a black-and-white tin-clad school and a former youth hostel at No 1036, but they thin out to the south. The fine Haverbeck works (1890) at No 1927 are now the Hotel Naguilán, although the bedrooms are all in the modern wings.

Valdivia's **museums** are across the bridge on the leafy **Isla Teja**, facing the city centre. First is the **Museo de la Exploración RA Philippi** (Museum of the Exploration of Rodolfo Amando Philippi; ⓦ www.museosaustral.cl ☉ winter 10.00–13.00, 14.00–18.00 Tue–Sun, summer 10.00–20.00 daily ⅊ can buy joint ticket with Museo Histórico) on the life and travels of the German botanist who directed the Natural History Museum in Santiago for over 40 years from 1853. Just beyond, the **Museo Histórico de Valdivia** (Historical Museum of Valdivia; same hours and prices), in the 1860s Casa Anwandter, has 19th-century furnishings plus displays on the German colonists and on the Hispanic and pre-Hispanic periods. The highlight is the collection of Mapuche

Towards the coast

Avenida Los Lingues leads south from Isla Teja across the Río Cruces, and after 18km reaches **Niebla**, at the mouth of the Río Valdivia. The **fortress of Niebla** (☉ 10.00–17.30 Tue–Sun, summer to 19.00 ☞ free on Wed) was built between 1645 and 1672 on a 35m cliff, its cannon covering an arc of fire across the bay. The former commanding officer's house is now a museum, with good information panels (Spanish only) and reproduction maps and prints. Ferries (and tour boats from Valdivia) cross the huge natural harbour to **Corral** and **Isla Mancera**, both of which have similar forts (mid-Nov to mid-Mar 10.00–19.00 daily, mid-Mar to mid-Nov 10.00–17.00 Tue–Sun). It's also possible to drive to Corral, and on to the **Reserva Costera Valdiviana**, a chain of parks run by their indigenous inhabitants.

Just before Km5 on the Niebla road is the **Kunstmann brewery** (Ⓦ www.cerveza-kunstmann.cl ☉ 12.00–24.00 Mon–Sat), where the one-room museum is just an excuse before heading for the souvenir shop and the family-friendly bar-restaurant. The Kunstmann family arrived in Valdivia in the early 1850s, setting up flour mills then diversifying into beer and yeast. In 1992, the current generation set up a microbrewery in Valdivia, replaced by the present out-of-town operation in 1996, now owned by Chile's leading brewery, CCU. Valdivia hosts Bierfests in January and November, and is home to several new microbreweries.

Heading north just beyond the brewery, or from Niebla, you can reach **Curiñanco**, where the 6km-long beach is popular at sunset. The **Punta Curiñanco Reserve** protects a very important and beautiful area of coastal rainforest. Not far north is the **Parque Oncol**, run by a forestry company and rather more touristic, with canopy rides and tour groups.

Immediately north of Valdivia, and reached by regular boat trips, the **Santuario de Naturaleza Carlos Anwandter** wetlands were formed when the area dropped 2m in the 1960 earthquake. Now perhaps the largest breeding population of black-necked swans is here, as well as three kinds of coot, slender-billed and austral parakeets, coypus and southern river otters.

silverwork and other artefacts, including displays of how the silverwork is worn. To the left, the **Museo de Arte Contemporaneo** also known as MAC (Museum of Contemporary Art; Ⓦ www.macvaldivia.cl ☉ Sep–Apr 10.00–14.00, 16.00–20.00 daily) was built in 1998 in the shell of the Anwandter Brewery, destroyed in the 1960 earthquake; now it's a superb exhibition space and one of Chile's most dynamic museums of modern art, with often challenging temporary shows.

Osorno

Entering Region X (the Lakes District), you'll soon come to Osorno, a hardworking commercial centre and transport hub. The railway arrived in 1898, and electric light in 1908, as it became a prosperous modern city. It has few attractions itself, but is a place to break the journey before heading inland to the **Parque Nacional Puyehue** and **Bariloche**, capital of the Argentine Lakes District, or west to the coast, where the new Mapu Lahuai system of indigenous-owned parks lies south of the fishing cove of Bahía Mansa.

Founded in 1558, Osorno was abandoned from 1603 until 1796; it only really grew with the arrival of German colonists from the mid-19th century. There's one surviving block of **historic German houses** a block south of the main plaza, a couple open as shops and restaurants and one (the Casa Schüller, at Mackenna 1011 and Cochrane) now a German cultural centre with an excellent café. Badly damaged by the 1960 earthquake, the city then found itself lumbered with two astonishingly ugly churches: the cathedral on the plaza, and San Francisco, just east by the market and bus terminals. Just north of the plaza, the Lutheran church is marginally less offensive.

The **Museo Histórico Municipal** (Municipal History Museum; ⊙ Mar–Dec 09.30–17.30 Mon–Thu, 09.30–16.30 Fri, 14.00–18.00 Sat, Jan–Feb 09.30–18.00 Mon–Fri, 14.00–19.00 Sat–Sun ⋑ free), a block south of the plaza at Matta 809, displays mastodon bones and a mummy from the Atacama; Mapuche crafts; and historic photos of German colonisation and the 1960 earthquake. Across the road, the **Museo Surazo** (ⓦ www. museosurazo.cl ⊙ 10.30–13.30, 15.30–18.30 Tue–Fri, 11.30–16.30 Sat ⋑ free) has changing art shows.

West of the centre, the **Reina Luisa fort** (1793) now houses dioramas and relics of the colonial period; just south, the old railway station (1917) is now the **Museo Interactivo** (Interactive Museum; Av Diego Portales 901; ⊙ 09.00–13.00, 14.30–17.00 Mon–Thu, 09.00–13.00, 14.30–16.00 Fri, 14.00–18.00 Sat ⋑ free), where children can discover science and technology.

Eating out in Osorno

Centro Cultural Sofá Hott (café in restored German colonists' house) Mackenna 1011 ① 64 331 804

Club Alemán (solid Chilean fare with a German touch) O'Higgins 563 ① 64 232 514

Parque Nacional Puyehue

From Osorno, Ruta 215 leads east through the **Puyehue National Park** to the Argentine border and on to Bariloche (paved all the way), passing between the relatively low volcanoes of Puyehue and Casablanca, with active fumaroles and hot springs. Since 2011, the **Cordón Caulle**, on Volcán Puyehue, has been erupting off and on.

The Puyehue National Park (pronounced 'poo-yay-way' and meaning 'Place of Puyes' – a kind of fish) is one of Chile's most popular, partly because of its location on the international highway and partly because it's free. At the far end of Lago Puyehue (Km76) is the Hotel Termas de Puyehue (see *Practicalities*, page 194), one of Chile's grandest hot springs resorts, with indoor and outdoor pools, spa, sauna and gym, and a five-star hotel. From the complex, a side road turns south to the ski resort of Antillanca (⊛ www.skiantillanca.cl) on the flank of Volcán Casablanca; 4km from the junction this passes **Aguas Calientes**, where there's cheaper accommodation, hot springs and the national park visitor centre.

Volcán Osorno seen across Lago Llanquihue from Puerto Octay. (RW)

The international road continues through dense Valdivian forest to the Anticura ranger station and campsite (Km93), with a half-hour trail to the **Salto del Indio Waterfalls**. It's another 4km (passing paths to more waterfalls) to the Pajaritos border post (95km from Osorno), and 22km more to the **border** itself at the Paso Cardenal Samoré (1,308m). When the Cordón del Caulle isn't erupting there's good **hiking** to the north from the El Caulle Church, just north of Anticura, with a good hut after 10km, below Volcán Puyehue (2,240m).

Lago Llanquihue

Ruta 5 (the Panamericana) from Osorno leads directly to Puerto Varas and Puerto Montt, but it's nicer to go via Puerto Octay, an hour to the southeast, and then follow the shore of **Llanquihue Lake**. This is the largest lake in the Lakes District, the second largest in Chile and the third largest in South America. It was 'discovered' by Pedro de Valdivia in 1552 but forgotten after 1604 when Osorno was abandoned; the

area was thickly forested and the indigenous people preferred to live in the hills. It was rediscovered in the 1840s, and from 1852 its shores were settled by German immigrants. By the 1870s there were settlements, linked by steamers, most of the way around the lake, although the only roads were from Puerto Octay to Osorno and from Puerto Varas to Puerto Montt. Its southern shore in particular is still lined with beautifully kept fields, wooden churches and shingle-faced farmhouses and watermills, many now offering accommodation and *kuchen* (German cakes) and *once* (high tea).

Puerto Octay

The first settlement on the lake, Puerto Octay became a backwater after being bypassed by the railway in 1912, and this has helped preserve many of its

colonists' houses and the Catholic **church** (1904). The little **museum** (Ⓦ www.museopuertooctay.cl ⊘ 10.15–13.00, 15.00–17.00 daily), a couple of blocks below the plaza at Independencia 591 is in one such house, built in 1920, and has displays on local archaeology and on the German colonists; there are also agricultural machines in a *galpón* (barn) just south on camino Centinela.

Frutillar

Midway along the lake's western shore, with great views of Volcán Osorno, Frutillar (Frutillar Bajo, strictly speaking) is a quiet village that trades on its German roots, with lots of cafés selling wonderful *kuchen*. It's dominated by the striking new Teatro del Lago which is home to the renowned Semanas Musicales de Frutillar (Ⓦ www.semanasmusicales. cl), a ten-day music festival at the end of January and the start of February.

Not far north, at Pérez Rosales and Prat, the **Museo Colonial Alemán** (Colonial Alemán Museum; ⊘ Mar–Dec 09.00–17.30 daily, Jan–Feb 09.00–19.30 daily) consists of four main preserved buildings set in beautiful gardens, with agricultural machinery and furniture used by the German colonists.

Puerto Varas

Stunningly located at the southwestern corner of the lake, with great views of the Osorno and Calbuco volcanoes, Puerto Varas (1,005km from Santiago) is renowned as the leading tourist resort of southern Chile and offers access to **Lago Todos Los Santos** and the **bus-boat**

Eating out in Puerto Varas

Balandra (elegant fine dining) Del Salvador 024 Ⓦ www.colonosdelsur.cl/balandra.htm

Café Dane's (empanadas, sandwiches and coffee) Del Salvador 441 Ⓣ 65 232 371

Club Alemán (solid fare with a German touch) San José 415 Ⓣ 65 232 246

La Gringa Bakery Café (superb breakfasts, lunches and kuchen) Ⓦ www.lagringa.cl

Mediterraneo (not especially Mediterranean, but the seafood and wine list are recommended) Santa Rosa 068 Ⓦ www.mediterraneopuertovaras.cl

Miraolas (excellent waterfront seafood restaurant) Santa Rosa 040 Ⓣ 65 718 316

Volcán Osorno, with Puerto Varas's German-style church in the foreground. (RK/A)

crossing to Bariloche in Argentina (see overleaf). Some of southern Chile's finest hotels and restaurants are also to be found here.

German colonists settled here from 1852, and Puerto Varas soon became the lake's principal port, with products being carried by oxcart to Puerto Montt. Tourism took off with the railway's arrival in 1911. Although the town's life centres on the beach and the plaza immediately inland from the pier and tourist office, the German **pre-war buildings** that make Puerto Varas distinctive stand mainly on the hill slopes a few blocks inland. The town centre itself is hardly attractive. It's dominated by the **church** of the Sagrado Corazón, built for German Jesuits between 1915 and 1918; based on the famous Marienkirche in the Black Forest, it has a corrugated iron exterior and a Baroque interior.

On the lakeside just south of the centre, the **Museo Pablo Fierro** (Pablo Fierro Museum; ⑭ www.pablofierro.cl ⊙ 10.00–14.00, 16.00–21.00 Mon–Sat) is the creation of a local artist, displaying his paintings of historic buildings and also his collection of furnishings rescued from local houses, all entertainingly thrown together.

Parque Nacional Vicente Pérez Rosales and beyond

The stunning Volcán Osorno (directly across Lago Llanquihue from Puerto Varas), Lago Todos Los Santos and the whole area leading to

Volcán Tronador and the Argentine border, are protected by the **Vicente Pérez Rosales National Park**, Chile's oldest, founded in 1926. Perhaps the best way to see it is the famous (and expensive) **Cruce de Los Lagos** (Ⓦ www.cruceandino.com, www.crucedelagos.com), which involves a bus from Puerto Montt or Puerto Varas to Petrohué, a boat across Lago Todos Los Santos to Peulla, a bus across the border and then two more boats and two more buses on the Argentine side, to finish in Bariloche; it's also possible to stop in the hotel at Peulla.

All excursions stop at the dramatic **Petrohué Falls**, at the entry to the park, where the Río Petrohué bursts through a dam of basalt from **Volcán Osorno**. It's possible to climb the volcano, although it's much harder and less popular than climbing Volcán Villarrica.

From Ensenada, at the southeastern corner of Lago Llanquihue, a road runs south to the head of the Estero de Reloncaví (Reloncaví Estuary), and down its east side to Cochamó, 94km from Puerto Varas.

Just south is the **Cochamó Valley**, which rivals Yosemite in its beauty and its potential for adventure. The only easily accessible classic U-shaped glacial valley in South America, it's also home to large stands of the biggest and oldest alerce trees yet found. In the 18th century the intrepid Jesuits of Chiloé pioneered a route to Argentina, used in the 20th century to give Argentine *estancias* (farms/ranches) an outlet to the sea. Its most notorious users were two gringos formerly known as Butch Cassidy and the Sundance Kid, who lived in Cholila between 1901 and 1905. Miraculously, the Cochamó Road still survives as a horse-track, with plans for road-building and logging thwarted. The valley has been discovered by adventure tourism (see opposite), and activities include horseriding, visits to hot springs and sea lion colonies, and hiking.

Climbing Osorno Volcano

Enshrouded in clouds and local legends, Osorno Volcano is a famed symbol of Patagonia. Its ascent is a magical experience, immersed in nature, which will test you to your limits. Rising out of surrounding fields and native forest, the Osorno also offers a perfect viewpoint of southern Chile. The climb towards the 2,656m summit starts before sunrise, with a trail through volcanic scree and glacier, which rewards us with a panorama of the Lakes region.

Patagonia Lakes District crossing

Puerto Varas is the gateway to the Patagonia Lakes District, a region south of Santiago dotted with alpine lakes, pines, volcanoes, and the occasional log cabin. The Patagonia Lakes District Crossing whisks you past Volcano Osorno and Mount Tronador. Along the way, stay in first-rate lodges with spectacular views of the lakes and mountains, dine on fresh trout or lamb *asado*, and enjoy a hike to Bride's Waterfall near Peulla.

It's another 25km south by the coastal road to the village of **Puelo**, from where a road is being built up the Puelo Valley towards Argentina, with a ferry along Lago Tagua-Tagua. The Río Puelo is known for huge salmon and trout, and there are some luxurious fly-fishing lodges (see pages 194–5 for details).

There's very little conventional infrastructure in either of these areas, but local adventure tourism outfit Campo Aventura (ⓦ www.campoaventura.com) owns the comfortable Riverside Lodge near the road at the mouth of the Cochamó Valley and the simpler Mountainside Lodge, 18km inland at La Junta and reached only on foot or horse.

Puerto Montt and surrounds

Twenty kilometres south of Puerto Varas, Puerto Montt is the transport hub of southern Chile and somewhere you are likely to pass through *en route* to Chiloé, Chaitén, the Laguna San Rafael, Puerto Natales or Punta Arenas. It's a working port, not a chi-chi tourist resort, but its setting between lush rolling hills and islands, with snow-capped volcanoes in the distance, and its quaint shingle- and tin-fronted buildings give it a Nordic charm of its own. It also offers the greatest variety of seafood in all of South America.

In 1852 the first Germans landed here to begin the colonisation of the Lakes District. The city served as a shipping point for goods brought across Lago Llanquihue by boat and then by cart from Puerto Varas. After completion of the railway in 1913, Puerto Montt continued to serve as a base for colonisation, this time to the south in Chiloé Continental (see page 220) and Aysén. The port and much of the city, including all its German pioneer buildings, were destroyed in the huge earthquake of 1960, but rebuilding was swift.

Eating out in Puerto Montt

Café Sirope (brilliant little café in the Diego Rivera Cultural Centre) Quillota 126 ⓣ 65 260 977

Club Alemán (quiet, traditional restaurant, good seafood) Antonio Varas 264 ⓣ 65 297 000 ⓦ www.elclubaleman.cl

Club de Yates (town's longest-established and best-known seafood restaurant) Manfredini 200 ⓣ 65 282 810

Puerto Montt's **waterfront promenade** and **plaza** have been attractively remodelled. On the north side of the plaza, the boxy wooden **cathedral** was begun in 1856, just three years after the foundation of the city itself. A couple of blocks north and west, the Jesuits built a more attractive wooden **church** in 1872, with a bell tower (1894) on the hill above it.

On the waterfront immediately east of the bus terminal, the **Museo Municipal Juan Pablo II** (Pope John Paul II Municipal Museum; ⊘09.00–19.00 Mon–Fri, 09.00–13.00 Sat) is currently closed for refurbishment, but has interesting displays on anthropology, natural history, the German colonisation and the aftermath of the 1960 earthquake, plus souvenirs of the Pope's visit in 1987. Even if it's closed, you can still see two steam locomotives and a crane preserved outside. One block east of the plaza, the **Casa del Arte Diego Rivera** (Quillota 116 ⓣ 65 482 638 ⊘ 10.00–19.00 Mon–Sat, 15.00–19.00 Sun and holidays) has excellent exhibitions and a good café (see below).

Beyond the bus terminal the Costanera leads west to the ferry terminal in the sheltered Canal Tenglo; just beyond this the **Angelmó market** carries an amazing range of fish and shellfish, with small seafood restaurants upstairs.

The **Ayaltue Cultural Park** (ⓦ www.ayaltue.cl), 25km southwest of Puerto Montt, illustrates the history, mythology, traditions, crafts, flora and fauna of this area, and of course its foods as well.

Parque Nacional Alerce Andino

Just east of Puerto Montt, the **Alerce Andino National Park** preserves groves of alerce trees about 2,000 years old. With up to 4.5m of rain a year, *quila* bamboo swallows up paths almost as soon as they are cleared, so hiking without a guide is difficult; you can stay at Alerce Mountain Lodge (see page 194 for contact information), an all-inclusive luxury eco-resort just outside the park.

In conversation with...

Chile seems huge; what are the best ways to see all the highlights and keep travel costs down?

Chile is a very long, narrow country and has an incredible mix of landscapes – from the Pacific coast to the Andes and the red sand of the Atacama Desert to the glaciers and lakes of the Torres del Paine National Park in Patagonia. To see all of these destinations visitors really need to take several domestic flights, which  can prove expensive but it is possible to arrange an air pass to keep the costs down. In the Lakes District and Patagonia, boat trips are a great way to get around and if you're feeling adventurous a boat from Punta Arenas around Cape Horn and into Argentina is really the only way to see the southern fjords.

What are the key places that no visitor should miss?

 No visit is complete without a stay in the Atacama Desert. It is the driest place on earth and home to some of the strangest and most beautiful landscapes in Latin America; there is plenty to explore. San Pedro de Atacama is a pretty town and an ideal base with some fantastic luxury accommodation. It is situated close to several natural wonders, including the Laguna Miscanti – a stunning blue lagoon set in a barren landscape which is not to be missed. Fit in a trip to the UNESCO World Heritage city of Valparaíso, a historic port full of quirky ancient architecture. It's a great place to soak up history, atmosphere and spectacular ocean views. Visitors should also not leave without sampling the amazing array of quality local wines on offer and many of the vineyards are conveniently located close to Santiago so can easily be visited on a day trip.

Can the Lakes District and Patagonia be combined? And should visitors travel to the Argentinian side of either?

The Lakes District and Patagonia are fantastic destinations with spectacular scenery and can easily be incorporated into one trip. Both are excellent gateways

to Argentina and travelling between the two countries can be an exciting and rewarding adventure. The Lakes District is arguably Chile's most beautiful region, with towering volcanoes, pristine lakes, waterfalls and forests. One of the best bases for exploring is Puerto Varas and we often recommend that visitors to the Lakes District hire a car for a few days to explore the national parks and picturesque villages. It is also possible to make the journey from Puerto Varas through the Andes and across a series of lakes to Bariloche in Argentina, a full day trip that takes visitors through some truly exceptional scenery. Patagonia is a great destination for those who love the outdoors and adventure – the best ways to discover this vast untouched wilderness are on foot or on horseback. Many hotels in Chilean Patagonia also offer complimentary transfer to El Calafate in Argentina, which is a base for trekking and exploring the Perito Moreno Glacier.

What tips would you give to people planning a trip to Chile?

Chile is a land of contrasts in terms of both landscape and culture; visitors to the northern regions will find an indigenous culture similar to neighbouring Peru and Bolivia, while those travelling to the south will find the country to be more modern and cosmopolitan, particularly Santiago. Visitors will also find that all this outdoor adventure and fresh air will leave them with a healthy appetite and Chilean cuisine is some of the best in the world. Choose from Patagonian lamb, succulent steaks and the freshest Pacific seafood on the coast, all washed down with fine Chilean wines.

Rainbow Tours Latin America specialists have been providing expert advice and tailor-made tours to the region for over a decade. Focusing on comfortable adventure, Rainbow's trips in Chile are aimed at enabling visitors to discover the very best of the region's natural wonders with opportunities to soak up the culture. We spoke with Amanda Sweeney of the company.

℡ +44 (0)20 7666 1272 Ⓔ info@rainbowtours.co.uk
Ⓦ www.rainbowtours.co.uk

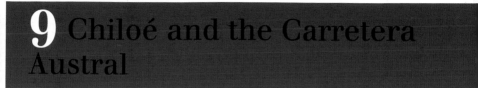

Only a narrow stretch of water separates Chiloé (the 'Place of Seagulls') from the mainland, but crossing it is like stepping into another country, and another century. The island's Pacific coast is almost uninhabited, but its sheltered northern and eastern sides are an emerald and gold patchwork of potato and wheat fields, with all the island's towns found here. To the east there's also an archipelago of islands with a scattering of attractive villages.

Until a few years ago the roadless wilderness on the mainland south of Puerto Montt remained virtually unknown and uninhabited except for a handful of isolated fishing villages. Only in 1988 was a road, the Carretera Austral, opened to Cochrane and then Villa O'Higgins. It's a rugged and very wet landscape, a cross between Switzerland, Scotland's west coast and a tropical jungle, with a few volcanoes thrown in; culturally it's like the Wild West, with the land still being tamed by hardy pioneers on horseback or wooden-wheeled oxcarts.

Chiloé

The green and fertile island of Chiloé was settled by Spanish colonists from 1567, and the indigenous population was soon decimated by European diseases. In 1598 the Spaniards were driven out of southern Chile, leaving Chiloé cut off and dependent for survival on an annual ship from Peru. The Spanish settlers were soon as poor as their neighbours and intermarried with them, producing a distinctive and homogenous society, with a vibrant folklore centred on sorcery and supernatural creatures.

The island finally joined independent Chile in 1826, and its economy began to improve. Many Chilotes left to work on Patagonian *estancias*, as they still do, and Chilote fishermen also established tiny settlements on the mainland just to the east, known as Chiloé Continental.

Chiloé is best known for its quaint *palafitos*, wooden houses built out over the water on stilts in order to avoid paying rent, and for its charming wooden churches. About 60 of these (of perhaps 150) remain, of which 16 were added to UNESCO's World Heritage List in 2000 (Ⓦ www.rutadelasiglesias.cl). Other attractions include its isolated islands and sheltered waters ideal for boating, its marine wildlife and national parks, as well as its friendly relaxed lifestyle.

Ancud

One of the island's two main cities, Ancud was only founded in 1767 to protect a huge natural harbour. It was the capital of the island between 1788 and 1982. Overlooking the bay southwest of the attractive plaza (and the

Fishing boats in Ancud harbour (SS)

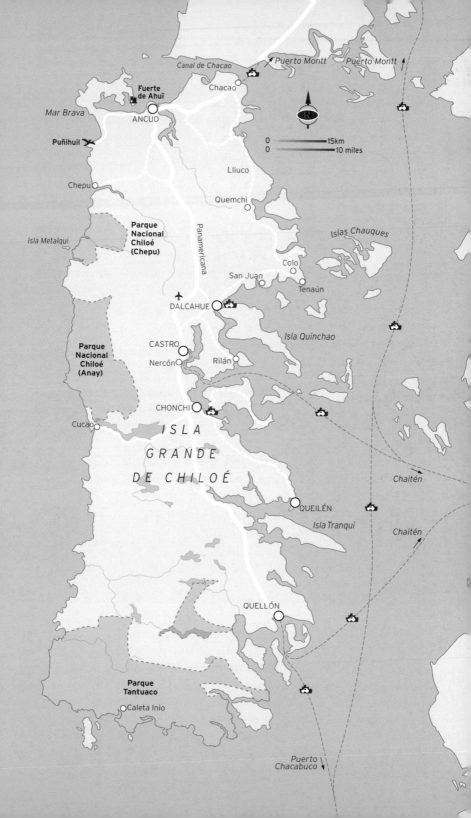

Practicalities

Ferries shuttle across the Canal de Chacao from the mainland, a delightful half-hour crossing with sea lions, dolphins, penguins, cormorants, gulls and petrels all visible. From the ferry at Chacao, it's 27km to Ancud. A brand new **airport**, opened early in 2012, has provided an alternative means of access.

It's about 70km down the **Panamericana** to the island's capital, Castro but it's more interesting to follow minor roads down the east coast via Lliuco,

Accommodation

Exclusive
Centro de Ocio (Castro) ⓦ www.centrodeocio.cl
Hotel Parque Quilquico (Castro) ⓦ www.hotelparquequilquico.cl
Hotel Refugia (Castro) ⓦ www.refugia.cl

Upmarket
Hostería Ancud (Ancud) ⓦ www.panamericanahoteles.cl/ancud.html
Hostería de Castro (Castro) ⓦ www.hosteriadecastro.cl
Hostería Quellón (Quellón) Pedro Montt 383 ⓣ 65 681 250
Hotel Galeón Azul (Ancud) ⓦ www.hotelgaleonazul.cl
Hotel Melimoyu (Quellón) Pedro Montt 369 ⓣ 65 681 310
Hotel Patagonia Insular (Quellón) ⓦ www.hotelpatagoniainsular.cl
Hotel Tierra del Fuego (Quellón) Pedro Montt 445 ⓣ 65 682 079
Hotel Unicornio Azul (Castro) ⓦ www.hotelgaleonazul.cl/unicornio

Moderate
El Chico Leo (Quellón) Pedro Montt 325 ⓣ 65 681 567
Hostel Palafito Cucao (Cucao) ⓦ www.hostelpalafitocucao.cl

modern cathedral) is the excellent **Museo Regional** (Regional Museum; ☉ Jan–Feb 10.00–19.30 daily, Mar–Dec 10.00–17.30 Tue–Fri, 10.00–14.00 Sat–Sun and holidays) – it's an amusing little building with all kinds of exhibits on the island's flora and fauna and human culture, notably religious art and the 1960 earthquake. Outside of the museum you will find a huge whale skeleton, a full-size replica of the schooner *Ancud*, which sailed from here to claim the Magallanes region for Chile in 1843, and wooden figures of characters from Chilote folklore such as the gnome-like Trauco and the mermaid La Pincoya.

Quemchi, Colo, Tenaún, San Juan and Dalcahue, tiny fishing villages with wooden churches. From the Chonchi junction the Panamericana continues south for 72km to end at Quellón, where the **ferries** to Chaitén leave.

The island's two main towns, Ancud and Castro, both make excellent bases with all **services**, as well as decent hotels and restaurants. However, the island's only really **exclusive hotels** are three stylish new places on the Rilán Peninsula, across a sound from Castro.

Hostal Vista al Mar (Ancud) Ⓦ www.vistaalmar.cl
Hotel Los Suizos (Quellón) Ladrilleros 399 Ⓣ 65 681 787
Hotel Madryn (Ancud) Ⓦ www.hotelmadryn.cl
Palafito Hostel (Castro) Ⓦ www.palafitohostel.com

Budget
Hospedaje El Mirador (Castro) Ⓦ www.hostalelmiradorcastro.cl
Hostal Lluhay (Ancud) Ⓦ www.hostal-lluhay.cl
Hostal Nuevo Mundo (Ancud) Ⓦ www.newworld.cl

Eating out

Kurantón (Ancud; seafood) Prat 94 Ⓣ 65 623 090
La Brújula del Cuerpo (Castro; lively café on the plaza) O'Higgins 308 Ⓣ 65 633 229
La Pincoya (Ancud; seafood) Prat 61 Ⓣ 65 622 511/622 613
Octavio (Castro; best and priciest seafood restaurant on the waterfront) Pedro Montt 261 Ⓣ 65 632 855

The **Ruta de las Iglesias (Wooden Churches Route)** has an interesting visitor centre in the attractively remodelled church of the **Inmaculada Concepción** (☺ 09.30–12.30, 15.30–19.00 Mon–Fri) at Errázuriz 227. There's interesting detail on the construction of the churches (based on shipbuilding) and the diseases that attack the wood, as well as church vestments and 18th-century baptism registers.

A little way north of the port, the **Fuerte San Antonio**, built in 1770, was the last royalist stronghold in Chile, and much of its stonework remains intact. To the west, a road runs right around the Bahía de

Lemuy Island, roots of Chiloé

Just a few minutes by ferry from the main island of Chiloé, you find the picturesque Island of Lemuy. Here Silvio and his wife will host you in their house and delight you with a delicious salmon, freshly fished. You spend the afternoon exploring the magnificent corners of the island, taking time to talk with their

inhabitants, meet the fishermen, and learn about the art of the loom and carpentry – a real journey to the roots of the Chiloé culture.

Ancud to three other **forts** (Balcacura, Chaicura and San Miguel de Ahuï), whose guns intersected with those of the Fuerte San Antonio, not far off as the crow flies but over 30km away by road, to close the entry to the bay.

Alternatively, it's a short distance across the neck of the Lacuy Peninsula to the wonderfully wild beach of **Mar Brava**. Minor roads wind south to **Puñihuil**, a fishing cove from where you can take a boat (⊘ every 20–30mins) to see the **penguin colonies** of the Islotes de Puñihuil Natural Monument – unusually, Humboldt and Magellanic penguins nest together here, from September to March.

Castro and surrounds

Castro is the third oldest town in Chile, having been founded in 1567, when it was the world's southernmost city, but there are few historic remains. Set on a plateau with distinctly steep hills down to the *costanera*, the town's centrepiece is **Plaza Prat**; on its north side is the **cathedral** (1912), which is on UNESCO's World Heritage List although it's hard to see that it has much in common with the traditional Chilote wooden churches. It has a wooden frame but is clad in metal, with moulded shingles on the front and corrugated sheets on the sides. There are better examples (also on the World Heritage List) in **Nercón**, 4km south of Castro (built between 1879 and 1895; ⊘ 10.00–18.00 daily) and **Chonchi**, 23km south (1893).

The **Museo Regional** (Regional Museum; ⊘ Jan–Feb 09.30–13.00, 15.00–19.00 Mon–Sat, 09.30–13.00 Sun, Mar–Dec 09.30–13.00, 14.00–17.50 Mon–Fri, 09.30–14.30 Sat ⪸ free) is in a small house at Esmeralda 205 (just south of the plaza). It has excellent displays on the construction of wooden churches and wooden boats, good photos of the railway to Ancud, and of the great fire of 1934, which destroyed most of the town. A striking new museum was built a decade ago on the waterfront on Lillo, but has never been occupied.

Castro may seem an unlikely site for a museum of contemporary art, but there is one – in a field 3km west and poorly signed. **MAM-Chiloé** (① 65 635 ⓦ www.mamchiloe.cl ⊘ Jan–Feb 10.00–18.00 daily, Nov, Dec, Mar 11.00–14.00 daily, rest of year telephone ahead) is a motley collection of barn-like buildings housing often excellent touring shows.

Castro is also known for its *palafitos*, although they're all post-1960 reconstructions: there are some northeast of the centre and more gentrified ones across the Puente Gamboa on the road south.

Traditional *palafitos* in Castro (RI/G)

Parque Nacional Chiloé

On the island's Pacific coast, the **Chiloé National Park** is in two parts, the main sector being directly west of Castro and reached by the newly paved road from Chonchi to **Cucao**. There's a wooden chapel here and a few guesthouses; across a footbridge is the park's Chanquín visitor centre, with excellent boardwalk trails through dense rainforest. You can also walk north for two hours along the superb beach to reach the Colo-Cole refuge and more rainforest.

To the north, the Chepu sector is reached from **Chepu**, 38km southwest of Ancud. After taking a boat across a river, it's a 24km coastal hike to the Río Refugio hut, not far north of Isla Metalqui, South America's largest sea lion colony.

Quellón and Parque Tantauco

The only town in the south of the island, Quellón is a run-down logging port that is notable only for the ferries to Chaitén and for one of Chile's most exciting new conservation projects. The **Parque Tantauco** (Ⓦ www.parquetantauco.cl), 118,000ha of very wet forest in the island's southwestern corner, is owned by Sebastián Piñera (currently president of Chilé, no less) and is recognised as a biodiversity hotspot.

The park has a visitor centre (Ⓣ 65 773 100 Ⓔ info@parquetantauco. cl ◷ 09.00–13.00, 14.00–18.00 Mon–Fri) in Quellón but its headquarters are in the tiny village of Caleta Inio, reached by boat (◷ mid-Mar to Dec 10.00 Wed, Jan to mid-Mar also Mon and Fri). There are guesthouses and camping plus a small **museum** (◷ 09.00–13.00, 14.00–18.00 daily).

Spectacular views in Chiloé National Park (MT/A)

Chiloé

Reached by ferry or by air from the mainland, these verdant windswept islands have forged their own culture and traditions. Visit Castro's most colourful Jesuit wooden church, one of over 60 on the islands, take snaps of the stilted houses – *palafitos* – that sit along the water's edge and make sure you sample the islands' prized oysters. If you have not got time to stay for a few days, take a day trip from your Lakes District base; it is well worth the detour.

There's also a rough road (40km) to the park's northern access at **Chaiguata**. From here it's a five-day hike to Inio (permitted in this direction only), sleeping in *refugios* or camping.

Recently blue whales have been gathering from December to April to the south of Chiloé, so **whale-watching** may offer Quellón a new road to recovery.

Aysén and the Carretera Austral

This is the wildest part of Chile, still being settled and developed – pioneer families are clearing fields for cattle and, increasingly, for guesthouses and fly-fishing lodges. The back-country is largely inaccessible, but you'll see huge forests and mountains, glaciers and waterfalls, and take boat trips to see wildlife on fiords and lakes.

Aysén (now Region XI) was only minimally populated by indigenous people, and then settled largely from Argentina. The Colonisation Law allowed settlers to claim land if it had been cleared, so from 1946 to 1953 huge fires raged across the province, clearing not only potential agricultural land but also inaccessible mountain slopes. Almost three million hectares, a third of the province's area, were burnt. Fields are still strewn with logs, rotting slowly in this cold climate.

The Chilean army began construction of the Carretera Austral (Southern Highway) in 1962, with the central section opening in 1983, the 1,028km from Puerto Montt to Cochrane (including ferry links) in 1988 and the final few kilometres to Villa O'Higgins in 1999. This was followed by side roads to isolated spots like Puerto Balmaceda,

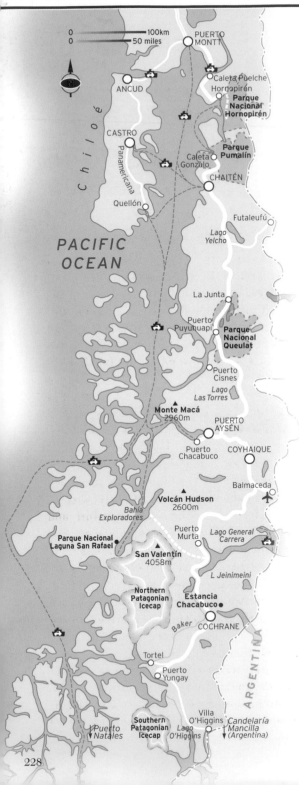

Bahía Exploradores and Tortel. It became known as one of the world's great wilderness routes, particularly popular with foreign cycle tourists, although much of it is now being paved.

The two main places of interest for tour groups are the Glaciar San Rafael, one of the world's most impressive tidewater glaciers, and Pumalín, a vast area of wilderness that's being preserved for sustainable tourism. Further south the draw is above all the experience itself, the long drive through the unfolding grandeur of this wet wilderness.

Hornopirén and Parque Pumalín

The Carretera Austral formally begins in Puerto Montt (see *Chapter 8*, page 213) and follows the coast for 46km to La Arena, from where a ferry shuttles across to Caleta Puelche; from here it's another 55km to the logging town of Hornopirén. Immediately to the east is the little-visited **Hornopirén National Park**, protecting a large

Lago General Carrera is the largest lake in Chile. (MR)

swathe of rainforest. People also come here to take the 50-minute boat ride to the Termas de Llancahue (⦿ www.termasdellancahue.cl), on an island in the mouth of the estuary.

A daily ferry links Hornopirén and Caleta Gonzalo, 56km north of Chaitén and the hub of the **Pumalín Park**, Chile's best known private conservation project. This is a huge expanse of wilderness that was bought by Californian millionaire Doug Tompkins, in the face of virulent opposition from nationalists and extreme right-wingers, who saw it as a foreign plot to cut the country in half (the park stretches from the sea to the Argentine border) and to steal its natural resources. The government accepts that it is a genuinely worthwhile conservation project, but negotiations dragged on for six years before Pumalín could be declared a Sanctuario de la Naturaleza in 2005, allowing Tompkins to hand it over to a Chilean foundation.

Pumalín covers a total of 270,000ha, an exceptionally wild area of fiords, mountains (including Volcán Michinmahuida, 2,404m) and above all untouched temperate rainforest including huge and ancient alerce trees, some as much as 3,600 years old. Much of the park is more or less inaccessible, and being left that way. Nevertheless visitors are welcome and there are good trails and campsites.

The northern half of the Parque Pumalín is less developed; by boat you can reach the **hot springs** of Cahuelmó and tiny fishing settlements.

Chaitén to Coyhaique

The main entry point to the Carretera Austral, Chaitén has a fine setting but even before the eruption of Volcán Chaitén in 2008 it was little more than a place to stay the night. At the time, it was evacuated and largely destroyed; now services are re-opening, but it's less appealing than it was previously.

Practicalities

To reach this remote region it's necessary to **fly**, to take a **ship**, or to **travel overland** through Argentina. The only **airport** with jet service from Santiago and other major cities is Balmaceda, near the regional capital of Coyhaique. The main **ferry** links to the Carretera Austral are provided by Navimag Cruceros (Ⓦ www.navimagcruceros.cl), shuttling from Puerto Montt and Quellón (and Castro in summer) to Chaitén, and Quellón to Puerto Chacabuco. Navimag sails twice a week from Puerto Montt to Puerto Chacabuco; drivers can also travel via Hornopirén with two other ferry crossings.

At the Carretera's southern end, another ferry crosses Lago O'Higgins to Candelaría Mancilla, from where it's possible to hike or ride (horse or bicycle) into Argentina – the route through Chile being blocked by the Southern Patagonian Icecap. In addition to ferries, Chaitén is also reached by **air taxis**.

Puerto Chacabuco is the main launch pad for the near-compulsory visits

Accommodation

Aysén has no luxury hotels, although some **fly-fishing lodges** are very comfortable (and you don't have to go fishing). South of Chaitén, tiny settlements such as Villa Santa Lucía and La Junta offer basic accommodation, and Puerto Puyuhuapi (195km from Chaitén) has a couple of nice guesthouses. It's possible to take a boat from here to the **Termas de Puyuhuapi** (Ⓦ www.patagonia-connection.com), a luxury spa resort offering packages that include catamaran trips to the San Rafael Glacier, as well as various activities and therapies.

There's plenty of superb **local seafood** in Aysén, but not a lot of haute cuisine otherwise. In Chaitén your best bet is the hotel restaurants.

Exclusive
Hotel Hacienda Tres Lagos (Lago Bertrand) Ⓦ www.haciendatreslagos.com

Upmarket
Hotel Dreams Patagonia (Coyhaique) Ⓦ www.mundodreams.com/hotel/hotel-dreams-patagonia
Hotel Termas de Llancahué (Isla Llancahué) Ⓦ www.termasdellancahue.cl
The Lodge at Valle Chacabuco (Cochrane) Ⓦ www.conservacionpatagonica.org/visit_wts_lodge.htm
Lodge Robinson Crusoe Deep Patagonia (Villa O'Higgins) Ⓦ www.robinsoncrusoe.com

to the San Rafael Glacier, although you can also fly in from Coyhaique. **Fast catamarans** have now made it possible to do a day-trip to the glacier. Most crucially, there's no road access to the Parque Nacional Laguna San Rafael, so those wanting to see the stunning glacier come by boat (or a few by air). In addition to Navimag Cruceros, Catamaranes del Sur (Ⓦ www. catamaranesdelsur.cl) sail from Puerto Chacabuco to Laguna San Rafael. The new road to Bahía Exploradores has allowed Turismo Río Exploradores (Ⓦ www.exploradores-sanrafael.cl) to reach the glacier in under three hours. Finally, **Skorpios** (Ⓦ www.skorpios.cl) provides luxurious cruises to the laguna, both three- and four-day itineraries from Puerto Chacabuco and a sixday trip from Puerto Montt, calling at remote and unspoilt hot springs.

Coyhaique is a relatively small and quiet town but as the regional capital it does have essential services and the closest decent hotels to the Laguna San Rafael. When **telephoning** in this region, note that many places use either mobile phones or a rural network with 08 or 09 codes.

Pasarela Sur Lodge (Lago Bertrand) Ⓦ www.pasarelasurlodge.cl
Terra Luna Lodge (Lago Bertrand) Ⓦ www.tinyurl.com/tierralunalodge

Moderate

Cabañas Brisas del Mar (Chaitén) Avda Corcovado 278 Ⓣ 65 731 284, 09 515 8808 Ⓔ cababrisas@telsur.cl
Cabañas Caleta Gonzalo (Parque Pumalín) Ⓦ www.parquepumalin.cl
Casa Ludwig (Puerto Puyuhuapi) Ⓦ www.casaludwig.cl
El Reloj (Coyhaique) Ⓦ www.elrelojhotel.cl
Hospedaje y Cabañas Pudú (Chaitén) Avda Corcovado 668 Ⓣ 08 227 9602/65 731 413 Ⓔ madera17@hotmail.com
Hostal Runín B&B (Villa O'Higgins) Pasaje Vialidad s/n Ⓣ 67 431 821
Hostería Coyhaique (Coyhaique) Ⓦ www.hotelcoyhaique.cl
Hotel Hornopirén (Hornopirén) Ignacio Carrera Pinto 388 Ⓣ 65 217 256
Hotel Schilling (Chaitén) Avda Corcovado 230 Ⓣ 65 731 295
La Casona de Puyuhuapi (Puerto Puyuhuapi) Ⓦ www.casonapuyuhuapi. aquinegocio.cl

Budget

Albergue las Salamandras (Coyhaique) Ⓦ www.salamandras.cl
El Mosco (Villa O'Higgins) Ⓦ www.patagoniaelmosco.com
Hospedaje Don Carlos (Chaitén) Riveros 54 Ⓣ 09 128 3328/65 731 287 Ⓔ doncarlos.palena@gmail.com

The Ventisquero Colgante (Hanging Glacier) is the centerpiece of the Queulat National Park. (DMP)

Stay in Queulat National Park

The Queulat Park is a wild and pristine territory where the temperate rainforest is topped with the Austral Andes glaciers and ice fields, and complemented with the rich biodiversity of the fjords and channels of the Austral Pacific. You can fully enjoy the park when staying at the Fiordo Queulat Ecolodge, close to all the park trails and to the Hanging Glacier. The lodge has five wood cabins and a very comfortable club house with regional and organic cuisine.

The Carretera Austral runs south through relatively undramatic scenery, passing **Lago Yelcho**, where there are some fine fly-fishing lodges, and a turning east to Argentina via **Futaleufú**, base for some of the world's most thrilling whitewater rafting. **Puerto Puyuhuapi**, 195km from Chaitén, was founded in 1935 by Sudeten Germans who opened a carpet factory, Alfombras de Puyuhuapi (® www.puyuhuapi. com), which is still going strong.

The Carretera continues south through the mountainous **Queulat National Park**, full of glaciers and waterfalls; at Km200 (214km from Chaitén), there's a turning to the viewpoint and information centre facing its main sight, the **Ventisquero Colgante** (Hanging Glacier). There's a turning to the west after 35km, which leads to **Puerto Cisnes**, a delightfully higgledy-piggledy little fishing port known for knitwear and trout-fishing.

From the Cruce Viviana junction, another 130km south from the Puerto Cisnes turning, a road runs west to **Puerto Aysén**, founded as the area's main port in 1914, and **Puerto Chacabuco**, built in the 1960s when Puerto Aysén silted up. Ferries and cruiseships call here, with excursions available to the interior. It's another 47km on the Carretera Austral to Coyhaique, capital of Aysén (region XI).

Parque Nacional Laguna San Rafael

The **San Rafael Glacier** discharges two million cubic metres of 30,000-year-old ice every day from its 3km face. It has been both retreating and advancing rapidly over a distance of 14km since 1871, but the present retreat (as much as 200m/year) is probably irreversible. The ice is astonishingly blue, and hard, because most of the air bubbles have been squeezed out.

San Rafael Glacier (r/S)

Most visitors just see it from inflatable boats, but there is 10km of boardwalk to a **viewpoint** over this glacier and another to the south. The *laguna* is visited by 20,000 visitors a year, but less than 200 land, so CONAF currently receives next to no fees. The rest of the 1,742,000ha **Laguna San Rafael National Park** receives virtually no visitors and is some of the most pristine terrain on Earth.

Coyhaique

Coyhaique only dates from 1929, when it was founded as part of the shift from large *estancias* granted concessions to raise cattle to a more general colonisation. It now has a population of almost 40,000 and a slightly disorienting layout, with a pentagonal plaza and ten radiating roads, supposedly based on the badge of the Carabineros!

Northeast of the plaza on Lillo at Baquedano, the **Museo Regional de la Patagonia** (Patagonia Regional Museum; ⊘ Jan–Feb 09.00–20.00 daily, Mar–Dec 09.00–13.00, 14.30–18.30 Mon–Fri) displays stuffed wildlife, explorers' maps, photos of the construction of the Carretera Austral and coverage of the forest burnings (which were denounced as early as 1870).

Outside the army base beside the main road to Puerto Aysén are a Sherman tank, troop carriers, and the earthmover which started work on the Carretera Austral in 1962. Continuing this way, it's about 1.5km to a junction to the **Reserva Nacional Coyhaique** (⊘ Dec–Mar 08.30–21.00 daily, April–Nov 08.30–18.30 daily), with a pleasant enough walk to the Laguna Verde and Cerro Cinchao, giving great views, although there's plenty of introduced pine.

South of Coyhaique

Some 40km south of Coyhaique, a junction forks left towards Argentina via the region's main airport at Balmaceda; keeping to the right, the Carretera passes through the Cerro Castillo Reserve, which should be one of southern Chile's best hiking areas. However, following fires, a considerable area has been planted with pines to prevent erosion. At Km197 (from Coyhaique) the Carretera passes Puerto Murta, a small resort on **Lago General Carrera**, the largest lake in Chile. Another 75km south there are various fancy fly-fishing lodges between Lago General Carrera and Lago Bertrand (see page 230).

It's 66km more to **Cochrane**, the last real town on the Carretera Austral, and base for a major new conservation project by Doug and Kris Tompkins, creators of the Pumalín Park (see page 229). Their 78,000ha **Estancia Chacabuco** is to be the centrepiece of the Patagonia National Park (⑭ www.conservacionpatagonica.org), linking with four national reserves to cover the whole area between Cochrane, the Argentine border and Lago General Carrera, and above all to protect the seriously endangered huemul deer.

Just over 100km beyond Cochrane a road leads a few kilometres west to **Tortel**, a unique little logging village with waterside walkways and no roads. It's another 32km to **Puerto Yungay**, where you have to take a free ferry a few kilometres upstream to reach the final section of the Carretera Austral (completed in 1999). **Villa O'Higgins** is another 100km away, but the highway's final terminus is 7km further on at **Bahía Bahamóndez**, at the end of a long narrow arm of Lago O'Higgins (shared with Argentina, which calls it Lago San Martín). From here a boat sails to the mighty **O'Higgins Glacier** (⑭ www.robinsoncrusoe. com; four days a week Jan–Feb, Sat only Nov–Dec, Mar).

Kayaking to the Capilla de Marmol

travel **Art**
C H I L E

The Capilla de Marmol ('Marble Chapel') is a hidden treasure located far down the Carretera Austral, the road traversing the thick forests, fjords, glaciers and mountains of Chile's south. On the shoreline of Lago General Carrera, time and water have carved out amazing shapes to create a unique natural wonder: a marble vault on slim pillars – a natural cathedral. Exploring it by kayak from Puerto Tranquilo or Puerto Sanchez makes the experience even more special.

10 Magallanes and Tierra del Fuego

For most visitors, the only reason to visit the far south of Chile is the fabulous scenery of the Torres del Paine. However, there is much more to see in the Magallanes region, especially in the wilder parts further south towards Cape Horn, visited mainly by boat. In these sheltered (but still rainy) waters you'll see many seabirds and sea lions, below huge glaciers coming off remarkably high and little-known peaks. Elsewhere you can visit sheep farms for horseriding with gauchos and massive teas. Meanwhile Punta Arenas has some remarkable historic buildings at the world's end.

To the west and south is some of the world's wettest terrain, and some of its most impenetrable forests, while the eastern side is a dry steppe; to the south is boggy tundra.

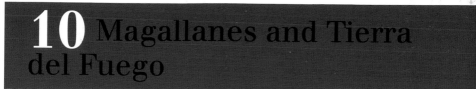

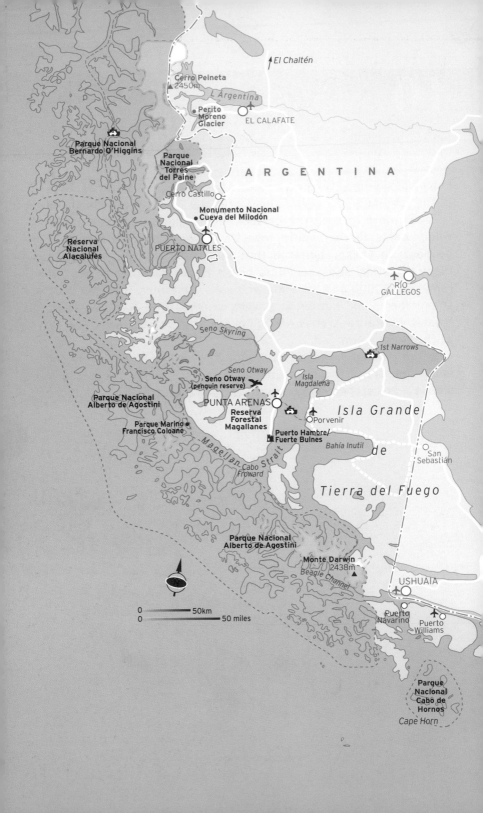

Magallanes

History

Ferñao de Magalhães (Ferdinand Magellan) discovered the straits that bear his name in 1520, and Cuidad del Rey Felipe was established by the Spanish in 1584; crops failed and supply ships never came, and when the English privateer Thomas Cavendish arrived in 1587 only 18 men were still alive. One man agreed to leave, the others stayed and starved to death. The site became known as Puerto Hambre ('Famine Port'), and there was consequently no non-indigenous settlement south of Chiloé until 1843, when Fuerte Bulnes was founded just south of Puerto Hambre. Amazingly, a French ship arrived the very next day, hoping to claim the area for France.

This settlement would have also failed without regular supplies by ship. In 1848 it was moved to a better site, now known as Punta Arenas. In 1876, the region's prosperity was assured when 300 sheep were brought from the Falkland Islands (Islas Malvinas); by 1900 there were a million of them here, producing seven million kilograms of wool a year. There was limited industrial development in the 20th century, but for the future, tourism will be key to the region's economy.

Punta Arenas

Founded as a penal colony in 1848, Punta Arenas supplied coal to steam ships from 1869, but it was sheep-farming that fuelled a boom from the 1890s to World War I. By 1902 this was a city of 10,000 with electricity, telephones, mains water and sewage, and a large British community. However, in 1914 the Panama Canal opened; by 1920 just three ships a month were calling, instead of three a day. Since 1945 oil production has provided more employment, followed by fishing and now tourism.

In the centre of Plaza Muñoz Gamero is a **statue of Magellan**, and below him a mermaid, a Patagonian native and a Selk'nam or Ona (from Tierra del Fuego) with a very shiny toe

Signpost at the Waldo Seguel viewpoint over Punta Arenas (EP/S)

Practicalities

Most visitors to Chile's far south will **fly** from Santiago or Puerto Montt to Punta Arenas. There's the ferry trip from Puerto Montt to Puerto Natales, or the long haul by road through Argentina. It's possible to make **excursions** around Punta Arenas, including to Tierra del Fuego, but most people will soon head north to the breathtaking Torres del Paine National Park, beyond Puerto Natales. There's a good, if unpaved, road through the park, and boat excursions are also possible, giving fantastic views. There are excellent hotels in and

Accommodation

Exclusive
Altiplánico (Puerto Natales) Ⓦ www.altiplanico.cl/en/altiplanico-hotel-puerto-natales

Hotel Dreams del Estrecho (Punta Arenas) Ⓦ www.mundodreams.com/hotel/hotel-dreams-del-estrecho

Hotel Salto Chico (Torres del Paine) Ⓦ www.explora.com/explora-patagonia

The Singular (Puerto Natales) Ⓦ www.thesingular.com

Tierra Patagonia Hotel & Spa (Torres del Paine) Ⓦ www.tierrapatagonia.com

Upmarket
Aquaterra Lodge (Puerto Natales) Ⓦ www.aquaterrapatagonia.com

CostAustralis (Puerto Natales) Ⓦ www.hotelcostaustralis.com

Eco-Camp Patagonia (Torres del Paine) Ⓦ www.ecocamp.travel

Hostería Lago Grey (Torres del Paine) Ⓦ www.lagogrey.cl

Hostería Las Torres (Torres del Paine) Ⓦ www.lastorres.com

Hostería Pehoé (Torres del Paine) Ⓦ www.pehoe.cl

Hotel Cabo de Hornos (Punta Arenas) Ⓦ www.hotelcabodehornos.com

Hotel José Nogueira (Punta Arenas) Ⓦ www.hotelnogueira.com

Hotel Río Serrano (Torres del Paine) Ⓦ www.hotelrioserrano.cl

Indigo (Puerto Natales) Ⓦ www.indigopatagonia.cl

Moderate
Hotel Finis Terrae (Punta Arenas) Ⓦ www.hotelfinisterrae.com

Hotel Isla Rey Jorge (Punta Arenas) Ⓦ www.islareyjorge.com

Hotel Lady Florence Dixie (Puerto Natales) Ⓦ www.hotelflorencedixie.cl

Hotel Martín Gusinde (Puerto Natales) Ⓦ www.hotelmartingusinde.com

Lodge de Montaña Paine Grande (Torres del Paine) Ⓦ www.verticepatagonia.cl

around the park, but no other restaurants, shops or ATMs – bring whatever you'll need with you.

The small town of **Puerto Natales** is the **entry point** to Patagonia for passengers on Navimag's wonderful three-day ferry trip from Puerto Montt (see box, pages 244–5), and for those coming from El Calafate and the Los Glaciares National Park in Argentina to visit the Torres del Paine National Park. It also provides a good range of facilities and activities for visitors. In Torres del Paine most refuges and hotels are closed from May to August.

Posada Río Serrano (Torres del Paine) ⓦ www.baqueanozamora.cl

Budget
Erratic Rock Hostel (Puerto Natales) ⓦ www.erraticrock.com
Hostal Amerindia (Puerto Natales) ⓦ www.hostelamerindia.com
Hostal La Estancia (Punta Arenas) ⓦ www.estancia.cl
Hostal Sonia Kuscevic (Punta Arenas) ⓦ www.hostalsk.cl
Hotel Isla Morena (Puerto Natales) ⓦ www.islamorenahotel.com

Eating out

There's been a foody boom in Puerto Natales in recent years, with some innovative new restaurants making the most of local produce.

Afrigonia (Puerto Natales; fusion of Chilean and Zambian cuisine) Eberhard 343 ⓣ 61 412 232
Cervecería Baguales (Puerto Natales; microbrewery with great beers and American-style pub food) Bories 430 ⓦ www.cervezabaguales.cl
Damiana Elena (Punta Arenas; excellent regional food in historic house) Magallanes 341 ⓣ 61 222 818
El Asador (Puerto Natales; grill-house on the plaza, local lamb a speciality) Prat 158 ⓣ 61 413 553
El Living (Puerto Natales; great vegetarian café on the plaza) Arturo Prat 156 ⓦ www.el-living.com
La Luna (Punta Arenas; friendly and busy, for lunch or dinner) O'Higgins 1017 ⓦ www.laluna.cl
Sotito's (Punta Arenas; seafood, renowned for its king crab or *centolla*) O'Higgins 1138 ⓣ 61 243 565

The municipal cemetery in Punta Arenas is full of amazing monuments. (TB/S)

– kissing this will supposedly ensure that you return to the city. Around the plaza are the **wool barons' mansions**, the two grandest being the Palacio Sara Braun on the north side (1905; now a hotel) and the Palacio Braun-Menéndez (1903) at Magallanes 949, housing the **Museo Regional** (Regional Museum; ⊘ Oct–Apr 10.30–17.00 Mon, Wed–Sat, 10.30–14.00 Sun and holidays May–Sep 10.30–14.00 Wed–Mon ⊛ free Sun and holidays). This preserves the mansion's opulent furnishings and interesting historic photographs and artefacts. On the east side of the plaza the Palacio Juan Blanchard is home to the **Chilean Antarctic Institute**, and there is a limited display on the city's role in Antarctic exploration here. Just east at Roca 864 is the site of the **former British Club** where Ernest Shackleton planned the rescue of his stranded expedition in 1916.

Three blocks west of the plaza along Waldo Seguel, the little Anglican church is fairly anonymous; behind it at Avenida España 959 is the baronial **house of Charley Milward**, the Victorian cousin who inspired Bruce Chatwin's *In Patagonia*. Waldo Seguel continues as steps to a **viewpoint** over the city and the Magellan Strait.

The enjoyable **Naval Museum** (⊘ 09.30–12.30, 14.00–17.00 Tue–Sat) at Pedro Montt 981 covers seafaring in this area, including the rescue of Shackleton's expedition. About a kilometre south, the beached hulks of various ships include the *County of Peebles*, the first four-masted iron-hulled ship, and the British frigate *Lord Lonsdale*.

Six blocks north of the plaza at Avenida Bulnes 636, by the ugly Salesian church, the **Museo Salesiano** (Salesian Museum; ⓦ www. museomaggiorinoborgatello.cl ⊘ 10.00–12.30, 15.00–18.00 Tue–Sun) is the city's best museum, with artefacts of indigenous peoples, settlers and the Salesians themselves, stuffed wildlife, and many fine maps and photographs.

Continuing two blocks north, the municipal **cemetery** (⊘ summer 07.30–20.00 daily, winter 08.00–18.00 daily ⚋ free) is one of Punta Arenas' great sights, full of the massive mausoleums of its richest families. There's a German plot (including those killed in the Battle of the Falklands) and an 'English' section (pretty Scottish, with names such as McIntosh, MacLeod and MacDonald). Right at the end of the cemetery is the Monument to the Unknown Indian, over the remains of the last Selk'nams.

At Km4.5 on Avenida Bulnes the **Museo del Recuerdo** (Museum of Memory; ⊘ 08.30–11.30, 14.30–18.30 Mon–Fri, 08.30–12.30 Sat) is a superb open-air museum of agricultural machinery and traction engines, and there are re-erected pioneer houses with some fascinating displays.

There's easy hiking in the **Reserva Forestal Magallanes**, on the edge of town; more exciting **excursions** include kayaking (possibly including whale-watching), visiting the Isla Magdalena and Seno Otway penguin colonies, and hiking to the San Isidro lighthouse and Cabo Froward, the southernmost point of the American mainland.

Magellanic penguins nest in burrows on Isla Magdalena, visited by tour boats from Punta Arenas. (PD/S)

Puerto Montt to Puerto Natales by ferry

South of Puerto Montt lies one third of Chile, inhabited by under 5% of its population. This is a remote region of desolate fiords, channels and uninhabited, thickly forested islands. Most traffic to Magallanes, the far south of Chile, goes by air or passes by road through Argentina, but it's also possible to take a ferry through this gloomy, storm-beaten archipelago to Puerto Natales, 1,460km from Puerto Montt. This is the equivalent of British Columbia's Inside Passage and the Alaska Marine Highway, but until recently its tourist potential was largely neglected. A couple of decades ago a few hardy backpackers joined the truck drivers in reclining seats in a container on an antique ferry that sailed to an erratic timetable. When the state company Navimag (Ⓦ www. navimag.com) took over they introduced the *Puerto Edén*, a larger ship with cabins, admittedly cramped, and the legendary *clase económico*, a dorm with bunks three high deep in the bowels of the ship. In 2001 a better vessel, the *Magallanes* (now renamed *Evangelistas*) was introduced, and the company is clearly trying to make the voyage more like a cruise, with staff to make the beds and empty the bins and two friendly guides who give lectures in Spanish and English.

Some things have not changed, such as the Chilean-style bingo and disco on the last night, and the open bridge policy, allowing you to chat to the officers and compare radar with chart (don't pay too much attention to your GPS, as this has been known to indicate you're on dry land). It can be disconcerting to find the officer of the watch dozing and the ship on autopilot – a helmsman appears only for docking and the passage through the three *angosturas* (narrows), Inglesa, Guia and Kirke, where there is as little as 2m of water under the keel even at high tide.

Puerto Natales and around

Until recently just a simple pioneer town (three hours north of Punta Arenas) where hikers stayed in family-run *residenciales*, Puerto Natales has boomed in the last decade as visitor numbers have rocketed. Nevertheless, it remains pleasant and unpretentious, with some very attractive metal-sided pioneer houses.

The main street, Bulnes, runs inland from the dock; a block north is the plaza, with the **church** (1930) and a narrow-gauge **steam engine** that used to run to Puerto Bories, the meat-packing plant 5km north. This operated from 1915 to 1970, processing 260,000 head of sheep a year; there's now a hotel at **Puerto Bories** but you can still visit the

You'll check in and leave baggage in the afternoon, boarding later for departure sometime in the early hours, depending on the tide. Again depending on tide and weather, the ship will detour up Fiordo Amalia to view a glacier such as the Skúa or Bruja, coming off the massive Southern Patagonian Icefield and calving small icebergs into the sea. There's a chance you'll see whales and dolphins, as well as plentiful birds such as black-browed albatross, South American terns, sooty shearwaters and various penguins and cormorants.

Sailing south, the usual route passes east of Chiloé and the Chonos (or Guaitecas) archipelago, down the Moraleda and Errázuriz channels and west usually by the Pulluche Channel to the Pacific, to pass around the Taitao Peninsula and across the Golfo de Penas. This is the one section where the ship is exposed to the Pacific swells and people can be sea-sick; southbound it's done overnight, northbound in the afternoon and evening.

Continuing down the Messier Channel, the ship passes the wreck of the *Capitán Leonidas*, stuck on a reef since 1968, and through the English Narrows (Angostura Inglesa) an hour before reaching **Puerto Edén**, a settlement of under 300 Kaweshkar and Huilliche people that was founded as a flying boat base in 1940. There's no jetty, but fishing boats come out with crafts such as baskets and bark boats to sell on board.

Capitán Leonidas was wrecked with a cargo of sugar in 1968. (SS)

The ship continues down the Ancho (Broad) and Sarmiento channels before swinging east to pass through the Angostura Kirke into the Golfo Almirante Montt (where mobile phones come back to life); the *angostura* is tackled in daylight only, after which it's two hours more to Puerto Natales.

machine rooms and the sheds used for drying hides. At Bulnes 285, the **Museo Municipal** (Municipal Museum; ⊘ Jan–Feb 09.00–12.30, 15.00–20.00 daily, Mar–Dec 09.00–12.30, 14.30–18.00 Mon–Fri) has an excellent and well-prepared collection, with quite a lot of information in English. It covers the region's fauna, flora, archaeology, native peoples and 20th-century colonists. There's a Yámana dugout and first settler Herman Eberhard's folding rowboat. The **Salesian College** at Padre Rossa 1456 has a one-room museum full of stuffed fauna.

To the north and west of Puerto Natales and the Torres del Paine, **Parque Nacional Bernardo O'Higgins** is Chile's largest national park (3.5 million ha). The only part that's open to tourism is the **Serrano**

Hiking Torres del Paine

travel Art
C H I L E

Torres del Paine National Park, in Chile's far south, is widely considered one of the most stunningly beautiful spots on earth. The park itself is easily reached from Puerto Natales, but the best way to experience the grandeur of the Torres and Cuernos peaks is on foot. The famous W-Trail trekking tour (five days and four nights) features close-up views of the mountains, glaciers and lakes, providing an incredible, once-in-a-lifetime experience.

Into Argentina

The only overland connection between Magallanes and the rest of Chile is through Argentina and many people choose to visit the Torres del Paine and the FitzRoy area (in Argentina's Los Glaciares National Park) together as both offer great hiking with fantastic views of soaring rock spires. In fact, FitzRoy is better for those who want shorter hikes without having to camp and carry heavy packs.

The base town for Los Glaciares is **El Calafate**, four hours from Puerto Natales on the semi-desert steppe on the south side of Lago Argentino, which has boomed in the last decade or so and now has a good airport and lots of over-priced shops and hotels. The compulsory excursion here (and rightly so) is to the **Perito Moreno Glacier**, 80km west, where the 5km-wide face of the glacier is just a couple of hundred metres from viewing terraces; it's highly active, with vast blocks of ice constantly cracking off and falling into Lago Argentino, setting off dramatic mini-tsunamis that threaten to swamp the tour boats.

From El Calafate it's another three hours to El Chaltén, starting point for treks to FitzRoy; accommodation here is oriented more to hikers and backpackers than in El Calafate, but there are still some very comfortable options.

Heading for El Calafate, the Cerro Castillo border post is 50 minutes north of Puerto Natales on the main road to the Torres del Paine; it's 7km to the Argentine post at Cancha Carrera, from where one road leads north to El Calafate and another east to Río Gallegos from where the highway runs north up the Atlantic coast towards Buenos Aires.

Heading towards Río Gallegos, it's better to take the Casas Viejas crossing (☉ Nov–Mar 24hrs, Apr–Oct 08.00–22.00), 16km southeast of Puerto Natales

Glacier, visited by boat from Puerto Natales; tour operators often include kayaking, hiking or horseriding in a remote corner of the Torres del Paine National Park. Just to the south (but outside the park) the **Fiordo de las Montañas** is a long fiord lined with stunning glaciers visited by fast boats (Ⓦ www.agunsapatagonia.cl ☺ Sep–Mar 08.00 Sat, Apr–Aug second Sat of the month).

North from Puerto Natales

The road north from Puerto Natales passes the turning to Puerto Bories and the airport, and after 16km reaches a junction where the asphalt ends. To the left it's 7km to the **Cueva del Milodón**, the cave (in fact three) that was the object of Bruce Chatwin's quest in *In Patagonia*. There are traces of human settlement from about 12,500 years ago, as

(on the Punta Arenas road), or the main highway from Punta Arenas. The Villa Dorotea crossing, nearer Puerto Natales, leads to the nearby coal-mining town of Río Turbio.

There are various minor crossing points back to Cochrane, Coyhaique and other points on the Carretera Austral (see *Chapter 9*, page 235), but most people will re-enter Chile via Bariloche, Argentina's main mountain sports centre, returning to Puyehue and Osorno.

The Perito Moreno Glacier near El Calafate, Argentina (GB/S)

well as of animals such as the milodon (ground sloth), which became extinct around 9,000 years ago.

There is a good visitor centre (⊘ 08.00–20.00 daily), and in the mouth of the cave (30m high, 80m wide and 200m deep) a tacky plastic model of a milodon.

Turning right at the junction, the classic route to the national park loops around by **Cerro Castillo**, but a shorter route via the Milodon Cave opened in 2006. It's much slower but more scenic.

Parque Nacional Torres del Paine

The Paine massif is one of the high points of any trip to South America. The granite **Towers of Paine** thrust up like giant fingers behind the Cuernos (Horns of Paine) while the monolithic Paine Grande, covered in snow and ice, rises to the west. These mountains appear suddenly on the horizon after miles of dry windswept plain – an astonishing sight. Twelve million years ago a mass of lava welled up into earlier marine sediments and was then eroded by glaciers. The area of lakes to the south is the bed of one huge lake which emptied into the Atlantic.

The area was settled from 1892, mainly by sheep-farmers, and today's landscape is in many ways the product of this activity. In particular they used fire to clear the land; this is still a a constant hazard so when cooking you must use a stove, and make sure cigarettes are completely extinguished. The national park was established in 1959 and currently

Torres del Paine National Park

If hiking is your thing, then the classic, three-to-six-day W-Trail is a must. Explore this iconic wilderness on foot, horseback or by kayak, and for those wanting a less strenuous experience, the scenic boat trips on Last Hope Sound or Lago Grey take in breath-taking hanging glaciers and panoramic views of snow-capped peaks. Splash out on a three-night package at one of the luxury lodges, but consider a low-season visit (Apr–Sep) when prices are lower and visitors fewer.

covers 242,242ha, and a range of altitudes from 20m to 3,248m. Some 115 bird species can be seen here, and 25 mammal species; the guanaco population has recovered from around 100 in 1975 to over 3,000 today.

Various **hikes** can be done on the park's 250km of well-marked trails, the most famous being the circuit which in eight days will take you right round the massif past Lagos Paine, Dickson and Grey. The most amazing view is the close-up of the Towers of Paine from the glacial lake below, a day-walk from the Hostería Las Torres. You will never forget it. There are also fine walks to **Glaciar Grey** and the **Valle del**

Paine Grande (left) and the Cuernos del Paine (right) from Laguna Verde (PBAG/A)

Francés, which can be combined with the hike to the Towers to form the 'W', now the most popular route (four to six days in total).

Visiting the park

The number of visitors to the park has shot up to around 140,000 (mostly foreigners), putting it under heavy pressure. Concessions have been granted to private businesses to run facilities – new refuges and hotels have been built, while some historically free huts and campsites are now subject to a charge. People are increasingly visiting out of season, even though the circuit is impassable in winter.

It can be bitterly cold and windy in any season; katabatic winds or williwaws rush suddenly off the ice cap at between 100km/h and 160km/h. Views are best at dawn; Paine Grande in particular is usually covered with cloud soon after.

Tierra del Fuego

When, in 1520, Ferdinand Magellan reached the great island at the tip of America, he observed smoke from the fires lit by the indigenous people to warn of strangers, so his patron, Charles V of Spain, later named the island Tierra del Fuego ('Land of Fire'). Three centuries later, Captain Robert FitzRoy arrived in the *Beagle* and met the island's 'savages' – the native Yámana, later virtually wiped out by measles and tuberculosis imported by white settlers.

Tierra del Fuego is divided more or less equally between Chile and Argentina, with the Argentine part being more developed. The north of the island is an arid steppe similar to the Patagonian plains, with vast sheep *estancias*, contrasting with the beautiful but largely inaccessible southern part where the Andes finally dive into the sea. Although not high, its peaks provide some of the world's hardest climbing, due mainly to foul weather and the impenetrable rainforest that fills the space between sea and ice. This area is best visited by boat from Punta Arenas.

Porvenir and surrounds

On the island's northern plain, Porvenir was established when gold was found nearby in 1880; the brief gold rush did not last long (although traces of it can still be seen), but the settlement survived by servicing the great sheep *estancias*. It was largely bypassed by their wealth and thus retains its metal-clad pioneer houses.

You'll see plenty of seabirds and maybe dolphins from the ferry, and Porvenir's sheltered bay, and two lagoons just north, are good for viewing cormorants, kelp geese, steamer ducks, black-necked swans and flamingos; at the **Parque Pingüino Rey** (Ⓦ www.pinguinorey.cl), 114km from Porvenir at the eastern end of Bahía Inutil ('Useless Bay', because it is so shallow) you can visit a king penguin colony.

The small **Museo Fernando Cordero Rusque** (◔ 09.00–17.00 Mon–Thu, 09.00–16.00 Fri, 11.00–14.00, 15.00–17.00 Sat–Sun), on the north side of the plaza at Padre Mario Zavattara 402, has displays on local fauna, archaeology and anthropology (with good photos of the Selk'nam), the gold rush and the wool industry, and an intriguing section on Porvenir's pre-World War I film industry.

Some people come here as a day trip, simply to say they've been to Tierra del Fuego, but it's mainly a stopover on the way to the wilder and more scenic parts of the archipelago.

Gaucho riding his horse, Patagonia (SS)

251

Practicalities

From Punta Arenas, **ferries** sail daily to Porvenir and weekly to Puerto Williams (leaving Wednesday and returning Friday; 28 hours). More frequent ferries to Tierra del Fuego shuttle across the First Narrows from Punta Delgada, off the Punta Arenas–Río Gallegos road. There may soon be a ferry service from Ushuaia to Puerto Williams, or possibly to Puerto Navarino, opposite Ushuaia. From Punta Arenas DAP **flies** to Porvenir (a 12-minute hop three times daily; Mon–Sat) and to Puerto Williams. Facilities are limited in this region, and Porvenir is the only real base in Chilean Tierra del Fuego.

Accommodation

Moderate
Hosteria Los Flamencos (Porvenir) Teniente Merino 1253 ⓣ 61 614 181

Budget
Hostería Yendegaia (Porvenir) Ⓦ www.hosteriayendegaia.com
Hotel España (Porvenir) Ⓦ www.hotelespana.cl

Eating out

Club Social Croata (Porvenir; standard Chilean cuisine with an emphasis on fish) Señoret 542 ⓣ 61 580 053

Southern and western Tierra del Fuego

In the more forested southern interior small lodges offer some of the world's finest **fly-fishing**, for huge trout including sea-run browns. These also give access to **Karukinka** (Ⓦ www.karukinkanatural.cl), one of Chile's largest conservation projects. Similarly, a very rough track continues a long way south to the vast **Estancia Yendegaia** (Ⓦ www.theconservationlandtrust.org/eng/proyectos_yendegaia.htm), on the Beagle Channel. There's an airstrip at Caleta María, from where you can take a boat to see the 40m-high **Marinelli Glacier**, as well as dolphins, elephant seals, sea lions, skuas, cormorants and Magellanic penguins.

The western extremity of the Isla Grande of Tierra del Fuego – all icefields, fiords and mountains – is unpopulated and inaccessible except by boat; the weekly ferry from Punta Arenas to Puerto Williams skirts it (although you pass it overnight southbound), but to really appreciate it you should take the luxury Australis cruise, sailing from Punta Arenas on Saturday nights (Oct–Apr) to Ushuaia and back. Inflatable boats take you close to glaciers and even (weather permitting) ashore on the island of **Cape Horn**, the last speck of land before Antarctica.

The naval base of **Puerto Williams**, across the Beagle Channel from the Argentine city of Ushuaia, is the world's southernmost town. It's on the north coast of Isla Navarino, an island of lakes, bogs and thick forest that offers excellent hiking.

The **Museo Martín Gusinde** (☉ 10.00–13.00, 15.00–17.00 Mon–Thu, 15.00–18.00 Sat–Sun) is easily recognised by the bow of the tug *Yelcho*, which rescued the Shackleton expedition, sticking out of the wall. It has well-organised displays on the indigenous peoples, missionaries, natural history, and photos of the town's development. The *Micalvi* carried supplies to remote settlements in the southern channels but eventually sank at her moorings here; in 1976 the upper decks were taken over as the yacht club, with a pleasant bar and restaurant. The other main sight is, sadly, the hamlet of Ukika, 2km east, where the last descendants of the Yámana survive.

Puerto Williams harbour, with the peaks of the Dientes de Navarino behind (CA)

In conversation with...

What are your top tips for visiting and travelling in Chile?

Travel during shoulder seasons – particularly in Patagonia – to avoid crowds of tourists and steeper prices. September and October are great, but my personal favourite month to visit Chile is April, when rich orange and red hues are emblazoned across the landscape. It's also a quiet time when you'll be able to enjoy the huge empty vistas and uncrowded trails without distraction, as well as offering a better chance of spotting wildlife. However, if you can't wait that long, March is still noticeably quieter than the peak months of November to February. I would also advise any visitor to give plenty of thought to the pace of the itinerary and how long they'll spend in each area; Chile is a huge country so it's important that a tour allows enough time to relax and enjoy each amazing place.

Which Journey Latin America holiday would you most recommend?

As the top specialists in travel to Central and South America, we are continuously seeking out new trips and new routes: our brochures and website are full to bursting with adventurous and unique trips. My current favourite Chile itinerary is a holiday we designed only last year that takes travellers off the beaten track to the pristine Aysén region. On this trip, you drive down Chilean Patagonia's frontier-breaching Carretera Austral, seizing the opportunity to explore one of the earth's most remote, wild and exquisitely beautiful regions with the freedom of your own hire car. I tried it out myself earlier in the year and the whole route was utterly mesmerising.

What makes your trips to Chile different?

For over 30 years we've been creating, tweaking and adapting trips to get them just right. Undoubtedly we couldn't have done it without the advice and suggestions from our 70-odd members of staff who all have a huge wealth

of knowledge and experience in this region. When you speak to a travel consultant you'll get a real sense of the passion and expertise that makes the company tick. We also have unparalleled experience in organising group tours in Latin America, and our award-winning tour leaders know just how to uncover the hidden sides to all our destinations that make your trip unique.

What are the absolute must-sees for first-time visitors?

Chile offers some of the most diverse and spectacular landscapes in all of South America. One such highlight is the Atacama Desert: imagine perfectly conical volcanoes turning from molten red to deep purple at sunset, valleys etched with jagged lunar rock formations, shimmering salt lakes dotted with pink flamingos, and geysers that shoot jets of steam high into the sky. And

of course no-one would want to miss Torres del Paine; it's famous for the triple-towered granite massif of the same name, but the sheltered glacial valleys, wildflower meadows and ice-strewn lakes to be found throughout the national park are equally impressive. The idyllic Lakes District, with its alpine feel, is another region you shouldn't miss. Finally, if you are able to visit Easter Island, it truly is one of the ultimate experiences in travel. Lying alone in seemingly endless ocean – its nearest neighbour is over 2,000km away – this rugged and haunting little Polynesian island is one of the most remote places on the planet.

Journey Latin America are the UK's number one specialists in travel to Central and South America. Having dealt exclusively with Latin America for well over 30 years, they offer practical advice based on personal experience. For the journey of a lifetime, let them show you the Latin America they know and love. We spoke to Product Manager David Nichols.

① +44 (0)20 8622 8376 ⓔ tours@journeylatinamerica.co.uk
ⓦ www.journeylatinamerica.co.uk

11 Easter Island

When Philip Larkin described fellow poet Ted Hughes as 'like a Christmas present from Easter Island', somehow everyone knew exactly what he meant. This tiny island, the remotest inhabited place on earth, is known worldwide for its *moai*, massive stone figures carved by members of a now virtually forgotten culture which developed in total isolation over many centuries.

After the collapse of the *moai*-carving culture, the island was left deforested and almost depopulated, but still dotted with *moai*, some standing in groups on *ahu* platforms, some overthrown nearby, and many abandoned at the quarry where they were carved. These remain today alongside petroglyphs and other relics. It's intensely evocative, largely because so little is known about their creators and the disappearance of their culture. Nowadays the native Polynesian culture is rebuilding well, but without tourism it would be a very limited subsistence lifestyle.

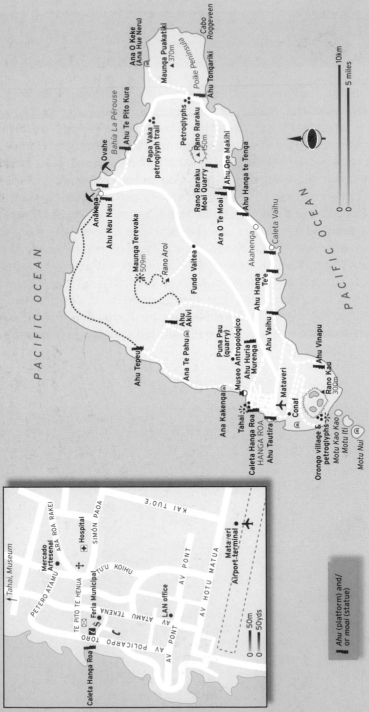

PACIFIC OCEAN

PACIFIC OCEAN

Ovahe

Bahía La Pérouse

Ahu Te Pito Kura

Ana O Keke
(Ana Hue Neru)

Maunga Puakatiki
▲ 370m

Cabo
Roggeveen

Poike Peninsula

Ahu Tongariki

Anakena

Petroglyphs

Rano Raraku
▲ 150m

Ahu Nau Nau

Papa Vaka
petroglyph trail

Rano Raraku
Moai Quarry

Ahu One Makihi

Maunga Terevaka
▲ 509m

Rano Aroi

Ahu Hanga te Tenga

Fundo Vaitea

Ara O Te Moai

Caleta Vaihu

Ahu Te Pahu

Ahu
Akivi

Akahenga

Ahu Hanga
Te'e

Ahu Tepeu

Puna Pau
(quarry)

Ana Te Pahu

Museo Antropológico

Ahu Huria
Murenga

Ahu Vaihu

Ana Kakenga

Tahai

Caleta Hanga Roa HANGA ROA

Mataveri

Ahu Vinapu

Ahu Tautira

Conaf

Rano Kau
▲ 300m

Orongo village &
petroglyphs

Motu Kao Kao

Motu Iti

Motu Nui

PACIFIC OCEAN

0   5 miles
0   10km

Tahai, Museum

PETERO ATAMU

ROA RAKEI
ARA

Mercado
Artesenal

Hospital

TE PITO TE HENUA

Feria Municipal

SIMÓN PAOA

TU'U KOIHU

ATAMU TEKENA

LAN office

KAI TUO'E

AV POLICARPO TORO

Caleta Hanga Roa

AV PONT

AV PONT

AV HOTU MATUA

AV PONT

Mataveri
Airport terminal

0   50yds
0   50m

Ahu (platform) and/
or moai (statue)

History

Easter Island (Isla de Pascua in Spanish, and Rapa Nui to its indigenous population) is an extinct volcano in the middle of the Pacific Ocean. It emerged from the waves three million years ago and remained empty, with just a few plant species managing to colonise it, until Polynesian settlers arrived around 1,600 years ago. They developed an elaborate culture, epitomised by the *moai*. These become ever bigger as competition developed between different clans developing into a mass obsession until the economy collapsed and civil war broke out. It seems that the trees were all felled to make rollers for moving statues which led to soil erosion, subsequent crop failure, and to a lack of wood to make canoes for fishing. Furthermore, the population of seabirds was almost wiped out.

Tangata Manu – the Birdman cult

Ancestor worship was normal in Polynesia but it became far more fervent here than anywhere else. Perhaps when the food supply failed, the survivors turned on the ancestors, pulling down the statues and then developing an entirely new religious system, based on the Tangata Manu or Birdman cult. The leader of each of the ten *mata* (clans) waited in low windowless houses made of grass-covered basalt slabs at Orongo (see pages 263-4) while their *hopu* (representatives) swam to Motu Nui, the furthest of the three rocky islets just offshore, and waited for the *manutara* (terns) to lay their eggs in early September. The leader whose *hopu* was the first to swim back (braving the sharks) and climb the cliffs with an intact egg became the Tangata Manu for the next year, giving his *mata* first claim on resources.

Petroglyphs at Orongo overlooking the three islets made famous at the Birdman cult. (GB/S)

Possibly, the survivors now turned on the ancestors, pulling down the statues and developing a new religious system based on the Birdman cult (see box, page 259), concentrating the competition into one annual event and ensuring stability for the next year.

It's unclear just when this occurred. The first European visitors, in 1722 and 1770, reported a prosperous society with plenty of food and no weapons. Captain James Cook's expedition in 1774 was the first to note toppled *moai*, damaged *ahu* (platforms), and hungry ill-clothed inhabitants. Certainly by 1838 it seems that only one *moai* was left standing on its *ahu*.

Introduced diseases meant that by 1877 the population had fallen to just 111; in 1888 Chile at last asserted its sovereignty, inherited from Spain. An airport opened in 1967, beginning the island's integration into the modern world. Tourism has boomed in recent decades, bringing some real prosperity at last and in 1995 the island was placed on the UNESCO World Heritage List.

Practicalities

Easter Island is the easternmost island of the South Pacific and the world's remotest populated spot, so not surprisingly transport options are limited. Unless travelling by sea, you are restricted to **flights** most days **from Santiago** (five hours away), and a couple a week from Papeete (Tahiti). Flights arrive at Mataveri Airport on the edge of Hanga Roa; there is **no public transport**, other than taxis, but hotels and guesthouses provide transfers.

The island's **main festival** is Tapati, lasting ten days in early February, when flights and guesthouses tend to be fully booked.

Dedicated tours are available, but Easter Island is usually an extension to a Chile tour, and you'll be booked into a hotel and taken around by your tour operator's guides or other local staff. There are many excellent guesthouses, and some luxury resorts which offer all-inclusive programmes similar to those in San Pedro de Atacama and Torres del Paine.

The island's only settlement is **Hanga Roa**, on its west coast. It's a small town but has standard **tourist facilities** including a post office, banks (and

Accommodation

The Sernatur office will be able to advise independent travellers on mid-range and budget options ⓦ www.sernatur.cl/buscador-de-servicios.

Easter Island highlights

The obvious circuit across the island to Anakena and back along the south coast (totalling some 50km) is almost entirely paved and it's possible to see the main sights in one day, although it's best to take three days to see all the important archaeological sites.

There's good **scuba-diving**, although being in the (coldish) ocean it's not for beginners. However, the water is wonderfully clear, with up to 50m visibility, and there is interesting coral and fish, as well as caves to explore. There's good **surfing** on the west coast (best in summer), mainly at Hanga Roa and Tahai, and on the south coast (best in winter) at Hanga Poukura and near Ahu Vaihu.

It's easy to arrange **horseriding**, mainly north of Hanga Roa. You can also **walk or cycle** along the north coast, through a very empty area with some virtually unvisited *ahus* and lava-tube caves. If you want to

ATMs) and an efficient hospital that's open 24 hours a day. US dollars can be used but you'll get a better rate in pesos; credit cards are accepted for car rental, but you should expect to pay a hefty premium. There's a **Sernatur tourist office** on Tu'u Maheke (① 32 2100 255 Ⓔ ipascua@sernatur.cl). Conaf, who run the national park, have their headquarters at Mataveri Otai, on the Orongo road (① 32 2100 236). Rangers are also on duty every day at Orongo, Anakena, Rano Raraku and Tahai.

The main **shopping** street is Atamu Tekena, south of Te Pito Te Henua. The best place for **fresh fish and produce** is the Feria Municipal (Ⓞ 08.00-12.00 daily), on Atamu Tekena at the junction with Tu'u Maheke. The best source for crafts is the Mercado Artesanal or **crafts market** (Ⓞ 09.00-19.00 Mon-Sat, 10.00-14.00 Sat), on Ara Roa Rakei opposite the church, with good selections also available in hotels. The best **bookshop** is at the museum. It's worth noting that there's almost nowhere to find **water** outside Hanga Roa, so take two or three litres with you (though bottled water may be for sale at Anakena and Rano Raraku). Use sunscreen and carry a long-sleeved shirt and sunhat - the air is amazingly clean and the sun strikes hard even on cloudy days.

Exclusive

Altiplanico Ⓦ www.altiplanico.cl/en/altiplanico-easter-island/
Hangaroa Eco Village & Spa Ⓦ www.hangaroa.cl
Posada de Mike Rapu Ⓦ www.explora.com

hike this track, it's best to take a taxi to Anakena and walk back; the scenery is at its best around Hanga Oteo, just before you swing to the south. There are many loose stones and you'll have to push, and even carry, a bike about 10% of the time.

Hanga Roa

A pleasantly Polynesian place, Hanga Roa is spread out with plenty of coconut palms and guayabas, and people going about their business on horses and trail bikes.

You'll probably see your first *moai*, at the foot of Te Pito Te Henua, right by the harbour, where Ahu Tautira (or Ahu Kopeka Tae Ati) is a platform with three *moai*. From here there's a very pleasant shoreside walk north to Tahai, a popular spot at sunset. Immediately north of

Fishing boats on the beach, Hanga Roa (MTO/A)

Easter Island cuisine

Naturally seafood is central to Easter Island cuisine and there is an endless supply of perfect tuna. Luckily there are other options – swordfish, remo-remo, toremo, nanue and lobster. Few restaurants make much use of Polynesian vegetables such as taro, manioc and sweet potato, but you may be able to enjoy a meal wrapped in banana leaves and cooked in an *umu ta'o* or earth oven; a particular speciality is *poe*, a bread made with banana or other fruits.

the harbour is another *moai*, then a track swings inland around the **cemetery** to Ahu Vai Uri, a particularly big platform bearing four *moai* (one with *pukao* – a hat or top knot) and eye discs of white coral), overlooking the **ceremonial centre of Tahai**. This is a wide open space with the oval foundations of a *hare paenga* or boathouse (ie: a house in the shape of an inverted boat), a slipway for launching rafts, earth ovens (for cooking on hot stones), and a couple of disused *ahu* just inland. By the coast just north are a couple more *ahu*, each with one *moai*, and five minutes' walk further north, beyond the end of Calle Tahai (or Ahu Akapu), two more, with a *moai* and a stump.

The next road north leads to the **Museo Antropológico Padre Sebastián Englert** (Father Sebastián Englert Anthropological Museum; ☺ 09.30–12.30, 14.00–17.30 Tue–Fri, 09.30–12.30 Sat, Sun and public holidays ⓦ www.museorapanui.cl), more commonly reached from the far side via Atamu Tekena. This houses an excellent balanced display on the controversies surrounding the island's history, as well as natural history and the development of the island's ten *mata* (or clans) and the Birdman cult. There's also a rare *moai* with female features, and wooden tablets carved in the mysterious *rongorongo* script which has only recently been deciphered (the tablets seem to record sexually explicit fertility chants). The only form of writing known in ancient Polynesia, it bears no resemblance to the spoken language.

To Orongo

Following the coast south from Hanga Roa past the airport, the road passes Conaf's headquarters, where *toromiro* trees (now extinct in the wild) are being cultivated, and rises steadily to the edge of the crater of **Rano Kau**, the **volcano** forming the island's southwestern corner. There's a modern visitor centre (☺ daily 09.00–18.00, summer to 21.00) at the entrance to the **Orongo ceremonial village**, 6km from central Hanga Roa.

In a fantastic site on a ridge between the crater and the ocean, this was the venue for the 'Birdman' (Tangata Manu) ceremony that regulated island life from around 1580 to 1866 (see box, page 259). At the site's southern end, looking out over the islets and the endless Pacific, there are rocks and houses (probably occupied by priests during ceremonies) marked with 150 **petroglyphs**.

To Anakena, Tongariki and Rano Raraku

The main road leads across the island to **Anakena**, the island's **main beach**, small but otherwise the epitome of the South Pacific with its white sand and palm trees. This is where the first settlers are said to have landed – although the 'wrong' side of the island for those coming from Polynesia, it is the easiest place to beach a boat. There are also two *ahu*, the main one, Ahu Nau Nau, with seven *moai*, descending in height from left to right. Some have unique 'tattoo' carvings on their backs. Just south beyond the headland is the island's only other beach, at **Ovahe**, even less frequented than Anakena.

A couple of minutes' drive to the southeast is **Ahu Te Pito Kura**, where the largest *moai* ever placed on an *ahu* (9.8m high and 82 tonnes in weight) now lies face down and broken in half. This may actually have survived the civil strife, only to be demolished by missionaries

in about 1838. Just north of it is the **Te Pito Te Henua** ('navel of the world'– also used as a name for the island itself), a big round stone, reputed to emit magnetic energy, surrounded by four smaller ones at the compass points. There are many *ahu* along this stretch of coast, and at Hanga Ho'Oru, beyond the bay, a 12m-long carving of a canoe forms part of the new **Papa Vaka petroglyph trail**. To the south, a dirt road leads into the Poike Peninsula, passing the main cone of Maunga

Exploration and tradition

travel Art CHILE

Photo © Pamela Pereira

Our most complete full-day excursion on Easter Island takes visitors to the famous *ahus* (stone statues) such as Tongariki and others, ancient caves, Ranu Raraku Volcano with its stunning view over the sea and its crater, and lovely Anakena Beach. It winds up in the evening with a traditional *umu* (earth oven) meal, accompanied by cultural treats including face-painting, storytelling and dance – wonderful!

Puakatiki (370m). A path leads down to the cliff-side **Ana O Keke Cave** (or Ana Hue Neru, known as the 'Cave of the Virgins') which shelters some great petroglyphs.

It's not far to the south coast and the great *ahu* of **Tongariki**, with 15 mighty *moai* in a row, just one with a *pukao* still on its head. They were knocked down by a tsunami in 1960 and restored between 1992 and 1994 by a Japanese crane company. To the west you'll also see the foundation of a boathouse and one more *moai*.

Just west is **Rano Raraku**, the volcano from which almost all the *moai* were quarried. Perhaps 300 *moai* were mounted on *ahu*, but 396 were left here after the *moai*-making cult collapsed. Hewn from volcanic tufa with basalt axes, these are perhaps the most finely carved *moai* (one has a three-masted ship carved on its chest, which could be European or perhaps Chinese) and the biggest is almost 21m long and at least 160 tonnes in weight.

Footpaths wind up the **volcano**, passing the unusual **kneeling Tukuturi** (or Tuturi) *moai*. From the crater rim you have great views, including Ahu Tongariki to the east and Ara O Te Moai, the 'Way of the Moai', to the west – this is the route by which the *moai* were taken to

Moai on the slope of Rano Raraku volcano (m/S)

their destinations, and dozens lie abandoned by the wayside.

Continuing west towards Hanga Roa, you'll pass the seaside Ahu One Makihi, with one big fallen *moai*, the end of the Way of the Moai, and then the ruined Ahu Hanga te Tenga, site of the largest *moai* to have fallen during erection and been abandoned, 9.94m long (but now in four pieces).

After passing the site of Akahenga village, a dirt track forks left to Caleta Vaihu. Just a minute down this track is **Ahu Hanga Te'e**, where eight *moai* have been left lying face down, their *pukao* lying nearby, as if a testimony to the cataclysm. Back on the main road, it's just a few minutes to the turning to Vinapu, with two main *ahu*, the first with amazing stonework and a sunken head in front. Dating from around 1200, this is one of the oldest complexes on the island, predating similar Inca masonry by a couple of centuries.

North of Hanga Roa

A shorter circuit continues north from the museum, passing **Ana Kakenga** (the 'Cave of the Two Windows'), a fine example of a lava tube that leads 50m to two openings in a cliff right above the sea (bring a torch/flashlight), and **Ahu Tepeu**, with fine stonework and the foundations of many boathouses – probably a school for students of the *rongorongo* script. The road swings inland across the flanks of **Maunga Terevaka** (509m), the island's highest peak, and comes to **Ana Te Pahu**, a spectacular lava tube, 150m long. Not far beyond is **Ahu Akivi**, one of the island's loveliest sites, with lichen-covered *moai* and relatively few visitors. The road continues past **Puna Pau**, the quarry where the red *pukao* topknots were carved, and soon reaches the paved road to Anakena.

Appendix 1

Language

Chilean Spanish is renowned as one of the fastest and most furious variants of the language, but it's not hard once you get used to it. Above all, Chileans drop terminal consonants, notably 's' – thus they say *bueno' día'* for good day (*buenos días*), and 's' can also be elided inside words – although it is sounded in *isla* ('island'); 'b' and 'd' also tend to vanish, while 'g' becomes an 'h'.

Stress is important in spoken Spanish, and words are written with an accent on the stressed vowel if it is not where a native speaker would expect it. There's also the *tilda* in 'ñ', like 'ny' (as in 'onion').

Vocabulary

Basic vocabulary

good morning	*buenos días*	from/to	*de/a*
good afternoon	*buenas tardes*	today/tomorrow	*hoy/mañana*
goodnight	*buenas noches*	yesterday	*ayer*
goodbye	*adiós*	sorry	*lo siento*
how are you?	*¿como está?*	very well	*muy bien*
well	*bien*	good, OK	*bueno*
yes/no	*sí/no*	of course	*claro*
hello	*hola*	what?	*¿qué?*
please/		when?	*¿cuando?*
thankyou	*por favor/gracias*	why?	*¿por qué?*
excuse me/	*con permiso/*	how?	*¿cómo?*
you're welcome	*de nada*	here/there	*aquí/ahí*
a pleasure to		open/closed	*abierto*
meet you	*mucho gusto*		*/cerrado*
bon voyage	*vaja bien/*	large/small	*grande/pequeño*
	buen viaje		

Basic phrases

Where is ... ?	*¿Dónde está ... ?*
What's this street called?	*¿Cómo se llama esta calle?*
Where are you from (your country)?	*¿De dónde es?*

How far is it to … ?	*¿A que distancia …?*		
How much does it cost?	*¿Cuánto vale?*		
May I … ? Is it possible … ?	*¿Se puede …?*		
I am English/American	*Soy inglés/norteamericano*		
I don't understand	*No entiendo*		
Please write it down	*Por favor, escríbalo*		
Do you speak English?	*¿Habla inglés?*		

Getting around

left/right	*izquierda/derecha*	return ticket	*pasaje*
north/south	*norte/sur*		*ida-y-vuelta*
east/west	*este* or *oriente/oeste,*	airport	*aeropuerto*
	occidente or *poniente*	I want to	*Quiero ir a…*
northeast/	*noreste/noroeste*	go to…	
northwest		cave	*cueva*
(easily confused)		dock	*muelle*
bus terminal	*terminal de buses,*	forest	*bosque/selva*
	rodoviario	hill	*cerro/cuesta*
bus stop	*parada*	lake	*lago/laguna*
train station	*estación de tren*	lookout/	*mirador*
boat	*barca*	viewpoint	
straight ahead	*todo recto/*	marsh	*bofedal*
	adelante	mountain	*cerro/pico/*
block	*cuadra*		*montaña*
(at the)		mountain	*cordillera/*
corner (of)	*esquina*	range	*sierra*
street/avenue	*calle/avenida*	ranger post	*guardería*
road/highway	*camino/*	river	*río*
	carretera		

Accommodation

single room	*sencillo*	key	*llave*
twin room	*doble*	sheets	*sábanas*
double	*matrimonial*	towel	*toalla*
en suite	*con baño (privado)*	soap	*jabón*
with shared	*con baño compartido*	toilet paper	*papel higiénico*
bathroom	*(comunal/general)*		
(electric)	*ducha*	air	*aire*
shower	*(eléctrica)*	conditioned	*acondicionado*
Do you have	*¿Hay un cuarto?*		
a room?			

Shopping

I want	*Quiero*	This one	*ésta/ésto*
I would like	*Quisiera (comer)*	(very)	*(muy) caro*
(to eat)		expensive	
How much is it?	*¿Cuánto cuesta?*	cheap(er)	*(más) caro*
shop	*tienda*	market	*mercado*

Food and drink

enjoy your		without meat	*sin carne*
meal	*buen provecha*	milk	*leche*
restaurant	*restaurante,*	potatoes	*patatas*
	comedor	wine	*vino*
bill	*cuenta*	cabbage	*repollo*
knife	*cuchillo*	squash	*zapallo*
fork	*tenedor*	sugar	*azucar*
spoon	*cuchera*	cheese	*queso*
beer	*cerveza*	mushrooms	*hongos*
bread	*pan*	orange	*naranja*
butter	*mantequilla*	apple	*manzana*
tea/coffee	*te/café*	plum	*ciruela*
	(usually *cafecito*)	water	*agua*
fish	*pescado*	peach	*peludito*
fruit	*frutas*	nectarine	*durazno*
beef	*vaca*		

Numbers

0	*cero*	16	*dieciséis*
1	*uno/a*	17	*diecisiete*
2	*dos*	18	*dieciocho*
3	*tres*	19	*diecinueve*
4	*cuatro*	20	*veinte*
5	*cinco*	21	*veintiuno*
6	*séis*	30	*treinta*
7	*siete*	40	*cuarenta*
8	*ocho*	50	*cincuenta*
9	*nueve*	60	*sesenta*
10	*diez*	70	*setenta*
11	*once*	80	*ochenta*
12	*doce*	90	*noventa*
13	*trece*	100	*cien/ciento*
14	*catorce*	500	*quinientos*
15	*quince*	1,000	*mil*

Chilenismos: Chilean slang

On the one hand Chileans are very formal people, and you should use formal greetings and the *usted* form of 'you' until it's agreed that you can *tutear*; on the other hand there is a very lively slang that can be pretty confusing, although plenty of tolerance is extended to obvious gringos. Thus *guagua* and *camion* which mean 'bus' in many countries mean 'baby' and 'truck' in Chile, and *colectivo* means a shared taxi; use *micro* for a city bus, or just *bus* or *autobus* for long-distance buses. *Lolo* and *lola* mean 'boy' and 'girl', and *pololo* and *polola* 'boyfriend' and 'girlfriend'; they might wear a *polera* or 'T-shirt' (originally meaning 'polo-shirt') and drink *piscola* (*pisco* with cola), to make them *piolo* or relaxed. *Piso* means 'stool' as well as 'storey', so you're not being invited to sit on the floor (as a rule). Chileans also add the diminutive '-to' or '-cito' to many words, so that *piscola* might be *piscolita* and a coffee is often *un cafecito*. Similarly, *un ratito* means both 'just a moment' and 'just a little way'.

'X' is used as an abbreviation of *por* (by, for), as in 4x4 (four-wheel drive) and the shop *Más x Menos* ('More for Less'); in bus routings *x* means 'via'.

Una pregunta (una consulta) no más	Just one question	*Cachai?*	understand?
		Ya vale	OK
Digame, caballero/señora	Can I help you, sir/madam?	*Ya se fue*	he/she/it has gone
		Filo	forget (about) it
Al tiro	straight away (literally, in a shot)	*Pasar lo bien*	to have a good time
		Paco	cop
Muy amable	very kind	*Taco*	traffic jam (also
Mucho gusto	my pleasure		high-heeled shoe)

Days of the week

Sunday	*domingo*	Thursday	*jueves*
Monday	*lunes*	Friday	*viernes*
Tuesday	*martes*	Saturday	*sábado*
Wednesday	*miércoles*		

Appendix 2

Further information

Natural history and field guides

Arraya, Braulio and Chester, Sharon *The Birds of Chile* (Latour/Wandering Albatross, 1993).

Couve, E and Vidal-Ojeda, C *Birds of Torres del Paine National Park/Aves del Parque Nacional Torres del Paine* (Fantástico Sur, 2004).

de la Peña, Martín R and Rumboll, Maurice *Birds of Southern South America and Antarctica* (HarperCollins, 1998). The birdwatcher's bible.

Dollenz Alvárez, Orlando *Los Arboles y Bosques de Magallanes/Guide to the Trees and Shrubs of Magallanes* (Universidad de Magallanes, 1995).

Donde Observar Aves en el Parque Nacional Torres del Paine (photographic guide) (Fantástico Sur, 1999).

Jaramillo, Alvaro *Birds of Chile* (Princeton UP/Helm Field Guides, 2003). Potentially definitive guide.

McEwan, Colin, Borrero, Luis A and Prieto, Alfred (ed) *Patagonia: Natural History, Prehistory & Ethnography at the Uttermost end of the Earth* (Princeton UP, 1997). Combines wildlife and human settlement.

Pearman, Mark *Essential Guide to Birding in Chile* (Worldwide Publications, 1995).

Rottman, J and Piwonka, N *Naturaleza de Chile* (Unisys/WWF, 1988); also Altiplano, *Bosques de Chile* – bilingual coffee-table books.

Wilcox, Ken *Chile's Native Forests* (NW Wild Books, Michigan, 1995).

Soper, Tony *Antarctica: A Guide to the Wildlife* (Bradt 2008).

History and politics

Aguilera, Pilar and Fredes, Ricardo (eds) *Chile: The Other September 11* (Ocean Press, 2002). The 1973 coup.

Aydon, Cyril *Charles Darwin* (Constable & Robinson, 2002). A balanced biography, placing Darwin in his social and economic context.

Beckett, Andy *Pinochet on Piccadilly: Britain and Chile's Hidden History* (Granta, 2003). On Chile's relations with Britain.

Boorstein, Edward *Allende's Chile: An Inside View* (International Publishers, 1977).

Browne, Janet *Charles Darwin: Voyaging* (Princeton UP/Cape, 1996); and *Charles Darwin: The Power of Place* (Princeton UP/Cape, 2002).

Highly acclaimed two-volume biography. Also *Darwin's Origin of the Species: A Biography* (Allen & Unwin/Grove Press, 2006).

Caistor, Nick *In Focus Chile* (Latin America Bureau, London, 2002). A guide to the economic, social and political background of Chile.

Constable, Pamela and Valenzuela, Arturo *A Nation of Enemies: Chile under Pinochet* (Norton, 1993).

Cochrane, Lord Thomas *The Autobiography of a Seaman* (reprinted by The Lyons Press, 2000).

Collier, S and Sater, W *A History of Chile 1808–2002* (Cambridge UP, 1996).

Cooper, Marc *Pinochet & Me: a Chilean Anti-memoir* (Verso, 2002).

Darwin, Charles *The Voyage of the Beagle* (1839; paperback editions by Penguin and Wordsworth Classics, UK, and NAL-Dutton, USA). Also *The Autobiography of Charles Darwin* (OUP/Dover, 1983); *The Origin of Species* (1859; paperback editions by Penguin, OUP World's Classics and Random House Modern Library).

Dinges, John *The Condor Years: How Pinochet and his allies brought terrorism to three continents* (New Press, 2004).

Franklin, Jonathan *The 33* (Bantam, 2011). First-hand account of the rescue of 33 miners after 69 days trapped underground.

Grimble, Ian *The Sea-Wolf: The Life of Admiral Cochrane* (Birlinn, 2001).

Harvey, Robert *Cochrane: the life and exploits of a fighting captain* (Constable and Robinson, 2000).

Kornbluh, Peter *The Pinochet File* (New Press, US, 2003). Declassified documents on the US's role in the coup.

Politzer, P and Brown, *C Fear in Chile: Lives under Pinochet* (New Press, 2001).

Timerman, Jacobo *Chile: Death in the South* (Picador, 1987).

Villalobos, S *et al Historia de Chile* (Editorial Universitaria, 1974); also *A Short History of Chile* – in English (Editorial Universitaria, 5/ed 2006).

Practical guides

Brennan, John and Taboada, Alvaro *How to Survive in the Chilean Jungle, an English Lexicon of Chilean Slang and Spanish Sayings* (Dolmen Ediciones, 2006).

Dawood, Dr Richard (ed) *Travellers' Health: How to Stay Healthy Abroad* (OUP, 5/ed 2012).

del Pozo, José *Historia del Vino Chileno* (Editorial Universitaria).

Guía Chiletur Copec, in three volumes (Copesa Editorial, Santiago, updated annually). Spanish-language guides to Chile; very detailed and up to date, with superb maps.

Ray, Leslie *The Language of the Land: the Mapuche of Chile and*

Argentina (Latin America Bureau, 2004).

Richards, Peter *The Wines of Chile* (Mitchell Beazley, 2006).

Romney, Jared *Speaking Chileno: A Guide to Spanish from Chile* (Language Babel, 2012).

Roraff, Susan *Cultureshock! Chile: A Survival Guide to Customs and Etiquette* (Marshall Cavendish, 2007).

Umana-Murray, Mirtha *Three Generations of Chilean Cuisine* (McGraw-Hill/Contemporary Books, 2/ed 1997).

Van Waerebeek-González, Ruth *The Chilean Kitchen* (HP Books, 1999).

Wilson-Howarth, Dr Jane *Healthy Travel: Bugs, Bites and Bowels* (Cadogan, 3/ed 2006); also *Essential Guide to Travel Health: Don't Let Bugs, Bites and Bowels Spoil Your Trip* (Cadogan, 2009).

Wilson-Howarth, Dr J and Ellis, Dr M *Your Child Abroad: A Travel Health Guide* (Bradt 2005).

Travelogues

Attlee, Rupert *The Trail to Titicaca* (Hindon, 1997, Summersdale Press, 1999). Cycling from Tierra del Fuego to Lake Titicaca.

Bridges, Lucas *The Uttermost Part of the Earth* (Hodder & Stoughton, 1947; Century Hutchinson, London, 1987).

Chatwin, Bruce *In Patagonia* (Cape/Picador, London, 1979). More in Argentina than Chile but still a classic.

Dixie, Lady Florence *Riding Across Patagonia* (reprinted by Southern Patagonia Publications). The first tourists in the Torres del Paine, in 1879.

Guevara, Che *The Motorcycle Diaries* (Routledge/Fourth Estate, 1995). Through Chile to Venezuela, with an awakening social conscience.

Jacobs, Michael *Ghost Train Through the Andes* (John Murray, 2006); also *Andes* (Granta, 2010).

McCarthy, John and Keenan, Brian *Between Extremes* (Black Swan/Bantam, 1999). The former Beirut hostages trace Keenan's heroes, Neruda and O'Higgins.

Pilkington, John *An Englishman in Patagonia* (Century, London, 1991).

Reding, Nick *The Last Cowboys at the End of the World: The Story of the Gauchos of Patagonia* (Crown, 2001). The gauchos of Alto Cisnes.

Sagaris, Lake *After the First Death: A Journey through Chile, Time, Mind* (Somerville House, Toronto, 1996); and *Bone and Dream: into the World's Driest Desert* (Vintage Canada, 2001). A Santiago-based journalist links modern Chile with the story of Inca princess La Tirana.

Thorpe, Nick *Eight Men & a Duck: an improbable voyage by reed boat to Easter Island* (Little, Brown/Abacus, 2002).

Wangford, Hank *Lost Cowboys* (Phoenix, 1996).

Wheeler, Sara *Travels in a Thin Country* (Little, Brown, 1994). The best recent book on Chile.

Literature

Allende, Isabel *My Invented Country: Life within and without Chile* (HarperCollins, 2003). A revealing insight into pre-Pinochet society. Of her novels, *The House of Spirits* (1985), *Of Love and Shadows* (1987) and *Daughter of Fortune* (1999) are largely set in Chile.

Bolaño, Roberto *By Night in Chile* (New Directions, 2003); *Distant Star* (Harvill, 2004).

Donoso, José *Curfew* (Weidenfeld & Nicholson, 1988). Set at the end of the Pinochet dictatorship.

Dorfman, Ariel *Heading South, Looking North: a Bilingual Journey* (Farrar, Straus Giroux, 1998). Written in English then translated into Spanish – an insightful memoir; also *Exorcising Terror: The Incredible Unending Trial of General Augusto Pinochet* (Seven Stories Press, 2002), and many plays, poems and novels, most dealing with human-rights abuses, notably the stunning play *Death and the Maiden*.

O'Brian, Patrick *The Unknown Shore* (HarperCollins, 1998); see also *The Golden Ocean* (HarperCollins, 1998), historical novel dealing with the continuation of Anson's around-the-world voyage; and his biography of Joseph Banks (Chicago UP/Harvill Press, 1997), who visited Tierra del Fuego as naturalist with Captain Cook.

Skármeta, Antonio *Burning Patience* (Knopf/Pantheon, 1987). Better known as *Il Postino* since the success of the film; also *I Dreamt the Snow was Burning* (Readers International, 1985), set in the last days of Allende.

Wilson, Jason *Traveller's Literary Companion to South and Central America* (In Print Publishing Ltd, 1993). Includes geographical, historical, political and literary comment on each country.

Pablo Neruda

By Neruda: *Isla Negra* (Souvenir Press, 1982); *Love* (Harvill Press, 1995); *Memoirs* (Penguin 1978).

Feinstein, Adam *Pablo Neruda: a passion for life* (Bloomsbury, 2004).

Kerrigan, Anthony *et al* (trans) *Selected Poems* (Penguin, 1988).

Merwin, WS (trans) *Twenty Love Poems and a Song of Despair* (Cape, 1976).

Otera Silva, Miguel, Sayers Peden, Margaret (eds) *Passions and Impressions* (Farrar, Straus & Giroux, 2001).

Schmitt, Jack; González Echevarria, Robert (trans) *Canto General* (University of California Press, 2000).

Stephens, Ilan (ed) *The Poetry of Pablo Neruda* (Farrar, Straus & Giroux, 2003). Almost 1,000 pages, with a good introducton.

Tapscott, Stephen (trans) *A Hundred Love Sonnets/Cien Sonetos De Amor* (Texas UP, 1986).

Teitelboim, Volodia *Neruda* (Texas UP, 1991). The standard biography.

Walsh, Donald (trans) *The Captain's Verses* (New Directions, 1972).

Websites

The most useful websites for tourists are: Ⓦ www.sitios.cl, Ⓦ www.gochile.cl and Ⓦ www.chileaustral.cl as well as Ⓦ www.interpatagonia.com which focuses on Patagonia. Others relevant to tourists are:

Ⓦ **www.chip.cl** Chip News (the Chilean Information Project)

Ⓦ **www.santiagotimes.cl/** English-language newspaper

Ⓦ **www.emol.cl** El Mercurio de Santiago

Ⓦ **www.tercera.com** *La Tercera* – Spanish-language newspapers

Ⓦ **www.elmostrador.cl** Online Spanish-language newspaper

Ⓦ **www.prochile.cl** ProChile

Ⓦ **www.sernatur.cl** Sernatur - tourist information

Ⓦ **www.amarillas.cl**, **www.blancas.cl** Phone directories

Ⓦ **www.cipma.cl** Database of 14,000 environmental documents

Ⓦ **www.codeff.cl** Conservation body

Ⓦ **www.conaf.cl** CONAF, in charge of national parks

General

Ⓦ **www.cdc.gov/travel** Medical advice

Ⓦ **www.lanic.utexas.edu** Academic links

Ⓦ **www.saexplorers.org** South American Explorers

Ⓦ **www.lab.org.uk** Politics and society

Ⓦ **www.patagonia-chile.com** Focuses on Ultima Esperanza (the Puerto Natales/Torres del Paine area) and Magallanes.

Ⓦ **www.lata.org** Latin American Travel Association.

Ⓦ **www.chilediscover.com**

Ⓦ **www.planeta.com/chile.html** Ecotouristic information and links

Ⓦ **www.gobiernodechile.cl** The government's portal

Ⓦ **www.ine.cl** Government statistics

Ⓦ **www.planos.cl** or **www.mapcity.com** For maps

Index

Entries in **bold** indicate major entries; those in *italic* indicate maps.

First published January 2013
Bradt Travel Guides Ltd, IDC House, The Vale, Chalfont St Peter, Bucks SL9 9RZ, England
www.bradtguides.com
Published in the USA by The Globe Pequot Press Inc,
PO Box 480, Guilford, Connecticut 06437-0480

ISBN: 978 1 84162 408 2

British Library Cataloguing in Publication Data
A catalogue record for this book is available from the British Library

Photographs Alamy: Cephas Picture Library (CPL/A), David A Barnes (DAB/A), Galen Rowell/Mountain Light (GR/ML/A), James Brunker (JB/A), Lee Foster (LF/A), LOOK Die Bildagentur der Fotografen GmbH (LDBFG/A), M Timothy O'Keefe (MTO/A), pkphotos.com (p/A), Prisma Bildagentur AG (PBAG/A), Russell Kord (RK/A), World History Archives (WHA/A); Alejandro Ulloa Díaz/DeutzHumslet (AUD/DH); Álvaro Franco (AF); Ana Druzian (AD); Antonio Ljubetic (AL); Archivo Fundación Pablo Neruda (AFPN); Arnoldo Riker (AR); Axel Kunzmann (AK); Ben Melbourne (BM); Bureau of Public Roads/US National Archives (BPR/USNA); Carlos Ivovic O (Carlos Ivovic O); Christian Bodadilla (CB); Claudio Bustos (CB); Corbis: Ivan Alvarado/Reuters (IA/R/C); Cristian Jara-Figueroa (CJ-F); Cristobal Palma/Museo de la Memoria y los Derechos Humanos (CP/MMDH); Cruceros Australis (CA); Daniel Aguilera Sánchez (DAS); Daniel Martínez Pereira (DMP); Dreamstime: Afagundes (Af/D), Anni54 (An/D), Bcarrillob (B/D), Dinobike (D/D), Hugoht (H/D), Jorisvo (J/D), Larshinksten (L/D), Solucionfotografica (S/D), Tifonimages (Tif/D), Titopix (Tit/D); Edison Zanatto (EZ); Eduardo Abásolo (EA); Eric Lafforgue (EL); Erfan Daliri (ED); Erwin Thieme L./www.erwinthieme.com (ETL); FLPA: Cyril Ruoso/Minden Pictures (CR/MP/FLPA), Dickie Duckett (DD/FLPA), Imagebroker (I/FLPA), Ingo Arndt/Minden Pictures (IA/MP/FLPA), Kevin Schafer/Minden Pictures (KS/MP/FLPA), Klaus-Peter Wolf/Imagebroker (K-PW/I/FLPA), Michael and Patricia Fogden/Minden Pictures (MF & PF/MP/FLPA), Nico Stengert/Imagebroker (NS/I/FLPA), Sandra Schänzer/Imagebroker (SS/I/FLPA), Tui De Roy/Minden Pictures (TDR/MP/FLPA), Yva Momatiuk & John Eastcott/Minden Pictures (YM & JE/MP/FLPA); Gabriela Andrea Silva Hormazabal (GASH); Getty: Fotografías Jorge León Cabello (FJLC/G), Rod Irvine (RI/G), Staff/AFP (STF/AFP/G); Ignacio Walker/www.ignaciowalker.com (IW); Ivan Zapata (IZ); James Lowen (JL); James Ramsay/Dibner Library (JR/DL); Jeremiah Thompson (JT); Jorge González Camarena (JGC); Jorge Zúñiga Vega (JZV); Julie Gosse (JG); Marcelo Dufflocq Williams (MDW); Matias Recondo (MR); Michel Gutiérrez (MG); Márcio Cabral de Moura (MáCM); Michael O'Regan (MO); Miguel Cáceres Munizaga (MiCM); MrFoxTalbot (MFT); NELRQJAR/Nelson Rojas Aracena (N/NRA); Orban López (OL); Otto Grashof/Instituto Nacional Sanmartiniano (OG/INS); Pablo Corvalan/Bancoimages. cl (PC/B); Pablo Octavio Azúa García (POAG); Pedro Montoya Alvarado (PMA); Pedro S Errázuriz/Museo National de Bellas Artes (PSE/MNBA); Rita Willaert (RW); Shutterstock: Alberto Loyo (AL/S), Alexander Chaikin (AC/S), Alexander Yu Zotov (AYZ/S), Anderl (A/S), Audrey Snider-Bell (AS-B/S), David Thyberg (DT/S), Eduardo Rivero (ER/S), Ekaterina Pokrovsky (EP/S), Galina Barskaya (GB/S), GlobetrotterJ (G/S), Grigory Kubatyan (GK/S), Ihervas (I/S), Ingrid Petitjean (IP/S), Jarous (J/S), jorisvo (j/S), Joshua Raif (JR/S), Lukasz Kurbiel (LK/S), ManxMan (M/S), modestlife (m/S), Nataliya Hora (NH/S), Neil Podoll (NP/S), Pichugin Dmitry (PD/S), ribeiroantonio (r/S), Rich Lindie (RL/S), Schmid Christophe (SC/S), steve100 (s/S), Tifonimages (T/S), Tomas Skopal (TS/S), Travel Bug (TB/S), Vinicius Tupinamba (VT/S); Stephen Cruise (SC); SuperStock (SS); Teri L Bertin (TLB); Thomas Somerscales (TS); Turismo Concepción; www.turismoconcepcion.com (TC); Víctor Pérez Pérez (VPP); Viña Casa Silva (VCS); Viña Mar (VM)

Front Cover (Top, left to right) Torres del Paine National Park (SS); Magellanic penguin (IA/MP/FLPA); Colourful houses in Valparaíso (SS); (bottom) Lake Miscanti (SS)
Back Cover Children dancing the *cueca* (AD); Vicuña (J/S)
Title page (Left to right) Moai on Easter Island (s/S); Viña Veramonte (GASH); Aymara musician (IZ)

Part & chapter openers Page 1: Alpacas graze in Lauca National Park, with Lago Chungara and Volcán Parinacota beyond. (K-PW/I/FLPA); Page 2: Portrait of Chile's Founding Fathers; from left to right: José Miguel Carrera, Bernardo O'Higgins, José de San Martín, Diego Portales (OG/INS); Page 3: Chile's national dance is the *cueca*. (AD); Page 24: Volcán Llaima over Lago Conguillío in Conguillío National Park (L/D); Page 25: Guanaco in Torres del Paine National Park (DT/S); Page 52: Picking grapes at Viña Casa Silva in the Colchagua Valley (VCS); Page 53: Touring cyclist looking across Lago Llanquihue to the imposing Volcán Osorno (PB AG/A); Page 77: Hikers in the Torres del Paine National Park (JG); Page 97: The Hostería Pehoé, with views across Lago Pehoé to Paine Grande (left) and the Cuernos del Paine (right) (JR/S); Page 98: Statue of the Virgin Mary, Cerro San Cristóbal, Santiago (Af/D); Page 99: View across eastern Santiago to the Andean foothills (T/S); Page 118: Valparaíso murals (ED); Page 119: Pacific coast near Viña del Mar (AC/S); Page 138: Aymara musicians at a festival in Colchane (IZ); Page 159: El Tatio geysers near San Pedro de Atacama (B/D); Page 172: Views of Volcán Osorno from Frutillar (LDBFG/A); Page 173: Petrohué Falls and Volcán Osorno (NS/I/FLPA); Page 218: The wooden church of Tenaún (J/D); Page 219: *Palafito* restaurants and fishing boats, Dalcahue (S/D); Page 256: Above Wulaia on Isla Navarino (CA); Page 257: Sea lions near the Marinelli Glacier, Tierra del Fuego (CA); Page 256: Spear-throwing competition at Tapati Festival, Easter Island (EL); Page 257: Solitary *moai* on the west coast of Easter Island, with Hanga Roa beyond (SC)

Maps David McCutcheon FBCart.S

Typeset from the author's disc by Chris Lane, Artinfusion (www.artinfusion.co.uk)
Production managed by Jellyfish Print Solutions; printed in Europe
Digital conversion by the Firsty Group